International Intervention and State-Making

This book analyses the changing dynamics of sovereignty resulting from contemporary international state-building interventions.

It aims to highlight how the exercise of 'exceptional' forms of power by intervening agencies impacts on the sovereign capacity of intervened states. Drawing upon in-depth analyses of three case studies – Kosovo, East Timor and the Kurdistan Regional Government, the book shifts the focus of the debate to the nature of contemporary intervention as an act of state-making, and argues that foreign intervention changes the dynamics of political power upon which sovereignty is structured. At the same time, it reveals how intervention reproduces the imposed conditions of international state-making, thus permanently internalising external regulatory mechanisms. International intervention, in other words, becomes the constitutive element of governance in the newly created state.

This book will be of much interest to students of state-building, war and conflict studies, global governance, security studies and IR.

Selver B. Sahin is assistant professor at Bilkent University, Ankara, Turkey, and has a PhD in Political Science from the University of Canterbury, New Zealand.

Routledge Studies in Intervention and Statebuilding
Series Editor: David Chandler

International Intervention and State-Making

How exception became the norm

Selver B. Sahin

Routledge
Taylor & Francis Group

LONDON AND NEW YORK

First published 2015 by Routledge

2 Park Square, Milton Park, Abingdon, Oxon OX14 4RN
711 Third Avenue, New York, NY 10017, USA

Routledge is an imprint of the Taylor & Francis Group, an informa business

First issued in paperback 2017

British Library Cataloguing-in-Publication Data
A catalogue record for this book is available from the British Library

Library of Congress Cataloging-in-Publication Data
Sahin, Selver B.
International intervention and statemaking : how exception became the
norm / Selver B. Sahin.
    pages cm
    Includes bibliographical references and index.
    1. Nation-building. 2. Intervention (International law) 3. Sovereignty.
    I. Title.
    JZ6300.S34 2016
    327.1'1–dc23   2015002436

ISBN: 978-1-138-77951-8 (hbk)
ISBN: 978-1-138-89326-9 (pbk)

Typeset in Times New Roman
by Wearset Ltd, Boldon, Tyne and Wear

To Anka

Contents

Acknowledgements

The writing of this book has truly been a long journey for me. Of the many people who helped me complete this challenging journey, one deserves special mention. Any words would indeed be insufficient to describe how grateful I am to Anka for always supporting and standing beside me in good and bad times. I therefore dedicate this work to him.

The idea of writing this book emerged out of discussions with Nevzat Soguk, Paul James and Manfred Steger during my time as a research fellow at Royal Melbourne Institute of Technology (RMIT) in Australia. I drafted the book proposal in early 2012 and received their encouragement and insightful comments. My sincere thanks are also due to Elizabeth Kath, Robin Cameron and Andy Scerri for their friendship and helpful suggestions.

My journey took a whole new turn in September 2013 when I started working at Bilkent University, Ankara, Turkey. I would like to express my gratitude for the research and technical assistance Eralp Semerci, Elizabeth Richter and Toygar Halistoprak provided me when writing the chapter on the KRG and producing the bibliography and footnoting.

I also would like to take this opportunity to thank the external reviewers for their constructive and helpful comments on this work, as well as the Routledge staff, especially Andrew Humphrys and Hannah Ferguson, as well as Hannah Riley and Steve Turrington, for their professionalism and practical assistance which helped this book come about.

Lastly, I would like to express my deepest gratitude to my parents Mesut and Emine and siblings Sevtap, Sevinc and Serdar for their love and support.

Introduction
State-building in international context

This book is about the effects of contemporary international state-building interventions on the power dynamics of the political space in states facing conflicts over sovereignty. International state-building has become the main strategic approach to the regulation of state 'failure' or 'fragility' associated with violent conflict. It refers to the long-term involvement of international agencies in the construction of democratic government capacities in 'fragile' or 'failing' countries in attempt to prevent the recurrence of violent conflict and contain the global security implications of their weak or non-existent governmental capacity through establishing and strengthening the institutional foundations of sustainable peace. It has been one of the widely addressed topics since the publication of Helman and Ratner's much-cited 'Saving Failed States' article in *Foreign Policy* in the early-1990s.[1] The conceptual origins of the contemporary 'state failure' phenomenon as a foundation of the discourse and act of international state-building can be found in the writings of English School theorists such as Bull and Watson,[2] and Jackson[3] on the governmental and institutional attributes of post-colonial states. However, Helman and Ratner were among the first to use the term 'failed state' as a 'disturbing new phenomenon' to describe the situations of the disintegration of formal government institutions and emerging dangers from the outbreak of violence in countries like Somalia, Liberia, Haiti, Sudan and former Yugoslav and Soviet republics in the immediate post-Cold War era. Their conceptualisation of failed state was premised on the understanding of the 'nation-state [that is] utterly incapable of sustaining itself as a member of the international community'.[4] Because they threaten the security of their populations and neighbouring countries, the argument follows, these states should therefore be 'saved' by other states.[5]

Since then, much has been written on the specific aspects of the state failure phenomenon and the outcomes of institutions-focused interventions rationalised as a necessary action to strengthen the capacity of states and regulate conflict. Much of the work has focused on how these interventions have been conducted or how they have impacted on the sovereign and functional capacity of intervened states. While 'exceptionalism' has constituted the discursive and operational basis of these interventions, it has either been excluded from these debates or referred to only to explain the exercise of 'exceptional' forms of power by international interveners or pursuit of extraordinary security policies in the face of 'exceptional' dangers posed by state failure. The role intervention has played in the creation of new 'exceptional' circumstances (such as autonomy and territorial secession) has received little attention. The argument this book makes is two-fold: foreign intervention changes the dynamics of political power upon which sovereignty is structured. At the same time, intervention reproduces the imposed conditions of international state-making, thus permanently internalising external regulatory mechanisms in the form of institutional capacity-development partnerships.

State failure as a humanitarian and security issue

The expanding academic and policy literature on state failure can be examined by breaking it down into two parts: as the humanitarian intervention literature of the 1990s and the global security literature produced in the post-September 11 period. The humanitarian intervention literature associated state failure with the emergence of a supposedly 'new' type of violence in the periphery countries (or the 'global borderlands' borrowing Mark Duffield's terminology[6]) and emphasised its potential to spread elsewhere in a rapidly globalised world.[7] Mary Kaldor, for instance, describes state failure by reference to the neo-liberal economic dynamics of contemporary globalisation that are 'breaking up the socio-economic divisions that defined the patterns of politics which characterized the modern period'.[8] From this perspective, the disruptive forces of globalisation which have further undermined the already weak capacity of many periphery states have also changed the nature of conflict, leading to the rise of 'new wars' characterised by a 'privatization of violence' and the emergence of 'a multiplicity of types of fighting units both public and private, state and non-state, or some kind of mixture'.[9]

The inability of the political leaderships of these states to effectively and democratically govern their societies was approached in terms of a regional security and humanitarian problem. The focus of policy discussions during that period was, to a larger extent, on addressing the implications of 'state failure' for local populations such as massive human rights violations, as well as its trans-boundary, 'spillover' effects such as the spread of fighting into neighbouring states, refugee flows and the emergence of regional black market economies.[10] The political turn the September 11 attacks generated, on the other hand, further reinforced the image of state failure as an existential threat and brought the dangers of limited or non-existent governance capacity to the centre of Western security policy-making. Due to their limited institutional ability to control their boundaries, enforce the rule of law, meet the basic needs of their citizenry and regulate conflict, failed states have come to be seen as providing 'safe havens' for non-state actors including terrorists, warlords and other illicit groups.[11] Underdevelopment of the 'borderlands', in other words, has now been perceived as a serious source of insecurity for 'metropolitan' or developed, Western nations.[12] This becomes apparent in a variety of security analyses offered in international policy documents and guidelines in which states with limited or non-existent institutional capacity to deliver security and welfare functions to their citizenry are often associated with a series of global security challenges ranging from irregular migration and pandemics to organised crime and terrorism.[13] Accordingly, improving the government capacity of the states in far away locations has been argued to be a necessary global security engagement towards controlling or containing the perils of ineffective government in an increasingly inter-connected world context.[14]

It is important to note that this distinction in the literature is made for analytical rather than practical purposes, as some overlaps can easily be observed. Indeed, both literatures are united by a series of overarching analytical and methodological approaches that have been applied to measure the institutional and operational capabilities of the world's states, despite the abundance of terms and adjectives used to describe the characteristics of 'state failure'.

First, 'failure' is analysed in terms of a continuum of stateness, along which the world's states are placed according to the degree to which they are perceived to 'deviate' from the Weberian ideal.[15] For instance, in an article published in *Third World Quarterly* in 1996, Gros offered a 'taxonomy' of five types of failed states on the basis of their central institutions' ability to exercise territorial control: anarchic states (such as Somalia which lacks an effective central government), phantom states (such as Mobuto's Zaire which had a semblance of authority employed to protect the security and wealth of the presidential dictatorship and its cronies), anaemic states (such as Haiti and Cambodia which were consumed by counter-insurgency), captured states (such as Rwanda in 1994 when a strong central authority was captured by members of insecure elites to intimidate or eliminate rival elites) and aborted states (such as Bosnia and Angola where state authorities failed before the process of state formation was even consolidated).[16] Rotberg, on the other hand, presented four stages of 'state failure' in a 'time of terror' by reference to the degree to which central government authorities are able to deliver a variety of public goods, including physical security, education, health care, transport and communication infrastructure, and a functioning banking and commercial system. These categories included weak, failing, failed and collapsed states.[17]

Similarly, the Failed States Index (or now the Fragile States Index) annually released by the US think-tank Fund for Peace and *Foreign Policy* since 2005, seeks to assess states' stability and their likelihood to become a failed state according to their performance along 12 criteria classified under three headings: as social indicators such as demographic pressures, large-scale displacement of the population, group grievance and brain drain; economic indicators involving uneven development and economic decline; and political indicators such as corruption, public services, human rights, security apparatus, factionalised elites and external intervention. Countries are then rated on a 1 to 10 scale, with 1 (lowest) being the most stable and 10 (highest) being the most at-risk of collapse and violence. The 2014 list classifies 34 states as 'high alert' and 'alert' and 92 states as 'very high warning', 'high warning' and 'warning' countries.[18]

Similar to Foreign Policy's approach, leading international development agencies such as the World Bank and the UK government's Department for International Development (DFID) have also adopted the term 'fragile states' in an attempt to avoid the essentially discriminatory and judgemental character of the 'failed state' discourse, as raised by some critical security analysts.[19] DFID classifies 46 developing states as 'fragile' where government authorities 'cannot or will not deliver core functions to the majority of its people, including the poor'.[20] The World Bank identifies around 30 countries as fragile states that are characterised by 'weak institutional capacity, poor governance, and political instability'.[21] As an interesting point to note, the World Bank's list does not include Pakistan, Kenya, Ethiopia, Democratic Republic of Congo, Niger, Egypt, Uganda, North Korea, Cameroon and Bangladesh which are listed in *Foreign Policy*'s index in the group of 'alert' countries. The Organisation for Economic Co-operation and Development (OECD), on the other hand, defines fragility in terms of states' 'weak capacity to carry out basic governance function', inability to 'develop mutually constructive relations with society' and vulnerability to 'internal or external shocks such as economic crises or natural disasters', and provides a list of 51 fragile states.[22]

Second, failure is usually associated with violent conflict, either as its cause or consequence. For instance, Helman and Ratner cited 'civil strife, governmental breakdown, and economic privation' among the factors precipitating state failure.[23] Similarly, the State Failure Task Force, commissioned by the US Central Intelligence Agency in the mid-1990s, defined state failure in terms of a 'wider range of civil conflicts, political crises, and massive human-rights violations that are typically associated with state breakdown'.[24] These included revolutionary wars, ethnic wars, adverse regime changes, and genocides and politicides.[25] Based on this definition, the State Failure Task Force reported 135 consolidated cases of state failure and identified four 'key drivers' for state failure: quality of life measured by infant mortality rates, regime type, openness to trade, and ethnic or religious diversity of the population. Collier, on the other hand, establishes a causal relationship between civil war and poverty in his 'conflict trap' theory: that is, civil war undermines countries' development process and failures in development increase the risk of violent conflict.[26] Similarly, Rotberg describes the persistence of civil conflict as a 'decisive' factor for state failure.[27] The World Bank also emphasises that three-quarters of fragile states are affected by ongoing armed conflicts.

Third, despite a lack of overall consensus on what exactly causes state failure or vulnerability to occur, it is often explained by reference to the internal political and social features of states such as patrimonial leadership behaviour and practices on the part of the political elites which are largely a legacy of the colonial past,[28] political exclusion,[29] mismanagement of resources[30] and social fragmentation.[31] Responsibility for failure or fragility, in other words, is attributed to the societies and their political leaders[32] situated along the 'unstable areas of the global margins'.[33] Gros, for instance, describes 'failed states' as 'perennial underachievers' or 'Bart Simpsons of the international economy' due to their low economic growth rates and increasing income disparities between the rich and poor within their societies.[34] Rotberg, on the other hand, stresses that when state officials are seen as working for themselves and their exclusive class or kinship groups, citizens turn to other sectional and community loyalties to meet their security needs and exploit economic opportunities.[35] From the perspective of these analytical approaches, the ability of state institutions to enforce the rule of law and property rights to underpin global markets[36] appears to determine the development outcomes associated with the opportunities of globalisation, such as access to new markets, investment, information and aid.[37] They therefore prioritise strengthening 'the ability of states to plan and execute policies and to enforce laws cleanly and transparently'[38] in an attempt to protect the state from predatory interests and promote a more effective use of its development resources.[39] While the effects of internal factors on states' government capacity need to be analysed, the exclusion from the analysis of wider contextual factors and historical dynamics (such as the use of state power in the global area including unequal trade relations, imposition of structural adjustment programmes and uneven patterns of capital accumulation) does not help explain what actually permits 'state failure' to occur in some parts of the world.[40]

Fourth, and most importantly, the emerging state failure paradigm has given rise to a widely held consensus on the need for external intervention. By intervention, I refer to the involvement of foreign agencies in the regulation of state failure or fragility through using military means such as deployment of troops and peacekeepers and/or non-military forms of interference such as diplomatic and political engagement, and non-governmental organisation (NGO) activities. Intervention has been justified as a necessary action to introduce and strengthen the institutional and social foundations of sustainable peace conceptualised by reference to the democratic governance capacity of societies. Zartman's rationalisation of externally led state reconstruction as a way of stabilisation and peace-building in the context of African countries illustrates this line of thinking:[41]

> It is necessary to provide a large, informally representative forum, and if the contenders for power do not do so, an external force to guarantee security and free expression during the legitimisation process may be required.

Democracy as solution to conflict and means of peace

The introduction of democratic modes of government is now treated as a solution to help break 'the vicious cycle of violence and conflict'[42] through addressing ethnic, religious and other lines of divisions. Democracy, in other words, has come to be viewed as one of the '*enabling conditions* for a functioning peacetime society'.[43] The rationale behind this optimism and confidence in the capacity of democratic institutions to regulate social conflict can be found in the prevailing mechanistic and procedural terms in which democracy is conceived. It is reflected in the policy emphasis placed on the potential of democratic government structures to encourage political groups and individuals to act on the basis of the rule of law, peacefully articulate public opinion and grievances into the political system, rely on conflict mediation mechanisms to resolve their differences, and hold their governments accountable through institutional and electoral frameworks.[44] This approach not only assumes the universality of democratic frameworks as a means of sustainable peace-building but advocates the transformation of conflict-affected countries by external agencies. In other words, 'peace as governance', which Richmond describes as an international engagement with reforming government institutions in the absence of local willingness or capacity, is prescribed as the solution to conflict.[45]

In addition to the potential of liberal democracy to promote social peace, liberal interventionism or the prescription of liberal democracy as the main strategy for conflict resolution is also based on other convictions. It reflects a 'belief that one model of domestic governance – liberal market democracy – is superior to all others'.[46] As mirrored in Fukuyama's 'end of history' thesis,[47] Western liberal democracy has indeed come to be viewed as 'the only model of government with any broad ideological legitimacy and appeal in the world' following the fall of socialist regimes in Eastern Europe.[48] Moreover, the revived democratic peace theory (i.e. democratic states do not wage war against each other)[49] has given rise to the idea that the worldwide spread of liberal democracies will contribute to international peace and security and foster sustainable global trade relations and economic prosperity.[50] Proponents of democracy promotion also acted upon a positive relationship established between democracy and development. For instance, in a report produced in 1998 by the International Panel on Democracy and Development (IPDD), chaired by Boutros Boutros-Ghali, it is suggested that democracy and development 'reinforce each other' because in order for political democracy 'to consolidate itself, [it] needs to be complemented by economic and social measures that encourage development, [and] similarly any development strategy needs to be ratified and reinforced by democratic participation in order to be implemented'.[51] Similarly, Nobel Prize Winner Economist Amartya Sen wrote in 1999 that 'no substantial famine has ever occurred in any independent and democratic country with a relatively free press' because 'a democratic government, facing elections and criticisms from opposition parties and independent newspapers, cannot help but make such an effort [to prevent famines]'.[52]

In addition to the conception of liberal democracy as a sustainable peace and development project, the representation of state failure as an ongoing process or a spectrum ranging from weakness to collapse in government capacity also suggests that it can be reversed. Indeed, the distinction between different degrees of state failure (such as weak, failing, failed and collapsed) defined in terms of the ability and willingness of state actors to overcome ineffective governance determines the type of international action, ranging from peace-keeping and electoral assistance to sector-wide capacity-development partnerships.[53] As a way of illustration, DFID identifies four groups of 'fragile' countries: 'good performers' with capacity and political will, 'weak but willing states' (i.e. states with limited capacity), 'strong but unresponsive states' (i.e. states ruled by repressive regimes) and 'weak-weak states' where there is neither capacity nor will.[54]

It is thought that, depending on their political will and institutional capabilities, 'fragile' or 'failing' states can be 'saved',[55] 'reconstituted',[56] 'repaired'[57] or 'fixed',[58] if early warning systems are put in place[59] and the right kinds of preventive measures are pursued to address the missing dimension of their statehood.[60] Another key aspect of this approach to 'state failure' is the depiction of weak or failing governance capacity as a pathological defect that needs to be remedied through forms of therapeutic governance interventions, including trusteeship-like arrangements.[61] Zartman, for instance, describes state failure in Africa as a 'long-term degenerative disease', and suggests that 'cure and remission are possible'.[62] In the same vein, Helman and Ratner compared 'failed states' to 'hapless' individuals incapacitated by mental or physical illness, broken families or bankruptcy,[63] and they argued that 'something must be done' about it.[64] Similar to guardianships put in place in domestic systems to assist people when they are incapable of managing their own affairs, Helman and Ratner proposed the idea of 'conservatorship' to 'enable' the United Nations to fulfil its 'nation-saving responsibilities'. Their proposed solution offered three models: governance assistance, delegation of governmental authority and the revival of the UN trusteeship system.[65] Conversatorship, according to Helman and Ratner, represented a 'novel', 'expansive' and 'desperately needed' solution because the 'traditional' methods of money grants, uncoordinated technical assistance and humanitarian relief proved to be insufficient to rescue states such as Somalia and Bosnia-Herzegovina from the 'brink of death'.[66]

Thus, the creation of international territorial administrations, according to Helman and Ratner, was not only the right kind of international response to the plight of failed states but 'consistent' with the principle of sovereignty. From their perspective, the domestic self-government capacity of states, rather than their exercise of full autonomy over policy-making, constitutes the true expression of sovereignty. Therefore, the establishment of conservatorships does not constitute an encroachment on state sovereignty but becomes a supportive measure for the state to 'resume responsibility for itself' and help 'advance popular sovereignty in the long-run'. What mattered in this context, according to Helman and Ratner, was the question of whether the UN and other international agencies were willing and capable of 'saving' failed states. In terms of the practicality of such administrative arrangements, they emphasised the international community's 'willingness' and 'responsibility' to promote democracy and human rights in conflict-affected countries as well as the UN's experience and ability to adapt itself to 'more complex demands of conservatorships' as a result of its supervision of Namibia and conduct of peace-keeping functions in Central America and former Yugoslav republics.[67]

The language of 'complexity', 'responsibility' and 'novelty', which presents 'remarkably intrusive forms of intervention' as an outcome of 'progressive evolution' in the policy and practice of international peace engagement,[68] has also shaped the course of policy discussions in the post-September 11 period. For instance, Krasner put forward the idea of 'shared sovereignty' as a 'new' form of institutional arrangement or an alternative framework to 'conventional' policy measures such as territorial administration and governance assistance.[69] Krasner's proposal for saving potentially failing or collapsed states was based on the conclusion of a capacity-development agreement with the political leaderships of these states. These agreements will allow the involvement of foreign agencies over some aspects of domestic governance for an 'indefinite period of time'.[70] Under such an arrangement, the target state is argued to only surrender its Westphalian/Vattelian sovereignty (i.e. the principle of political autonomy) with the purpose of improving its domestic governance capacity, as it will maintain its international legal identity as a political community.[71]

Intervention, in other words, is prescribed as an objective solution to a technical problem – that is, the governance or 'good governance' problem.[72] The governance problem is understood in terms of the lack of local institutional ability to deliver any governance activity or exercise political authority, as illustrated by the cases of refugee camps run by the UN High Commissioner for Refugees (UNHCR) in poor and conflict-affected countries or the deployment of the United Nations Operation in the Congo (ONUC) between 1960 and 1964. The problem of 'good governance', on the other hand, is concerned with the quality of governance associated with local institutions' ability to exercise liberal democratic practices.[73] In this situation, the task becomes replacing existing administrative authorities that are deemed to be unable or inappropriate to operate in a manner that is advocated by international agencies.[74]

Exceptionalism

The contemporary policies and practices of regulatory interventions are premised on the 'exceptionalism' argument. The use of military force and involvement of foreign agencies in the domestic institutional and policy-making processes of these states are argued to be a necessary exception to the norms of non-intervention and sovereign equality of states because it is brought about by the need to contain or control global security risks (such as terrorism, crime, irregular migration) arising from the weak or non-existent governance capacity of fragile or failing states. This is reflected in the description of military intervention for human rights protection as an 'exceptional and extraordinary measure' in the 'Responsibility to Protect' (R2P) report of the International Commission on Intervention and State Sovereignty Intervention (ICISS).[75] The ICISS report, released in December 2001, specifies the following situations as 'exceptional' circumstances characterised by 'serious and irreparable harm occurring to human beings':[76]

> A. large scale loss of life, actual or apprehended, with genocidal intent or not, which is the product either of deliberate state action, or state neglect or inability to act, or a failed state situation; or

> B. large scale 'ethnic cleansing', actual or apprehended, whether carried out by killing, forced expulsion, acts of terror or rape.

These 'exceptional' situations of human risk and insecurity are then referred to in the context of a 'modern understanding of the meaning of sovereignty'.[77] Rather than the exercise of unlimited power by state authorities, sovereignty is now conceptualised in terms of a 'dual responsibility: externally – to respect the sovereignty of other states, and internally, to respect the dignity and basic rights of all the people within the state'.[78] That is, sovereignty is associated with the accountability of domestic authorities to the wider community of states as well as with their ability or willingness to 'protect' citizens from the perils of ineffective and non-democratic government. This shift in the meaning of sovereignty from 'control' to 'responsibility' simultaneously changes the meaning of intervention, including the threatened or actual use of military force and other coercive measures including sanctions, criminal prosecutions and trusteeships. Because intervention, as noted above, is now framed as a solution to the good governance problem, the purpose of intervention appears to become the creation of a model of government that is 'compatible with the sovereignty of the state in which the enforcement has occurred – not undermining that sovereignty'.[79] Looked at this way, intervention is claimed as a necessary action that 'suspends sovereignty claims to the extent that good governance – as well as peace and stability – cannot be promoted or restored unless the intervener has authority over a territory'.[80] Indeed, the non-intervention rule becomes an irrelevant concept in 'extraordinary' cases of widespread violence and state failure:[81]

> Where a population is suffering serious harm, as a result of internal war, insurgency, repression or state failure, and the state in question is unwilling or unable to halt or avert it, the principle of non-intervention yields to the international responsibility to protect.

The 'responsibility to protect' principle, as noted in the ICISS report, represents a shift away from the claims of intervening agencies and the 'act of intervention' to the urgent needs of those seeking assistance and empowerment. In doing so, the often neglected issues of preventive measures and subsequent follow-up assistance after military interventions, the authors of the report emphasise, receive more attention.

However, the act of military intervention, rationalised on the basis of the exceptionalism argument, determines the emerging conditions of governmental capacity-development, as it creates new situations of exception. These new exceptional situations include the establishment of trusteeship-like administrations, deployment of foreign security staff, and the operation of foreign civilian agencies to support the development of democratic self-government capacities in the intervened states. Exceptionalism has therefore both discursive and operational aspects that shape the emerging state of political and institutional affairs in the aftermath of military or coercive interventions. As reflected in the declaratory statements by intervening powers, the use of military force and other coercive measures is rationalised as a necessary action to respond to an emerging humanitarian and security crisis on the ground (such as in the case of Kosovo) or as an outcome of diplomatic consensus on the need for undertaking a military intervention to restore security (as during the Gulf War and the deployment of the Australian-led multinational force in 1999). The operational aspects of exceptionalism include the imposition of new institutional arrangements and exercise of intrusive powers by foreign agencies to prevent the recurrence of humanitarian and security problems associated with the democratic quality and functional sovereign capacity of states. Based on this, exceptionalism can be defined as the employment of interventionist policies and practices that are claimed to be necessary exceptions to the norm of non-intervention.[82]

While exceptionalism has constituted the discursive and operational basis of contemporary interventions, it has either been excluded from policy and academic discussions on state capacity-building or referred to only to explain the pursuit of such policies in the context of the 'war on terror' following the September 11 attacks. This has been manifest in the analytical focus of the current state-building literature. The debates have centred on either the situations of 'exceptional' dangers or the 'exceptional' forms of power assumed by international interveners. Proponents of international intervention as a global security engagement[83] approached the effects of intervention as a 'problem-solving' exercise, and emphasised the importance of 'local ownership' in relation to the achievement of good governance objectives. Their focus, in other words, has been on the question of how the so-far-patchy institutional capacity-building outcomes can be improved in fragile or failing states associated with a range of trans-national security risks from human trafficking to terrorism. Critics,[84] on the other hand, pointed either to the exercise of excessive regulatory powers by intervening agencies and how this undermines the sovereign capacity of the newly constructed state structures or to the denial of political choices to domestic authorities due to the transnationalisation of certain state functions.[85] They therefore conclude that because foreign interveners dominate local decision-making processes and prevent the development of home-grown solutions within a national framework, interventions are immoral and bound to fail.

These critical analyses provide significant insights into the essentially power-driven nature of contemporary interventions. However, they do not fully highlight the shifting dynamics of sovereignty as a result of increasing military and political pressures. The effects of intervention are rather analysed in terms of a critique of contemporary state-building approaches in three major respects. This includes the normative architecture of these approaches rooted in the liberal peace thesis,[86] the ways in which interventions are framed and practised,[87] and the political underpinnings of interventions.[88] Bellamy and Richmond, for instance, criticise the design of institutional capacity-building frameworks which are premised on certain assumptions made about the construction of liberal democratic polities and the specific institutional and political context of the countries where they are applied. Regarding the assumptions about the post-conflict policy spaces, Lemay-Hébert criticises international agencies' 'empty-shell approach' evidenced by their description and treatment of war-affected countries such as Kosovo and East Timor as a *tabula rasa* or places where everything needs to introduced from the outside, and representation of their mandate as a challenging engagement with inventing forms of governance and authority from scratch.[89] This approach, he adds, neglects local social processes and indigenous sources of authority and undermines the legitimacy of newly created institutional structures on the basis of Western models in the eyes of local populations.[90] Chandler, on the other hand, theorises international state-building as a 'paradigm' through which the world's problems are understood and responded to.[91] These analyses describe the relations between intervening and domestic parties in dualistic terms as occurring between powerful foreigners and resistant locals.[92] Lemay-Hébert, for instance, points to an emerging social 'gap between the 'international' and 'local' ways of life' created by top-down state-building interventions.[93] This gap that becomes apparent in income disparities and differentiation of lifestyles between the internationals and locals such as expatriate officials receiving tax-free high salaries, staying in overpriced hotels, driving four-wheel vehicles and dining in expensive restaurants, while local populations live in poverty, often fuels resentment and resistance.[94]

Thus, the formulation of alternative solutions[95] or the pursuit of 'participatory'[96] and locally driven 'bottom-up' strategies[97] is often emphasised to better serve the needs of local populations. These strategies are thought to help prevent the perpetuation of hierarchies of power[98] and overcome the operational limits and contradictions of international democratic state capacity-building activities encountered in the context of the 'sustainability' and 'ownership' of these institutional reforms.[99] On the other hand, those who sought to examine the inherent political underpinnings of contemporary interventions concentrated their analysis on the responses of domestic groups to the reorganisation of political power, such as the formation of internal alliances between the state bureaucracy and powerful social groups benefiting from the economic reform policies promoted by international actors.[100] From this analytical perspective, interventions do not seek to rebuild the state but transform it because the formal-legal sovereignty and territorial integrity of intervened states is preserved 'without exception', while some of its functions are transnationalised.[101]

However, these generalised conclusions are contested by specific country experiences. For instance, the international recognition of the secession of Kosovo and East Timor and the de facto exercise of state identity by the Kurdistan Regional Government (KRG) in northern Iraq exemplify the unique role of intervention as an act of state-making.

Research setting

The analysis offered in this study is based on a synthesised analytical approach that is focused on the role of intervention as an act of state-making. It follows a comparative case study to illustrate the political effects of contemporary interventions on the way in which state power is redistributed in states facing sovereignty-related conflicts. The selected case studies represent different geographical settings. It examines the current practices of state-making in Kosovo, East Timor and Northern Iraq and places the analysis of the emerging political, institutional and social dynamics into a historical context. The cases are intended to highlight the changes in the conditions of political power brought about by foreign intervention and illustrate the symbiotic relationships of foreign and local actors that permeate the subsequent process of state-making.

Before providing an overview of the specific aspects of the cases of intervention it might be helpful to distinguish among the terms state-making, state-building and state formation referred to in this study. State-making, following Tilly's analysis of the processes of elimination and neutralisation of internal rivals and Wendt and Barnett's analysis of post-colonial states' dependency on security assistance, can be defined as a political process through which competing social groups acquire and exercise power within a territory and establish and secure their existence and identity as a member of the community of recognised polities.[102] State-building which reflects an architectural and purposeful understanding of institutional structuring is used in this book in the sense of creating and strengthening the capacity of formal organisations.[103] State formation, on the other hand, can be described as a historically driven and negotiated, dynamic process of centralisation of administration and social integration.

These three cases illustrate the current practices of state-making through intervention that also indicate what I call 'incomplete state formation' as described in the following way.

Kosovo, Kurdistan and East Timor were all peripheral parts of past empires (i.e. Ottoman and Portuguese Empires) and the peoples of these territories were denied the right to determine on their political future following the disintegration of these empires. In all these three cases, nationalism as an organising political social movement for establishing an autonomous territorial unit came as a belated development (emerging in the late nineteenth century for the Kosovo Albanian and Kurdish cases and the mid-twentieth century for East Timorese nationalism). However, these movements failed to achieve their objectives. Kosovo was incorporated into the Kingdom of the Serbs, Croats and Slovenes at the end of the First World War, Kurdish-populated lands were partitioned amongst Syria, Iraq, Iran and Turkey following the dissolution of the Ottoman Empire, and East Timor was annexed by Indonesia following the departure of the Portuguese in 1975. None of these communities, on the other hand, were ever fully integrated into the central state structures to which they were forced to belong. Indeed, their conception of distinct collective identity developed in opposition to foreign rule. The peoples of these localities received unequal treatment, repression, discrimination and a denial of their cultural and political identity. They sought autonomy or separation. Their resistance strategy, on the other hand, was dependent on the availability of foreign patronage and support to achieve their 'national cause'. The escalation of violence and deteriorating human rights conditions in these places in the 1990s were followed by military interventions rationalised on the basis of the exceptionalism argument. These military interventions were also followed by political intervention in the form of institutional capacity-development that sought to experiment with the creation of democratically functioning governance systems in places with little or no such prior experience.

These three cases illustrate the symbiotic relationship between foreign interveners and domestic social groups. On one hand, the involvement of foreign military and non-military agencies has enabled previously oppressed local groups (i.e. Kosovo Albanians, East Timorese and northern Iraqi Kurds) to pursue their political objectives such as territorial autonomy and separation. On the other hand, the conditions of state-making created by external forces as an 'exceptional' state of affairs have turned into routines over time. Due to structural and operational weaknesses of their newly established institutions, these political entities remain heavily dependent on external governance and development assistance particularly in the areas of poverty alleviation, rule of law, anti-corruption and fighting against organised crime. The long-term involvement of foreign agencies in key areas of the domestic policy domain has made intervention a near permanent practice.

This book incorporates 'exceptionalism' into the analysis of contemporary interventions and seeks to address the following questions:

1 How are the internal dynamics of sovereignty reconfigured through prolonged practices of exceptional state-making?
2 How do these expanded practices of exceptional state-making produce and reproduce the conditions of political intervention as the constitutive element of governance in intervened states?

Rather than looking at the ways in which intervention takes place, this book pays attention to its unique role as an act of state-making, an act that is rationalised and operationalised on the basis of the 'exceptionalism' argument. It situates the rise of 'exceptionalism' as a discourse and practice of contemporary global security policies in a historical context. Its origins can be found in the first Gulf War which has often been described as an action undertaken in 'exceptional circumstances'. This process of 'exceptionalism' turned a new corner during the Kosovo and East Timor conflicts, which came onto the international agenda following the outbreak of violence in the late-1990s. The military action of the North Atlantic Treaty Organization (NATO) against Serbia in 1999 was defended by the intervening powers as an 'exceptional' operation and the subsequent placement of Kosovo under the administration of the United Nations (UN) was put forward as an 'exceptional' institutional arrangement. Similarly, East Timor, where the UN assumed all sovereign powers to supervise the territory's transition to independence, is also viewed as an exceptional case of intervention.

Structure of the book

In the next two chapters, theoretical and conceptual dimensions of contemporary state-building interventions justified from the perspective of exeptionalism are investigated in detail. A synthesised analytical framework is also offered to examine the emerging political environment in Kosovo, East Timor and northern Iraq. This analytical framework draws upon McAdam's discussion on 'political opportunity structures'[104] and Agamben's theory of 'exception-as-the-rule'.[105] This framework demonstrates how the involvement of foreign actors in the domestic sphere has created new 'opportunity structures' for local interest groups in an opened up political landscape, while, at the same time, setting intervention as the 'dominant paradigm of government' in the newly emerging political environment.

Chapter 4 examines the international involvement in the Kosovo conflict rooted in the opposing sovereignty claims of Belgrade and Pristina over the territory of Kosovo and its population. It focuses on NATO's launch of military action against Serbia in March 1999 and the subsequent conversion of Kosovo into a UN protectorate. A critical analysis of the key background events, including the international recognition of Slovenia and Croatia, is also provided. This includes the evolution of the Kosovo Albanian leadership's strategic approach to internationalise the conflict and attract support for an independent Republic of Kosovo. The chapter explores how NATO intervention rationalised as an 'exceptional' event produced new 'exceptional' political and social realities in Kosovo. An in-depth analysis of these developments demonstrates how intervention created 'new opportunity structures' for the Kosovo Albanians and paved the way for the territory's formal secession from Serbia that was argued to have been conditioned by the 'irreversible realities' on the ground.

Chapter 5 provides a discussion of the discursive and operational aspects of the international military interventions in Iraq in 1991 and 2003. It addresses the 'enlargement' of the Kurdish question by analysing key aspects of the post-military intervention political process in northern Iraq such as the establishment of the KRG and its de facto exercise of state identity in its designated territory. It pays particular attention to the strategic interactions between the intervening powers and local Kurdish groups and how this impacted on the trajectory of sovereignty. It also provides a discussion of how the exercise of extensive autonomy by the Kurdish political leadership has become a contentious issue for the central government in Baghdad. The KRG's formation and control of its own military forces (the Peshmerga), establishment of diplomatic representations in European capitals and the United States (US) as well as its plans to create a free trade zone with Turkey are seen by the central government as a step towards independence. Indeed, KRG President Massoud Barzani's latest independence referendum announcement in Washington on 6 May 2015 following meetings with President Obama and Vice-President Biden attests to the Iraqi Kurdish leadership's efforts to garner international support for the exercise of formal statehood status 'as soon as the war [against the Islamic State] ends'.[106]

Chapter 6 discusses the major political developments leading to the deployment of an Australian-led multinational security force to East Timor in late-1999 and the establishment of a large, 'exceptional' UN state-building mission entrusted with all sovereign powers to supervise the territory's transition to political independence. It also examines the structural transformations (including operational, political and ideological) the East Timorese resistance movement experienced from the mid 1980s onwards. This helps evaluate how the East Timor conflict which remained a peripheral question to the international community for years started attracting international attention in the 1990s. A detailed analysis of the reorganisation of the Timorese resistance in association with the changes in the wider international context becomes instrumental to understand the symbiotic relationship between foreign and domestic actors of political change.

Concluding remarks are discussed in the final chapter, which summarises the contemporary policy and practice of international intervention as an act of state-making. The key points made in relation to the shifting dynamics of sovereignty in intervened states are recapped.

Notes

1 Helman and Ratner, 'Saving Failed States'.
2 Bull and Watson, *The Expansion of International Society*.
3 Jackson, 'Quasi-States, Dual Regimes, and Neoclassical Theory'; Jackson, *Quasi States: Sovereignty, International Relations, and the Third World*.
4 Helman and Ratner, 'Saving Failed States', 3.
5 Ibid.
6 Duffield, *Global Governance and the New Wars*.
7 Helman and Ratner, 'Saving Failed States'; Atwood, 'Suddenly Chaos'; Kaplan, 'The Coming Anarchy; Dorff, 'Democratization, Failed States and Peace Operations'; Kaldor, *New and Old Wars*.
8 Kaldor, *New and Old Wars*, 92.
9 Ibid.
10 Helman and Ratner, 8. See also Deng, 'State Collapse'; Woodward, 'Failed States'.
11 Fukuyama, *State-Building*; Rotberg, *When States Fail*; Ottaway and Meir, 'States at Risk and Failing States'.
12 Duffield, 'Social Reconstruction and the Radicalization of Development'.
13 See for example, DFID, *Why We Need to Work More Effectively in Fragile States*; UK Government, *Building Stability Overseas Strategy*, (2012), accessed 6 June 2014, www.gov.uk/government/uploads/system/uploads/attachment_data/file/32960/bsos-july-11.pdf; USAID, *Fragile States Strategy*.
14 Fukuyama, *State-Building*; Rotberg, *When States Fail*; Rice, 'The New National Security Strategy'; Dobbins *et al.*, *America's Role in Nation-Building*; Dobbins *et al.*, *The UN's Role in Nation-Building*.
15 Milliken and Krause, 'State Failure, State Collapse and State Reconstruction'; Bilgin and Morton, 'From "Rogue" to "Failed" States?'; Hameiri, 'Failed States or a Failed Paradigm?'.
16 Gros, 'Towards a Taxonomy of Failed States in the New World Order'.
17 Rotberg, *When States Fail*.
18 For details, see *Foreign Policy*, 'Fragile States Index 2014'.
19 See, for example, Bilgin and Morton, 'From "Rogue" to "Failed" States?'.
20 DFID, *Why We Need to Work More Effectively in Fragile States*, 7.
21 World Bank, 'Definitions of Fragility and Conflict, 2009'.
22 OECD, *Fragile States 2014*, 16.
23 Helman and Ratner, 'Saving Failed States', 3.
24 State Failure Task Force, *State Failure Task Force: Phase III Findings*, 3.
25 Ibid.
26 Collier, 'Breaking the Conflict Trap'.
27 Rotberg, *When States Fail*, 11.
28 Chabal and Daloz, *Africa Works*; Reno, *Corruption and State Politics in Sierra Leone*; Zartman, 'Introduction: Posing the Problem of State Collapse'; Rotberg, *When States Fail*; DFID, *Why We Need to Work More Effectively*.
29 Holsti, *The State, War, and the State of War*; Gros, 'Towards a Taxonomy'; Rotberg, *When States Fail*.
30 Gros, 'Towards a Taxonomy'; Di John, 'Oil Abundance and Violent Political Conflict'.

31 Migdal, *State in Society*.
32 Wilde, 'Representing International Territorial Administration', 89.
33 Duffield, 'Social Reconstruction', 1050.
34 Gros, 'Towards a Taxonomy', 462.
35 Rotberg, *When States Fail*, 9.
36 World Bank, *The State in a Changing World*.
37 See, for example, Ghani *et al.*, 'Closing the Sovereignty Gap'; Ghani and Lockhart, *Fixing Failed States*; AusAID, *Australian Aid*.
38 Fukuyama, *State-Building*, 9.
39 World Bank, *The State in a Changing World*; World Bank, *Capacity Building in Africa*.
40 Bilgin and Morton, 'From "Rogue" to "Failed" States'; Barkawi and Laffey, 'The Imperial Peace'; Duffield, *Global Governance and the New Wars*; Berger, 'From Nation-Building to State-Building' (2006).
41 Zartman, 'Putting States Back Together', 270.
42 Annan, *Support by the United Nations System of the Efforts of Governments to Promote and Consolidate New or Restored Democracies*, para. 15.
43 World Bank, *Post-Conflict Reconstruction*, 4.
44 Boutros-Ghali, *An Agenda for Democratization*; Annan, *The Causes of Conflict and the Promotion of Durable Peace and Sustainable Peace in Africa*; Gurr, *Peoples Versus States*; Rummel, 'Democracy, Power, Genocide, and Mass Murder'.
45 Richmond, *The Transformation of Peace*, 69–73.
46 Paris, 'International Peacebuilding and the "Mission Civilisatrice"'.
47 Fukuyama, 'The End of History?'.
48 Diamond *et al. Democracy in Developing Countries*, vol. 2, x. See also Sen, 'Democracy as a Universal Value'.
49 See, for example, Doyle, 'Kant, Liberal Legacies, and Foreign Affairs'.
50 Clinton, *A National Security Strategy of Engagement and Enlargement, 1995–1996*.
51 Boutros-Ghali, *The Interaction between Democracy and Development*, 12.
52 Sen, 'Democracy as a Universal Value', 7–8.
53 See for example, Torres and Anderson, 'Fragile States'; François and Sud, 'Promoting Stability and Development in Fragile and Failed States'.
54 DFID, *Why We Need to Work*.
55 Helman and Ratner, 'Saving Failed States'.
56 Zartman, 'Putting States Back Together'.
57 Rotberg, *When States Fail*.
58 Ghani and Lockhart, Fixing Failed States.
59 DFID, *Why We Need to Work*
60 Fukuyama, *State-Building*.
61 Pugh, 'The Political Economy of Peacebuilding', 34.
62 Zartman, 'Introduction', 9.
63 Helman and Ratner, 'Saving Failed States', 12
64 Ibid., 3.
65 Ibid., 13.
66 Ibid., 7–12.
67 Ibid, 12–18.

68 Wilde, 'Representing International Territorial Administration', 71–5.
69 Krasner, 'Sharing Sovereignty', 114.
70 Ibid., 119.
71 Ibid., 108.
72 Wilde, 'From Danzig to East Timor and Beyond'.
73 Ibid., 592–3.
74 Wilde, 'Representing International Territorial Administration', 85.
75 ICISS, 'The Responsibility to Protect', xii.
76 Ibid.
77 Ibid., 8.
78 Ibid.
79 Ibid., 44.
80 Ibid.
81 Ibid., xi.
82 This definition draws upon the distinction Neal makes between the 'exception' (events and situations that are designated as 'exceptional') and exceptionalism (i.e. those policies and practices that are legitimated through claims about necessary exceptions to the norm). For details, see Neal, 'Foucault in Guantánamo'.
83 See, for example, Fukuyama, *Statebuilding*; Ghani and Lockhart, *Fixing Failed States.*
84 See, for example, Bickerton *et al.*, *Politics without Sovereignty*; Chandler, *Empire in Denial*; Chandler, *International Statebuilding.*
85 Hameiri, *Regulating Statehood.*
86 Bellamy, 'The "Next Stage" in Peace Operations Theory'; Richmond, *The Transformation of Peace.*
87 Chandler, *Empire in Denial;* Chandler, *International Statebuilding.*
88 Hameiri, *Regulating Statehood.*
89 Lemay-Hébert, 'The "Empty-Shell" Approach'.
90 Ibid.
91 Chandler, *International Statebuilding.*
92 Chopra and Hohe, 'Participatory Intervention'; Richmond, *Peace in International Relations*; Richmond and Franks, *Liberal Peace Transitions.*
93 Lemay-Hébert, 'The Bifurcation of the Two Worlds'.
94 Ibid.
95 Pugh, 'The Political Economy of Peacebuilding'; Paris, *At War's End.*
96 Chopra and Hohe, 'Participatory Intervention'.
97 Richmond and Franks, *Liberal Peace Transitions*; Mac Ginty, 'Indigenous Peace-Making Versus the Liberal Peace'.
98 Pugh, 'The Political Economy of Peacebuilding'.
99 Paris and Sisk, *The Dilemmas of Statebuilding.*
100 Hameiri, *Regulating Statehood.*
101 Ibid.
102 Wendt and Barnett, 'Dependent State Formation and Third World Militarization', 337.
103 See, for example, Fukuyama, *State-Building.*
104 McAdam, 'Conceptual Origins, Current Problems, Future Directions'.
105 Agamben, *The State of Exception.*
106 Saeed, 'Barzani: Independence Will Come, and Peacefully'.

1 The myth of exceptional state-building

State-building operationalised in terms of exceptionalism, as discussed in the previous chapter, has become central to the discourse and practice of contemporary international intervention. The intrusive and long-term involvement of foreign agencies in domestic policy and institutional processes is justified as a necessary engagement conditioned by exceptional security and development challenges facing 'fragile' or 'conflict-affected' states. Bellamy, for instance, suggests that international intervention is not a discrete act with a clear beginning and end because international attempts to legitimise the use of military force on humanitarian grounds should be accompanied by longer-term programmes directed at conflict prevention and post-conflict reconstruction.[1] In this way, intervention becomes a means to transform these countries through near permanent engagement with the construction of the institutional and societal foundations of liberal democratic, market-oriented government models as part of a global security strategy.[2]

The intrusive and extended involvement of foreign state and non-state actors in the regulation of the domestic affairs of fragile states is now treated as a necessary action that seeks to prevent emergencies or crisis situations associated with domestic governance capacity of states. In this conception of prevention, intervention is argued to foster the sovereignty of states rather than challenging their political independence and territorial integrity. When foreign intervention is followed by territorial secession, rise of autonomous power centres or emergence of violent insurgencies, international agencies tend to argue that these situations are exceptional cases of state-building or unintended consequences of intervention. For instance, it was frequently emphasised by the Australian political leadership at the time that the 1999 military intervention resulting in an independent East Timorese state was a 'special case' that 'no parallels' could be established with other secessionist movements in the region such as Aceh and West Papua.[3]

Similarly, the recognition of internationally 'supervised independence' to Kosovo in 2008 was rationalised by leading Western governments as an exceptional method of conflict resolution. The outbreak of sectarian violence and insurgency in Iraq following the 2003 intervention, on the other hand, was explained by Western leaders as an unforseen development.[4] While the rest of the country was engulfed in violence and insecurity, northern Iraq ruled by the Kurdish Regional Government (KRG) has consolidated its existence as a 'de facto'[5] or 'quasi' state[6] following the US-led military intervention in 2003.

The centrality of exceptionalism to the discourse of intervention reflects intervening powers' efforts to avoid an operational framework that may force them to resolve or respond to similar situations in the same way in the future.[7] It is also important to acknowledge that while discourses or declaratory statements of international agencies cannot be accepted at face value, a critical analysis of the actions or decisions of state officials requires us to take into account these discourses or the justifications offered, as they constitute their 'representational practices' to legitimise their actions[8] or construction of a particular 'reality' that helps marginalise alternative understandings of such situations.[9] However, their justifications for their violation of certain norms (such as non-use of force or territorial integrity) by reference to other norms (such as human rights),[10] at the same time, are likely to give rise to a new rule or practice and produce new states of political and social affairs in intervened states.

Taking these into account as to the analysis of the effects of contemporary state-building interventions, I therefore would like to point to two kinds of effects which the policies and practices of intervention operationalised on the basis of the exceptionalism argument tend to produce: (1) normalisation or acceptance of the creation of states through intervention (or the normalisation of the idea that separatist movements are more likely to achieve their preferred statehood objectives through obtaining the support of the most powerful states); (2) normalisation of the involvement of foreign actors in domestic processes through longer-term intervention in the form of institutional capacity-building.

This being noted, foreign military intervention helps challenging local groups (such as self-determination movements and rebels) to achieve their political aspirations. This chapter investigates contemporary international interventions as a myth of exceptional state-building to demonstrate that the creation of new states through foreign interference is nothing exceptional. By new states, I refer to both recognised (Kosovo, East Timor and South Sudan) and non-recognised (or 'informal states')[11] (such as Northern Iraq, South Ossetia and Abkhazia) political entities that have established their existence as a result of great power intervention justified on humanitarian and security grounds. Rather than being exceptions, these cases illustrate how states are now created through foreign intervention and supervision.

In elaborating on this trend, the chapter examines the processes leading to the formation of new states by reference to the features of the relationships between intervening and local actors developing in the context of power struggles and mutual dependencies. After all, as noted earlier, the formation of states is essentially a power-driven process, as it entails not only the construction of competent government institutions for territorial control but also the acquisition of political power by one of the competing social groups and consolidation of their identity as an autonomous entity.[12] Therefore, the creation and distribution of political power as the basis of statehood is subject to constant contestation and negotiation by competing social groups. The key questions that need to be investigated in this regard are those that are concerned with the implications of interventions for the existing local power structures upon which sovereignty is based: How do the use of military force and the subsequent involvement of foreign agencies in the institutional and policy domain affect the dynamics of political power? How does the long-term involvement of foreign agencies in domestic policy-making transform the conditions of institutional and governmental order in intervened states? To be able answer these questions, it is essential to investigate the features of the relationships between intervening agencies and domestic groups developing in the context of a liberal peace framework, as discussed below.

Interveners and locals locked in the liberal peace paradigm

The interplay between interveners and local agencies remains as one of the under-investigated topics in relation to the construction of democratic state capacities in failing or fragile countries. In the 1990s, some scholars, inspired by Foucault's work on power, examined foreign development assistance as a discourse of power and control that objectified and instrumentalised Western interventionism.[13] These studies were focused on the hidden or subtle forms of power, surveillance and discipline behind international development policies, despite their seeming benign and well-meaning at first glance. A brief review of this literature may provide helpful insights into the contemporary forms of power exercised by foreign agencies to promote 'good governance' in fragile or post-conflict countries.

James Ferguson, for instance, applies Foucault's concept of discourse as a structured and power-ridden practice of constituting knowledge to examine the operation of the international 'development apparatus'.[14] His analysis is centred around a Canadian government-funded rural development project implemented in the African state of Lesotho in the 1970s and 1980s. One of the key points Ferguson emphasises is that even though numerous donor-funded projects consistently failed to achieve their intended objectives of agricultural development or poverty alleviation in Lesotho and elsewhere, these projects became instrumental in expanding the 'bureaucratic state power' and depoliticising the exercise of that power by political authorities.[15] Development assistance, in other words, emerged as an 'anti-politics machine' in that it has produced powerful constellations of control through seemingly apolitical projects. This becomes apparent in the rise of a discourse that depicts countries like Lesotho and others all in the same way: 'less developed countries' whose populations are classified as a collection of subsistence peasants that are 'isolated' from global markets.[16] The representation of former colonies in such terms helps rationalise planned social interventions in the name of modernising or bringing these 'isolated' societies into a closer relationship with the world economy, although in reality they were already in contact with global markets for a long time even before they became independent.[17] In addition to this, political and structural conditions of poverty such as inequalities in resource distribution, unemployment or low wages are excluded from the analyses of their economic and social underdevelopment. From these studies rather follows a reductionist strategy that treats poverty alleviation as a matter of technical improvements such as educating people, improving livestock and soil quality, and devising medium to long-term development plans.[18] In this way, international agencies present their role as politically neutral, technical missions seeking to improve the provision of services to the rural poor. In reality, however, development projects reshape rural social relations and create new bureaucracies and facilities such as administrative offices, roads or health services which are often appropriated as a powerful resource by governments and elites.[19]

In a similar fashion, Arturo Escobar looks at development as a historical construct or 'invention' that turned poor countries into objects of knowledge and management.[20] Escobar locates the origins of development as an instrument for Western capitalist domination in the rearrangement of world power that occurred during the immediate post-Second World War period. The decline of the colonial order and the 'discovery' of mass poverty on a global scale were some of these rearrangements.[21] Before the 1940s, Western governments' concern with poverty was conditioned by a conviction that any attempt to stimulate economic development in colonies was pointless because the natives did not have the capacity for science and technology needed for socio-economic progress.[22] Following the war, however, the chronic conditions of poverty or 'underdevelopment' in these now newly independent states came to be regarded as a threat not only to their populations but to the liberal, capitalist international order because it was commonly accepted that if poor countries were not rescued from their poverty, they would be lost to communism.[23] The recognition of poverty as a domestic and global social problem meant that it should be managed. The management of poverty, on the other hand, was dependent on new ways of intervention in almost every aspect of social life including education, health, sanitation, morality and employment.[24]

Behind the seemingly humanitarian concern and positive outlook of this development strategy, Escobar suggests, new forms of power and control were put in place. These mechanisms are framed in the language of development that presents Western societies' experience with industrialisation and economic prosperity as an objective, universal pathway that was supposedly to be followed by all others. The emerging development discourse also changed the characteristics of the relations between the rich, Western countries (now referred to as the 'first world') and poor countries (or the 'third world'). The 'third world' was defined relatively by reference to the wealth and material possessions of Western societies including their per capita income, technical expertise and management skills.[25] The definition of the 'third world' in terms of what it did not have also created the image that it is like a child in need of adult guidance.[26] These representations turned poor countries into an 'other' that should be monitored by the West on the basis of a 'secular theory of salvation'.[27] In this discourse, the 'third world' is presented as a homogenous bloc and its development is treated as a matter of transition from the status of poor to rich countries. With the erasure of differences between people, an Indonesian peasant, a Bedouin woman in Egypt, a Vietnamese child worker and a Liberian miner all appear the same: that is, poor and underdeveloped. Moreover, their poverty is articulated in a pathological manner as the source of instability and disorder that requires outside intervention. In this representation of the 'third world' as a monolithic entity, caught in a chronic pathological condition, experts of the West, like a good doctor, intervene to cure the diseased or dysfunctional social body.[28] The formula for success was also argued to be available to all countries, which means that any country that is willing to accept the guidance of its saviour can achieve development.[29] In this way, intervention is legitimised as a necessary action to alleviate the suffering of 'third world' people such as hunger and malnutrition. In fact, intervention is prescribed not only as a solution to their problems but as an opportunity to become like 'advanced' capitalist countries by replicating their modes of economic development such as industrialisation and urbanisation, rapid growth of material production and living standards, and the widespread adoption of modern education and cultural values.[30] This discourse of development as an instrument of regulation, Escobar concludes, has become the basis upon which policy frameworks are structured. Similar arguments about the role of discourses of sovereignty, democracy promotion and human rights protection in the construction and reproduction of a hierarchy of international identities (such as 'modern/traditional' or 'first world/third world') can also be found in the International Relations literature.[31]

More recent contributions to the development debate, on the other hand, have focused on the agency and capacity of both foreign and local actors. These actors-oriented analyses point to the reconfiguration of aid relationships in the rhetoric of 'partnership', 'participation' and 'ownership',[32] and investigate the creation and socialisation of knowledge as an outcome of interactions and negotiations between different actors.[33] In this approach, intervention is analysed in terms of the changing dynamics and differential interpretations of development operations, and local actors are viewed as strategic agents rather than passive recipients of externally designed interventionist policy frameworks.[34] Mosse, for instance, looks at domestic actors (such as policy elites, bureaucrats, businesses, technicians, NGO staff, aid workers, etc) as 'beneficiaries' or 'consumers' of development assistance who re-interpret and strategise ways of manipulating the rhetorics and rules of aid programmes.[35] He criticises deconstructionist analyses such as those offered by Escobar and Ferguson for situating power 'too vaguely' in the West and the state organisation, and relying 'so much' on donor policy texts as representations of discourse.[36] Policy models privileged in donor texts as 'good governance' or 'empowerment', Mosse suggests, can only be understood in terms of the characteristics of institutions and social relationships surrounding these institutions.[37] From the perspective of actors-focused analyses, deconstructionist approaches, in other words, appear to overstate the capacity of international agencies to objectify and dominate 'third world people' and portray locals as a homogeneous group of actors resisting foreign domination.[38]

Another key aspect of donor-recipient power relations, as discussed in the more recent literature, is the internalisation of the adjustment agenda by aid-dependent countries.[39] The language of 'partnership' and 'ownership', as noted earlier, is now invoked frequently to indicate that national governments are the ones sitting in the driver's seat, even though in reality donors exercise a great deal of influence and power over the setting of development priorities. Country development strategies or poverty reduction action plans, for instance, are prepared by domestic officials in conjunction with internationally advocated administrative reforms to secure donor funding.[40] Intervention is therefore conducted in ways that blur distinctions between external and internal boundaries and interests. This is exemplified by the establishment of co-staffed policy offices within the Ministries of Finance and other key public departments in many aid recipient countries as well as by the portrayal of these countries as 'best reformers' in policy evaluation reports. What distinguishes these 'post-conditionality' regimes from conditionality regimes is that, rather than threatening to withdraw funding, donors now selectively employ aid programmes to encourage the adoption of neo-liberal economic policies and institutional mechanisms (such as anti-corruption measures) that underpin global market transactions.[41] Through 'post-conditionality', donors become 'part of the state itself' not just because the budgeting process becomes fully dependent on foreign funding but because international agencies are closely involved in every aspect of policy-making from economic planning and budget execution to information management.[42] The power wielded by international financial institutions and development agencies, in other words, is not exercised externally to the state but integrated into its machinery through capacity-building initiatives. Moreover, today's donor-recipient relationships are based on mutual but unequal dependencies that reflect a convergence of interests. On one hand, the presentation of some countries as success stories is relevant for continued practices of neo-liberally informed 'good governance' frameworks as they provide an important point of reference to promote the idea that adjustment reforms work and they should be implemented no matter how painful and disruptive they might be in the first place.[43] The elites of aid recipient nations, on the other hand, continue to receive the necessary financial resources and political support they need in their efforts to consolidate their hold on state power.

Thus, the types of relationships between international and local actors shape the conditions and outcomes of state-building interventions. What is not much discussed in this regard, however, is the political and social context within which these relationships are formed and develop. The interactions between internationals and locals are rather depicted in dualistic terms in the critical literature on international state-building. Interventions are examined in terms of coercively introduced alien institutions and values, while locals are analysed as homogenous actors resisting the policy frameworks imposed from the outside.

Critiques of the liberal peace

The above domination/resistance dichotomy, however, does not fully reflect the dynamics of interveners–locals relationships, even though the power dimensions of contemporary state-building interventions, presented as technical, administrative projects, are well demonstrated in the critical literature. The key points raised in the critical literature can be summarised under three headings:

1 *Objectives*: that is, contemporary state-building interventions represent the specific preferences of the most powerful members of the international community, as evidenced in the projection of a particular type of state (i.e. liberal democratic market-oriented state structures) as a universal model of governance through a mixture of coercion and consensus.[44]
2 *Motives*: that is, the liberal peace thesis upon which these interventions are based is driven by a desire to achieve a radical societal transformation in non-Western societies.[45]
3 *Assumptions*: that is, the essentially interventionist state-building approaches are premised on certain assumptions about the transferability of the Western state to non-Western societies and the capacity of Western agencies to transform them.[46]

The focus of these critical analyses has therefore been largely on the ways in which state-building interventions have been conducted. For instance, in his analysis of the limits of liberal interventionism, Roland Paris describes contemporary post-conflict operations as 'social engineering' projects due to their experimentation with installing Western forms of political and economic organisation. He criticises the methods employed by the UN and other international agencies (i.e. the organisation of elections and introduction of market-oriented economic reforms following the conclusion of formal settlements) to achieve a rapid societal transformation through resting on the assumption that democratisation will shift conflict away from the battlefield to the electoral landscape and marketisation will promote economic growth and reduce the likelihood of conflict. Paris questions the validity of such policy assumptions by addressing the potential 'destabilising side effects' of rapid liberalisation such as the intensification of political rivalries and ethnic, religious or other divisions in an increasingly competitive environment as experienced during the course of peace operations in Angola, Rwanda, Bosnia, Croatia, Cambodia and El Salvador in the 1990s. These 'pathologies', Paris concludes, can be neutralised through an 'institutionalization before liberalisation' strategy which envisions a long-term regulatory mandate for international agencies.[47] This institutions-focused approach has been practised in many conflict-affected countries from Kosovo, East Timor and Sierra Leone to Iraq, Afghanistan and the Solomon Islands, where the UN and other international agencies have been actively involved in the construction of democratic state institutions through security sector reform, justice reform, public sector reform and other institutional capacity-development programs. However, the results on the ground have been less than successful, evidenced by the resumption of violence, authoritarian tendencies, high rates of poverty, social inequalities, inefficient service delivery and communal tensions in many post-conflict countries.

In a more recent work with Sisk, Paris explains the shortcomings of contemporary interventions as an outcome of 'insufficient understanding of state-building's complexities – in particular, its intrinsic tensions and contradictions'.[48] These contradictions, according to Paris, produce a series of policy dilemmas for international state-builders that are impossible to resolve due to them arising from 'competing (and sometimes contradictory) imperatives'[49] but may be 'better managed' through careful analysis of their roots.[50] Somewhat in contradiction to his previous analysis of contemporary peace operations as a present-day reincarnation of the colonial-era 'mission civilisatrice',[51] Paris cautions the critics of the liberal peace against equating it with imperialism and rejects their call for a radical shift in the policy and practice of peace-building.[52]

Focusing on meeting the human security needs of the people in post-conflict countries is one of the approaches formulated by some commentators to reform the current state-based approaches to post-conflict reconstruction.[53] Human security, as discussed in detail in UNDP's 1994 global human development report, symbolises a normative shift in the conception of security that has traditionally been associated with the protection of states from armed threats.[54] The concept indicates a broadening of security to include threats to personal, community, economic, political and environmental safety, as well as its deepening that is illustrated in the inclusion of social groups, communities and individuals in the subject matter of security policies.[55] Proponents of human security advocate its integration into post-conflict operations that would prioritise securing the human rights and well-being of the populations in conflict-affected countries rather than merely focusing on the creation of institutional capacities.[56] While this may seem to provide an attractive strategy to avoid the discouraging results of state-building interventions and 'emancipate' suffering individuals, critics such as Chandler point to the co-option of human security approaches by Western governments and perpetuation of hierarchies of power rather than producing real outcomes for the targeted populations, most of whom continue to live in poverty and dismal humanitarian conditions.[57]

A similar point is also taken up by Oliver Richmond, who, drawing upon Homi Bhabha's theorisation of resistance as hybridisation in the colonial encounter, proposes the concept of 'post-liberal peace' as another alternative approach.[58] The liberal peace, Richmond argues, is a highly interventionist project, as it includes the notion of 'victor's peace', which derives from the Realist idea that 'a peace that rests on a military victory, and upon the hegemony or domination of a victor peace is more likely to survive'.[59] In addition to its projection through power, the legitimacy of the liberal peace is further undermined by its focus on the construction of a global and state-level order and failure to engage with the local context ingrained in a plurality of concerns, customs, identities and day-to-day life activities. The liberal peace, in other words, tends to distance individuals in post-conflict societies, as it fails to negotiate with local actors in political terms. Peace, however, Richmond emphasises, cannot be achieved without engaging with 'the everyday', which can be described as a dynamic space 'where local individuals and communities live and develop political strategies'.[60] The neglect of 'the everyday', on the other hand, provokes open or hidden forms of reactions and resistance from the population such as direct opposition, limited co-operation, civil disobedience, co-option or manipulation of newly crafted institutions, and the articulation of public demands for the nationalisation of governance structures as illustrated in the 'Kosovanisation', 'Timorisation' and 'Afghanisation' campaigns initiated against state-building administrations.[61] From these reactions and resistance emerges a 'hybridity' that combines the elements of liberalism with indigenous traditions and governance practices. The emerging liberal-local hybridity, according to Richmond, constitutes a shift towards a 'post-liberal peace', where citizenship, rights and duties carry an everyday meaning and a new social contract is achieved. Through this contract, localised models of peace-building are recognised, customary processes are incorporated into governance systems, and social welfare and justice are prioritised. With this new contract established through resistance, Richmond concludes, individuals are also connected to state institutions and politics.[62]

The concept of 'life welfare' outlined by Pugh *et al.* stands as an alternative to the liberal peace.[63] Pugh discusses elsewhere that neo-liberal economic policies (such as macro-economic stability, privatisation and trade liberalisation) promoted by the liberal peace project as a solution to the problems of post-conflict societies not only serve hegemonic interests of Western powers but reproduce the conditions of conflict (such as poverty, inequalities and divisions) in these countries.[64] Rather than resorting to revisionism (or trying to address the problems faced in contemporary interventions through introducing global policy reforms without questioning the assumptions of the liberal peace paradigm), Pugh calls for an 'inclusive/emancipatory' approach that would generate greater 'participation of local actors' and discussion of alternative options.[65] One of the possible ways that may facilitate the emancipation of local communities, according to Pugh *et al.*, is incorporating alternative notions of life into peace-building models that would encompass the individual, community, the biosphere and planetary environment. This is what they define as 'life welfare' that provides an alternative framework not only to the liberal peace but human security. For these writers, human security has emancipatory potential in itself but the way it has been operationalised serves the interests of global capitalism, as illustrated by the securitisation of local political economies to legitimise Western military interventions and institutions-focused disciplinary programmes and the prioritisation of macroeconomic stability over social welfare in poverty reduction programs.[66] Life welfare, on the other hand, they emphasise, is conceptualised in an 'unsecuritised language' that takes the individual as a social being, connects environmental, physiological and biological processes to economic processes, and rejects the imposition of Western principles as universal models of social organisation.

The underlying assumptions of the current state-building paradigm formulated within the liberal peace framework have also been challenged in other critical studies focusing on state sovereignty. Bellamy *et al.*, for instance, conceptualise contemporary interventions as 'post-Westphalian' operations based on the notion of 'sovereignty as responsibility' as opposed to 'traditional' peace missions of the Cold War that sought to maintain a 'Westphalian' society of states on the basis of the non-intervention principle.[67] This normative shift from sovereignty as immunity from foreign interference to sovereignty as responsibility (i.e. the idea that states can enjoy non-interference so long as they protect the human rights of their citizens), Bellamy emphasises elsewhere, is closely associated with certain assumptions made about the relationship between war and peace, global politics, and the capacity and role of international agencies to act as neutral peace-builders.[68] These assumptions, Bellamy notes, shape the contours of prevailing instrumentalist approaches, which are concerned with identifying the functional problems encountered in peace operations rather than addressing their political aspects, such as the making of decisions on when and how to intervene and what objectives should be pursued in humanitarian crises situations. Such 'problem-solving' approaches, framed by interveners as a series of responses to seemingly objective problems that exist exogenously to them, not only fail to produce the necessary conditions for emancipation and the eradication of human insecurity but complicate the long-term effects of relations between global cores and peripheries.[69]

For Chandler, however, these analyses of the liberal peace and its basic assumptions are not really critiques of current interventionist practices but apology for the limited success of state-building projects, as they imply that these policies have not been properly implemented due to interveners' lack of knowledge about the 'everyday life' in non-Western countries.[70] In these studies, Chandler suggests, the binary oppositions between a liberal West and non-liberal Other are also reinforced because they not only overemphasise the liberal character of current institutions-focused interventions but also portray intervened societies as an obstacle to the spread of Western aspirations of social peace and progress or as a resistant subject whose identity is threatened by liberal peace policies. Thus, the expression of 'post-liberal', according to Chandler, signals that the classical liberal rights-based conceptions of state–society relationships are now transformed through the state-building paradigm: that is, in the past, autonomy of individuals was treated as the basis upon which democratic government institutions are constituted, while today's state-building paradigm problematises autonomy as it insists that the capacity of individuals should be built first.[71] The current state-building approaches, in other words, frame intervention as a necessary course of action to construct sovereignty by constructing capacity, as sovereignty is now equated with capacity rather than the right to political autonomy and self-government.[72] This project of democratisation, Chandler concludes, is bound to fail because democracy cannot be achieved without exercise of policy-making autonomy and paying attention to local demands and pressures. By abstracting sovereignty from society, regulatory mechanisms rather result in the erosion of sovereignty and institutionalisation of 'phantom states' whose governing institutions may enjoy extensive external support but have little or no legitimacy in the eyes of their populations.[73]

Another important point that Chandler makes in this regard is that the language of 'empowerment', 'partnership' and 'ownership' advocated in donor guidelines for improved capacity-development outcomes masks the extent of powers and influence international agencies exercise over domestic policy-making without any accountability to domestic populations.[74] The OECD, for instance, sets out ownership as a key pillar of successful institutional reforms by reference to an emerging 'consensus' between donor and host countries that leaves capacity development 'primarily [with] the responsibility of partner countries, with donors playing a supportive role'.[75] This approach is also advocated by the World Bank which defines capacity development in terms of a

> locally driven process of learning by leaders, coalitions and other agents of change that brings about changes in sociopolitical, policy-related, and organizational factors to enhance local ownership for and the effectiveness and efficiency of efforts to achieve a development goal.[76]

While 'there is much talk of ownership', in practice, however, locals are treated as agents who are 'supposed to own what outsiders tell them to'[77] in relation to the implementation of seemingly technocratic but essentially 'social engineering' projects[78] based on the policy objectives designed and prioritised according to donor preferences, their timetables and strategies. For intervening states, local ownership therefore appears to be a matter of finding 'importing elites' who could be trusted to take 'ownership of 'our' ideas'.[79]

In addition to donors' conditioning of aid or organisational membership on the adoption of certain policies,[80] this form of international regulatory controls presented as 'partnership' is also exemplified by the placement of foreign officials as co-workers or line managers in critical state institutions such as the police service, finance and justice departments to proceed with implementation of counter-terrorism measures and neo-liberal institutional reforms in almost all developing countries.[81] Even where intervention is conducted in 'conventional' ways such as invasion and occupation, Chandler notes, interveners still tend to cast their role as facilitators of democratic self-governance. Despite the rapid transfer of formal administrative powers to the Afghan and Iraqi authorities shortly following the military operations, significant powers, however, still resided with foreign civilian and military agencies. This is what Chandler calls an 'empire in denial', which refers to a non-territorial kind of domination that enables Western actors to exercise intrusive powers while escaping from responsibility for outcomes of interventions. When their policies fail to deliver the stated objectives of transforming fragile countries into effectively and democratically functioning liberal sovereign polities, international agencies rather resort to a highly well-known defensive argument: that is, 'we tried but they failed'.[82]

While providing significant insights into the power dimensions of state-building interventions, Chandler's analysis of the reproduction of sovereign incapacity as an outcome of the marginalisation of the domestic political process and of distancing of local populations from internationally regulated governing institutions obscures the essentially symbiotic relationships between external and local actors that shape and reshape the dynamics of power upon which sovereignty is based. Sovereignty is often taken to mean the authority states exercise over their territory and their recognition by other states, even though its meaning is inscribed and re-inscribed through the practices of states.[83] Its contested nature, according to Cynthia Weber, is exemplified by the co-existence of different forms of state sovereignty (e.g. democratic, authoritarian, capitalist, socialist regimes) in modern global politics and changing elements of state power that include particular privileges and competencies states have had over time.[84]

In his analysis of sovereignty as an example of 'organised hypocrisy' (which refers to rulers' violation of sovereignty depending on their calculations of interests despite their formal acceptance of it as a foundational principle of contemporary international politics), Krasner highlights four ways in which the term has been employed: *international legal sovereignty*, referring to state practices associated with mutual recognition between territorial entities that exercise formal juridical independence; *Westphalian sovereignty*, referring to a political organisation that is based on the exclusion of external actors from domestic authority structures; *domestic sovereignty*, referring to the formal organisation of authoritative decision-making structures and the ability of public authorities to exercise effective control within their borders; *interdependence sovereignty*, referring to the ability of public authorities to regulate the flow of people, goods, ideas, pollutants or capital across their territorial boundaries.[85]

Notwithstanding diverging views on what it actually entails, the idea of sovereignty has had a strong emotional and political appeal, as reflected in the struggle of many national groups to 'earn' sovereign statehood status.[86] The appeal of sovereignty associated with 'imagined communities' as the main source of political legitimacy[87] following the French Revolution and industrialisation[88] derives from certain material and ideational benefits and opportunities it provides.[89] First, sovereignty is considered as a 'ticket of general admission to the international arena', as the acquisition of sovereign statehood status through recognition brings entitlement to certain international rights such as expropriation, diplomatic immunity and national jurisdictions.[90] Second, recognition enables territorial rulers to receive external resources to stay in power and pursue the security and economic interests of their constituencies such as participation in international organisations and access to capital markets.[91] On the other hand, aspiring nations' ability to 'earn' sovereignty has often been dependent on the availability of external support, as mirrored in the experience of many state-seeking nations such as the successor states of the Ottoman Empire in the nineteenth century including Egypt, Greece, Serbia and Bulgaria.[92] A closer look into their path to statehood also reveals that in their search for recognition as sovereign entities through foreign military and political intervention, these nations became vulnerable to continuing external interference and regulation.[93] Moreover, the experience of Egypt is particularly illustrative for showing how the conditioning of the recognition of sovereign status on certain state behaviour is indeed an old practice. Following its acquisition of semi-independent status from the Ottoman Empire during the 1840s, Egypt was invited by European powers to join the 'Public System of Europe' as an equal power. However, later in the 1870s it was excluded from European organisations due to Egyptian leaders' 'barbaric' behaviour and inability to meet the 'standard of civilisation'.[94]

Regarding the centrality of external support to the attainment of statehood status, the process of decolonisation has occupied a particular place in the sovereignty debate. According to Robert Jackson, for instance, the sovereign status former colonies have enjoyed is 'primarily juridical' because they were created through extension of the self-determination principle, while being unable to demonstrate the de facto attributes of statehood defined in terms of internal self-government capacity such as law enforcement, provision of public security, welfare promotion, and application of science and technology.[95] Deriving his analysis of sovereignty from Isaiah Berlin's distinction between positive and negative liberty, Jackson's conception of juridical and empirical statehood informs the ideational foundations of contemporary state-building interventions. Negative sovereignty (or juridical statehood), for Jackson, represents a 'formal-legal condition' that enables the exercise of a right to 'freedom from outside interference … upon which a society of independent and formally equal states fundamentally rests'.[96] Positive sovereignty (or empirical statehood), on the other hand, refers to a 'substantive rather than a formal condition' that designates not only states' entitlement to non-interference but their possession of governmental capacity to provide political goods to their citizens, advance development objectives and take part in alliances and other international arrangements.[97] Most of the post-colonial states, according to Jackson, are 'quasi states' whose existence is propped up through international recognition, even though they possess limited or no functioning institutions and government capabilities.

Jackson's conception of quasi states often referred to in the context of contemporary state-building interventions has been challenged by many scholars including those who have focused their analysis on unrecognised states whose origins lie in self-determination conflicts. Kolsto, for example, suggests that the term 'quasi states' applies to those entities that have seceded from another state and gained de facto control over the territory they claim to rule but failed to obtain recognition from other states, for example South Ossetia, Abkhazia, Nagorno-Karabakh, Somaliland, Taiwan and the Turkish Republic of Northern Cyprus (TRNC).[98] In their search for recognition, the leaderships of these polities often strive to demonstrate their institutional effectiveness and democratic credentials to 'earn' external sovereignty. Most of these entities also maintain their existence through external patronage and assistance. For instance, Abkhazia and South Ossetia rely on Russian support and military presence, while the TRNC is heavily dependent on Turkey's military, economic, diplomatic and political backing. In some other cases of conflicts over sovereignty such as Kosovo and Kurdish-controlled lands in Iraq, international organisations such as the UN and NATO functioned like an external patron.[99] Regarding the settlement of secessionist conflicts through recognition, as Kolsto notes, international agencies' 'sympathies' have played a key role; however, the international engagement has been marked by inconsistency. While in some cases, international actors have been in favour of recognition (such as the admission of new states during the dissolution of the Soviet Union and Yugoslavia), in some others they chose to freeze conflicts through long-term peacekeeping operations and negotiations (such as Cyprus). However, the settlement of quasi state conflicts has implications for other cases of secession. For instance, a parent state's recapturing of its lost territory through military action or the granting of international recognition to one quasi state on an 'exceptional' basis is likely to encourage leaders of remaining parent states and seceding entities to 'try the same solution'.[100] From the perspective of secessionist groups, this denotes the importance of finding a strong and resourceful external patron state that will help protect them from intervention and collapse or achieve the preferred outcome of recognised sovereign status.[101] Sovereignty and its co-existent principle, non-intervention, can therefore be conceived as an 'instrument of politics'[102] that determines both the scope and outcomes of claims to power and authority.

A synthesised analytical approach to investigate the symbiotic relationships between intervenors and locals

As discussed above, the critical literature on state-building examines the effects of interventions on the sovereignty of intervened states in terms of the imposition of alien institutions and values and denial of policy-making autonomy to local agencies[103] or the emergence of hybridised political orders as a result of negotiation and co-option of internationally advocated state-building projects.[104] Clearly, the asymmetries in power and resources shape the interactions between foreign and local actors. Their ability to resist or subvert liberal peace frameworks is also limited. However, these analyses of interventions do not tell us how the involvement of foreign agencies in essentially sovereignty-related conflicts impacts on the dynamics of political power upon which state institutions are structured. Because actors try to achieve their objectives through engaging in symbiotic relationships rather than simply relying on their material capabilities, a synthesised analytical approach may provide a helpful approach to investigate the transformative effects of state-building interventions on the ways in which power is distributed and exercised.

Power operates within relationships that develop in a dynamic political context, as power, Elias points out, is 'not an amulet possessed by one person, and not another; it is a structural characteristic of human relationships – of *all* human relationships'.[105] Because power is relational rather than a thing, actors are involved in different levels and alignments of relationships that are determined by the relative strength of others and moves to control or constrain their ability.[106] This means that power is a matter of degree because if 'we are more dependent on others than they are on us, more directed by others than they are by us, they have power over us'.[107] The configurations of power that parties form operate in a dynamic context. From these dynamic processes different patterns of power and outcomes emerge, as the kinds of constraints actors exert on each other result from the 'particular nature of their relatedness and interdependence as players'.[108]

A critical analysis of the processes through which state capacity-development programmes are executed in fragile countries therefore requires a closer look into the political context within which actors make their claim for power and rule-making authority in light of converging interests and inter-dependencies. This entails untangling the dynamics of the state targeted by these programmes. The classical definition of the state offered by Weber as 'a human community that (successfully) claims the *monopoly of the legitimate use of physical force* within a given territory'[109] indicates an ideal type of statehood. This image of the state as a supposedly 'coherent, controlling organization in a given territory' sits uneasily with the actual practices of its various parts.[110] Thus, rather than being a static, 'integrated and autonomous' entity that controls 'all rule making', the state is 'embedded' in a social framework that determines its claim to create and maintain the rules that structure and govern political and social life.[111] The engagement of its fragments (e.g. legislators, bureaucracies, political parties) with other 'social forces' such as clans, tribes, families, domestic businesses, political parties and multinational corporations produces coalitions and networks between various parts of the state and social actors, which affect the formulation and actual practice of policies in terms of a mutually transformative dynamic. These forces may accept or resist state policies and initiatives, depending on the material and ideational incentives these coalitions generate. Understood as such, the state can be conceptualised as a 'field of power', where competing social forces, including state agencies, are involved in mutually transformative struggles over the definition of rules governing their day-to-day behaviour.[112] Thus, the types of relationships between the state organisation and powerful social actors embodied in dynamic alliances of interests determine the outcomes of policy-making processes.

When applied to the analysis of the political space in intervened states, it appears that the symbiotic relationships between foreign state-builders and local political groups are determined by their agendas. In this relationship, the former are concerned with the implementation of capacity-development programmes which requires their embracement by local constituencies, while the latter seek to attain international support to achieve their ultimate political aspirations. The policy sphere turns into a site of mutually reinforcing agendas where international and local political objectives are brought into some sort of mutually supporting balance. Practices of positive remarks and praising become a key feature of this process. International agencies need success stories for the justification and legitimisation of their presence and the policy reforms they advocate. Loudly praised accounts of developing local performance and publically expressed stories about progress with stability and democratic governance serve to continue with implementation of capacity-building strategies and provide a reference point for promoting neo-liberal policy agendas in other fragile or conflict-affected countries. Expressing their commitment to democratic governance principles such as human rights and capacity to cooperate against global security threats associated with state failure such as terrorism, local groups, on the other hand, strive to achieve the endorsement of international actors for formal recognition of statehood. The mutually reinforcing different agendas of international and local actors are also accommodated by efforts to design the institutional setting in such a way that facilitates particular political objectives. This includes the designing of electoral structures, organisation of elections and drafting of constitutions that reflect the conditions of local balance of power and preferred state-making outcomes. The way in which policies are made in intervened states, in other words, privileges certain interests and outcomes over others.

The policy sphere in intervened states can therefore be conceptualised as a contentious 'field of power' where different groups of actors engage in symbiotic relationships to exert political authority over the definition of rules that govern the day-to-day functioning of politics and society. Viewed as such, international agencies, national elites, local community leaders and other power holders all appear to be competing 'social forces' that are involved in mutually transformative negotiations and struggles over the rules of the exercise of political authority across multiple arenas of this 'field of power'. In this context, the resources which international state-builders provide create opportunities (as well as constraints) for domestic actors to access the reins of power or consolidate their hold on power. For a sustainable intervention, on the other hand, external agents require the cooperation and support of local stakeholders who possess the necessary knowledge, competencies and connections to advance preferred policy objectives. This makes it clear that the types of relationships between international and domestic actors embodied in dynamic alliances of interests determine the way in which the capacity of the state is created.

It therefore becomes clear that a synthesised analytical approach may help clarify the emerging conditions of the political space and types of opportunities created through foreign intervention, and the practices and processes of state-making that are rationalised and operationalised on the basis of exceptionalism, as detailed in the next chapter.

Conclusion

The current state-building approaches are premised on the claim that the involvement of foreign agencies in the domestic affairs of fragile or failed states does not challenge the territorial integrity and political independence of host states. The situations of territorial secession, insurgencies or rising power centres following the use of military force are rather explained by reference to the exceptional nature of these cases of state-building or unintended consequences of intervention. Such references, however, tell us little about the relationships between intervening agencies and domestic groups that actually shape the outcomes of intervention premised on the liberal peace paradigm. International and domestic actors are involved in a symbiotic relationship that is rooted in mutual dependencies and converging interests.

These interventions have been rationalised from a perspective of exceptionalism, as manifested by the justification of wide-ranging powers and authority exercised by intervening agencies. The patchy results in the creation of democratic state capacity as a foundation of sustainable peace in many 'reconstructed' states have also encouraged the questioning of the motives and assumptions of the liberal peace paradigm and given rise to some alternative approaches such as human security, 'post-liberal peace' and 'life welfare'. These critical analyses highlight the inherent limits of, and also contradictions in, state-building interventions and the specific aspects of the international–local interactions that are characterised by asymmetries in power and resources. However, they tend to examine the relations between intervening agencies and local groups through a mere dichotomy of domination/resistance. The policy environment in intervened states rather indicates a 'field of power' where competing 'social forces' including international state-builders and local factions are involved in a symbiotic relationship.

Notes

1 Bellamy, 'Humanitarian Responsibilities and Interventionist Claims in International Society', 331.
2 Paris, 'International Peacebuilding and the "Mission Civilisatrice"'.
3 Dupont, 'The Strategic Implications of an Independent East Timor', 197. On the operational aspects of the Australian military involvement in East Timor as an 'exceptional' case, see Cotton, *East Timor, Australia and Regional Order*.
4 For instance, former British Prime Minister Tony Blair writes in his memoirs published in 2010:

> I can say that never did I guess the nightmare that unfolded, and that too is part of the responsibility. The truth is we did not anticipate the role of al-Qaida or Iran. Whether we should have is another matter; and if we had anticipated, what we would have done about it is another matter again.
>
> (Blair, *A Journey*)

5 Charountaki, 'Turkish Foreign Policy and the Kurdistan Regional Government'.
6 Natali, *The Kurdish Quasi State*.
7 Roberts, 'NATO's "Humanitarian War" over Kosovo'.
8 Campbell, *Writing Security*.
9 Weldes, 'Constructing National Interests'.
10 Krasner, *Sovereignty*.
11 Isachenko, *The Making of Informal States*.
12 Wendt and Barnett, 'Dependent State Formation'.
13 See, for example, Ferguson, *Anti-Politics Machine*; Escobar, *Encountering Development*.
14 Ferguson, *Anti-Politics Machine*.
15 Ibid.
16 Ibid.
17 Ibid.
18 Ibid.
19 Ibid.
20 Escobar, *Encountering Development*, 17.
21 Ibid., 24–6.
22 Ibid.
23 Ibid., 34.
24 Ibid., 23.
25 Ibid.
26 Ibid., 30.
27 Ibid.
28 Ibid., 159.
29 Ibid.
30 Ibid., 4.
31 See, for example, Doty, *Imperial Encounters*.
32 Mosse, 'Global Governance and the Ethnography of International Aid'.
33 Mudege, *An Ethnography of Knowledge*.
34 Ibid.
35 Mosse, 'Global Governance and the Ethnography of International Aid'.
36 Ibid.
37 Mosse, 'Is Good Policy Unimplementable?'.
38 Mosse, 'Global Governance'.
39 Harrison, 'Post-Conditionality Politics and Administrative Reform'.
40 Ibid., 669.
41 Ibid., 658–60.
42 Ibid., 669.
43 Ibid, 661.
44 See, for example, Paris, 'International Peacebuilding and the "Mission Civ- ilisatrice"'; Paris, *At War's End*; Bellamy, 'The "Next Stage" in Peace Operations Theory?'.
45 Duffield, *Global Governance and the New Wars*; Paris, 'International Peacebuilding'; Richmond, 'The Problem of Peace'.
46 Paris, *At War's End*; Bellamy, 'The "Next Stage" in Peace Operations Theory?'.

47 Paris, *At War's End*.
48 Paris and Sisk, 'Introduction: Understanding the Contradictions of Postwar Statebuilding', 13.
49 Ibid.
50 Ibid., 18.
51 Paris, 'International Peacebuilding'.
52 Paris, 'Saving Liberal Peacebuilding'.
53 See, for example, Kaldor, *Human Security*.
54 UNDP, *Human Development Report 1994*.
55 Paris, 'Human Security', 97.
56 Kaldor, *Human Security*.
57 Chandler, 'Human Security'.
58 Richmond, 'Resistance and the Post-Liberal Peace'.
59 Richmond, 'The Problem of Peace', 293.
60 Richmond, 'Resistance and the Post-Liberal Peace', 670.
61 Richmond, *A Post-Liberal Peace*.
62 Richmond, 'Resistance and the Post-Liberal Peace', 686.
63 Pugh *et al.*, *Whose Peace?*.
64 Pugh, 'The Political Economy of Peacebuilding'.
65 Ibid., 24.
66 Pugh *et al.*, *Whose Peace?*, 395–7.
67 Bellamy *et al.*, *Understanding Peacekeeping*.
68 Bellamy, 'The "Next Stage"'.
69 Ibid.
70 Chandler, *International Statebuilding*.
71 Ibid.
72 Ibid.
73 Chandler, *Empire in Denial*.
74 Ibid; see also Bickerton, 'Exporting State Failure'.
75 OECD, *The Challenge of Capacity Development*.
76 Otoo *et al.*, *The Capacity Development Results Framework*, 3.
77 Boege *et al.*, 'On Hybrid Political Orders and Emerging States', 29.
78 Suhrke, 'Reconstruction as Modernisation'.
79 Ibid., 1292.
80 Chandler, *International Statebuilding*.
81 Bickerton, 'Exporting State Failure', 116.
82 Chandler, *Empire in Denial*, p. 79.
83 Weber, *Simulating Sovereignty*.
84 Ibid.
85 Krasner, *Sovereignty*.
86 Caspersen, *Unrecognized States*.
87 Anderson, *Imagined Communities*.
88 Osiander, 'Sovereignty, International Relations, and the Westphalian Myth'.
89 Krasner, *Sovereignty*.
90 Fowler and Bunck, *Law, Power, and the Sovereign State*, 12.
91 Ibid.
92 Ibid.

93 Ibid.
94 Mazower, *Governing the World*, 71.
95 Jackson, *Quasi States: Sovereignty, International Relations and the Third World*.
96 Ibid., 27.
97 Ibid.
98 Kolsto, 'The Sustainability and Future of Unrecognized Quasi-States'.
99 Ibid.
100 Ibid.
101 Caspersen, *Unrecognized States*.
102 Kurtulmus, *State Sovereignty*, 147.
103 Chandler, *Empire in Denial*; Bickerton, 'Exporting State Failure'.
104 Richmond, 'Resistance and the Liberal Peace'.
105 Elias, *What is Sociology?*, 74, emphasis in the original.
106 Ibid., 75.
107 Ibid., 93.
108 Ibid., 96.
109 Weber, *From Max Weber: Essays in Sociology*, 78, emphasis in the original.
110 Migdal, *State in Society*.
111 Ibid.
112 Ibid.

2 Theorising exceptional state-making[1]

As discussed in the previous chapter, the analyses of the relations between intervening and local agencies have tended to focus on the forms and ways of intervention rather than their specific role in the making of exceptional states that establish their existence as a new political entity through foreign interference. Interventions often rationalised as a necessary action to respond to exceptional dangers and threats are not neutral undertakings. Intervention changes the dynamics of power and the features of the political space in intervened states.

Exceptionalism has become a key element of the contemporary security discourse that has instrumentalised certain policies and practices as 'necessary exceptions to the norm'[2] particularly when dealing with failed states. The term 'failed state', as noted earlier, was coined by Helman and Ratner in the early 1990s to describe the breakdown of central authority structures and eruption of violence in places like Somalia, Liberia, Haiti and former Yugoslav and Soviet republics.[3] Since then, the failed state phenomenon has gained currency despite the lack of general agreement on what it is and what causes it. Deriving their views from the Western conceptions of statehood and a subjective interpretation of the institutional capabilities of the world's states a number of observers – politicians, journalists, policy analysts and scholars – have divided the world conceptually into zones, placing states along an imaginary scale starting with successful states and ending with failed states.[4] The latter, most of which are former colonies in Africa and Asia, are alleged to have failed to meet the criteria for successful statehood; the observers have labelled them 'weak', 'fragile', 'dysfunctional', 'failed' or 'collapsed' states.

The classification of the states under such headings provides a powerful rationalisation for external interference. State failure is often identified as the underlying cause of economic and political underdevelopment and a serious threat to regional and global security. Incapable public institutions are frequently singled out as the cause of state failure, while the factors behind institutional weaknesses, and their regional and international dimensions, are not often addressed. Indeed, the construction of democratic institutions of government capable of providing citizens with security and basic services by international agencies has been promoted as an achievable policy objective throughout the post-Cold War era. Depending on the ability and willingness of the domestic leaderships of these states, the state failure problem has been addressed through selectively undertaken state capacity-building interventions, ranging from peace-keeping, conditional use of foreign aid and forced regime change to the establishment of UN trusteeships and insertion of foreign civilian staff into key state institutions.[5]

Foreign intervention, however, bring about shifts in the dynamics of power in intervened states and these changes in the political space produce mixed outcomes. This chapter provides a synthesised theoretical framework to analyse these changes and their effects on the way in which sovereignty is organised in intervened states.

Conflict, opportunities and exceptions in state-making

It is now commonplace to argue that state-building interventions do not violate sovereignty, which has come to been defined in terms of states' 'good governance' capacity. Informed by a technocratic understanding of capacity, good governance is associated with states' institutional ability to function as effective and democratic entities in order to regulate conflict. From this perspective, conflict is understood as the breakdown of societies' supposedly 'natural' state of peace and harmony caused by weak or non-existent governance capacity. Intervention is prescribed as an early prevention strategy to address state failure symptoms such as declining wealth, political instability and criminal violence.[6] The introduction of right kinds of institutions and policies informed by a liberal understanding of peace (such as accountability, responsiveness, anti-corruption strategies, effective fiscal and budget management, etc) are thought to facilitate their transition to sustainable stability and development.[7] The extension of regulatory state-building mechanisms into almost all developing countries, both in conflict and peace,[8] in the name of capacity-building is a reflection of this approach.

Such an understanding of intervention as a continuous activity also constitutes the basis of the policy instruments put forward in the 2001 'Responsibility to Protect' report. The authors of the report set out a three-stage operational framework for international actors: that is, the international community has not only a 'responsibility to react' but a 'responsibility to prevent' and a 'responsibility to rebuild' those states whose leaderships are unable or unwilling to 'protect their own citizens from avoidable catastrophe – from mass murder and rape, from starvation'.[9] In the report, the use of military force is depicted as just 'one element in a continuum of intervention, which begins with preventive efforts and ends with the responsibility to rebuild'.[10] The policy measures that are available to international agencies, it is argued, range from constitutional power-sharing arrangements, deployment of good-offices missions, peace-keeping operations and development assistance to the use of sanctions and diplomatic isolation, human rights monitoring, prosecution of war crimes and crimes against humanity before the International Criminal Court and reforming state security institutions.[11] It is important to note that the principle of 'responsibility to protect' formulated from a holistic conception of intervention was formally endorsed by the UN General Assembly in 2005. By adopting the report, member states agreed to assist states with building 'capacity to protect their populations', help 'those which are under stress before crises and conflicts break out' and establish an 'early warning capability'.[12]

The involvement of foreign agencies in domestic institutional processes as part of a preventive policy agenda is framed as an action that helps close a 'sovereignty gap'.[13] The gap is claimed to arise where, though legally equal to other nation states under international law, fragile or failing states are functionally incapable of achieving security and development goals domestically. Intervention in the form of capacity-building 'partnerships' is therefore argued to facilitate the 'co-production' of sovereignty[14] rather challenging it.

The debate on sovereignty as an organising principle revolves around different opinions on the nature of the relationship between the states and their citizens. Some view it as the states' right to exercise autonomy over their territory and population. Morgenthau, for instance, defines sovereignty as 'the supreme authority to enact and enforce legal rules within that territory'.[15] According to Hinsley, sovereignty refers to 'the idea that there is a final and absolute political authority in the political community ... *and no final and absolute authority exists elsewhere*'.[16] Rather than defining sovereignty in terms of autonomous territorial authority, more recent conceptualisations are focused on states' functional ability to deliver public services such as security, education, health care and transportation.[17] For some others, sovereignty is not absolute but conditional on states' ability to meet certain criteria such as respect for human rights.[18] Proponents of a contingent understanding of sovereignty argue that the definition of sovereignty has changed in the post-Cold War era. For instance, Kofi Annan wrote in 1999 that sovereignty was 'being redefined' by the forces of economic globalisation, international cooperation and a rising human rights agenda that privilege the 'freedom of individuals' and instrumentalise the state as an actor 'at the service of their peoples'.[19] Sovereignty, according to some others, can be 'shared',[20] 'transferred',[21] 'contracted'[22] or 'pooled'.[23] From Morgenthau's perspective, however, attempts to 'share' or 'divide' sovereignty represent 'a significant symptom of the discrepancy between the actual and pretended relations existing between international law and international politics in the modern state system'.[24]

Indeed, sovereignty has always been a contested concept and its meaning has historically been 'fixed' or 'stabilised' through practices of intervention, as Cynthia Weber points out.[25] Sovereignty and intervention, in other words, co-exist and are defined by reference to each other, as any intervention is always followed by justifications offered by intervening states to legitimise their action. These justifications resolve the questions about the 'true' meaning and location of sovereignty and the boundaries between 'domestic' and 'international' spaces and communities constructed in the speeches of diplomats and state officials of intervening states.[26] These practices also produce an 'interpretative community' that will judge the legitimacy of intervention activity based on a set of assumed norms, define who the sovereign authority in the target state is and draw the sovereignty/intervention boundary.[27]

When applied to the analysis of contemporary state-building interventions justified as exceptional operations undertaken to contain the security threats supposedly inherent in fragile or failed states (such as terrorist groups, irregular migration and humanitarian emergencies), states' capacity to govern themselves (rather than the right to exercise political autonomy) is constructed as the true meaning and location of sovereign authority. In the same way, the meaning of intervention is 'stabilised' as an action that helps strengthen rather than violate sovereignty.

This method of meaning stabilisation is exemplified by the work of the Canadian government-chaired International Commission on Intervention and State Sovereignty (ICISS) which put forward the concept of 'responsibility to protect' (R2P) to replace the term 'humanitarian intervention' in 2001. The rationale behind this conceptual change, emphasised by the authors of the R2P report, was to shift the focus of the debate away from the right of intervention (which revolves around the question of when it is permissible to take military action against another state) to the urgent needs of the populations seeking protection and assistance. According to the authors, the focus on the right of humanitarian intervention was 'unhelpful' because it privileges the claims of intervening states rather the needs of potential beneficiaries of coercive action.[28] This conceptual shift produced the judgement about the 'true' meaning of sovereignty as responsibility by defining it in terms of the ability or willingness of states to protect their populations from 'avoidable catastrophe' rather than the right to self-government.[29] When a state is unable or unwilling to so protect its population, it is noted, this responsibility is assumed by the 'broader community of states'.[30] The authors of the report, in other words, 'fix' the meaning of sovereignty as responsibility and construct an international community that has a 'residual responsibility' and makes a judgement about the 'true' meaning and location of sovereignty: that is, the states that are able and willing to protect and promote the rights of their populations. States that are perceived to fail to do so are no longer treated as sovereign. The meaning of intervention is 'stabilised' in terms of coercive actions taken by other states to fulfil this responsibility of human rights protection on behalf of the governments and populations in failed states. When it comes to the meaning of military action, it is 'fixed' in terms of exceptionalism: that is, actions authorised in 'exceptional' or 'extreme cases' that involve situations of violence which 'genuinely 'shock the conscience of mankind', or which present such a clear and present danger to international security, that they require coercive military intervention'. The questions of what makes a particular case exceptional that should be responded to with military action and what levels of violence amount to an emergency situation that 'shocks the conscious of mankind' become a matter of interpretation and judgement by a supposed 'community of responsible states' that is implied in the speeches of the chairs of the ICISS. Moreover, the report sets out engagement after military action (such as construction of security and judicial institutions) within a framework of 'post-intervention obligations' to prevent the recurrence of conflict. These definitions draw the boundaries between sovereignty and intervention in terms of claimed capacity-development objectives for human rights protection and promotion that are again left to the judgement of a responsible community of states.

While framed as an objective, technical engagement with strengthening sovereignty defined in terms of governance and conflict regulation capacity, intervention does change the internal dynamics of political power upon which sovereignty is actually structured. The use of military force and other forms of intervention by foreign agencies creates a new state of political affairs in intervened states. The political space that is opened up through inclusion of new actors as a result of intervention

becomes a 'field of power' where a variety of competing societal interests struggle to dominate the control of power and resources.[31] After all,
politics is organised around 'bias' and 'scope of conflict'.[32] This means
that the structure of all political systems is structured in favour of the
'exploitation of some kinds of conflict and the suppression of others'.[33]
Conflicts, in other words, are organised to favour particular interests and
their outcome is determined by who gets involved in the political process
and who cannot: 'The number of people involved in any conflict determines what happens'.[34] Any change in the status of conflict is therefore
dependent on the ability of dominant political actors to isolate rival
groups and push them to the margins of the political landscape. It is also
linked to the capacity of challengers to define and socialise the conflict as
an issue with a broader involvement of actors because the inclusion of
new actors helps increase their bargaining power.[35] For instance, states
facing separatist movements or revolutionary wars try to keep the scope
of the conflict as narrow as possible in an attempt to restrict the operational ability of rival organisations to achieve their preferred outcomes,
while opposing groups strive to widen it through forming alliances[36] or
internationalise it through appealing to foreign agencies.

The success of social movements is therefore dependent on changes in
the 'structure of political opportunities'. Political opportunity structures
can be conceptualised as a set of formal institutional arrangements and
informal power relations in a given political system that may enhance or
constrain the ability of political groups to mobilise and make their claim
for power.[37] Their key elements include the relative openness or closure
of the institutionalised political system, stability or instability of political
alignments, presence or absence of allies, and the state's capacity and
propensity for repression.[38] Political opportunity structures have also an
international dimension. International trends and events such as changes
in trade and economics and proliferation of civil society and solidarity
networks (e.g. Amnesty International and Greenpeace) and pressure
groups lobbying for policy change also affect the dynamics of domestic
political opportunity structures.[39]

According to McAdam, 'any event or broad social process' such as
wars, international realignments and unemployment that are likely to
'undermine the calculations and assumptions on which the political establishment is structured' can be described as a structural change.[40] This,
however, does not necessarily mean that the shifts in the political status
quo and existing power relations automatically produce social movements. The formation of social movements is also dependent on the
strength of organisations, which is closely related to the availability of

resources to the aggregate population that enables them to capitalise on the opportunities created by the changes in the political system. These organisational resources range from leadership attributes and the existence of formal and informal group associations to solidarity incentives and developed communication networks. Another key factor in the formation of social movements, McAdam suggests, is 'cognitive liberation' which refers to the political consciousness of excluded groups about their circumstances and their ability to change them. That is, insurgent groups must recognise that the oppressive conditions they are facing are unjust and believe that they can be redressed through collective action.

In addition, divisions among elites, opening of political access points, the presence or absence of elite allies, the stability or instability of elite allies,[41] states' policy implementation capacity,[42] as well as ambiguities within states' political, ideological and institutional underpinnings[43] create new windows of opportunities for social movements. Expanding political structures entail not only structural changes but people's perceptions of these changes and power shifts as an opportunity. Indeed, regardless of 'how momentous a change appears in retrospect, it only becomes an "opportunity" when defined as such by a group of actors sufficiently well organized to act on this shared definition of the situation'.[44] Any changes in the opportunity structure can become an opportunity when groups identify it as a chance for mobilisation. Thus, opportunities can be missed if agencies are unprepared, disconnected or unable to interpret and use political and social developments in their favour.

When this conceptual framework is applied to analyse the political environment in intervened states, it becomes clear that external intervention in situations of ethnic, political or other conflicts brings shifts in conditions and structures of power. The use of military force and the establishment of international administrative arrangements result in a partial or complete removal of the political landscape from the jurisdiction of the respective central governments. These shifts in the balance of power relations are exemplified by the stationing of foreign troops, creation of transitional administrations (such as in Kosovo and East Timor) and the imposition of a no-fly zone (northern Iraq). These territories are transformed into an 'exceptional' site of governance or a 'zone of indeterminacy' where the boundaries between the inside and outside are blurred.[45] On the other hand, the forced withdrawal of the dominant state authorities enables challenging groups to exercise territorial control and operate in an environment that is secured by foreign military forces. They also take advantage of the flow of post-conflict recovery and reconstruction assistance provided by a plethora of donor agencies.

The political space is also opened up, with international agencies (e.g. the UN, United Nations Development Programme (UNDP), World Bank, aid workers, etc) acting as institutional capacity-builders. These zones remain within the geographical boundaries of intervened states but operate outside their legal and political reach. International actors are closely involved in the constitution of a new legal order based on democratic participation, accountability and international human rights standards. However, they maintain no organic connection to it, as foreign staff enjoy full immunity from any local criminal and international monitoring mechanisms.

Clearly, the shifts in the balance of power relations create fluidities over the political status of these zones and the exercise of political power there. With their newly set up democratic government institutions and adopted political symbols such as the flag and national anthem, these territories appear to function like a sovereign entity. Their existence, on the other hand, is not internationally recognised in legal terms. The populations in these territories find themselves part of a quasi state or protectorate-like authority.

Yet, these fluidities simultaneously open new windows of opportunity for previously oppressed social and political movements. Indeed, a 'zone of indeterminacy' created as a result of intervention can also be conceived as a 'zone of opportunities' where surrounding uncertainties can be utilised by local agencies to form a new political order and arrangement of sovereignty. Rather than a 'negation of sovereignty', intervention, in other words, becomes a 'necessary component of sovereignty', as it helps these agencies establish and sustain particular structures of power and interest.[46] This is evidenced in the creation of democratic self-government institutions in pursuit of 'earned sovereignty'. Referring to a 'conditional and progressive devolution of sovereign powers and authority from a state to a substate entity under international supervision', earned sovereignty is defined in terms of three elements: shared sovereignty, institution-building and a determination of final status.[47] During the stage of shared sovereignty, the substate entity exercises sovereignty with the host state or international organisations and begins construction of new institutions with the assistance of the latter. In the second phase, the substate entity continues working with the international community to develop the capacity of the newly created institutions. The third element entails the resolution of the final status of the substate entity through referendum or negotiated agreement with the host state, often with international mediation.[48] The determination of the final status issue is conditioned on the consent of the international community in the form of formal recognition.[49]

Earned sovereignty has become the main strategic approach of the leaderships of many unrecognised states from Taiwan, Somaliland and the Turkish Republic of Northern Cyprus to Nagorno-Karabakh and Kosovo. The newly established democratic institutions encourage discussion of the conflicts over sovereignty and present a manoeuvring space to expand the previously oppressed movement's sphere of influence at home and abroad. Operating in a relatively autonomous and freer political environment, formerly oppressed groups can also capitalise on their resources and surrounding ambiguities to legitimise and materialise their claim to statehood in the form of earned sovereignty. Through coalitions and alliances they form with domestic and international groups, they also may seek 'remedial secession' as a way of correcting or compensating for past deficiencies and wrongdoings of their parent states. Remedial secession, as described by Buchanan, entails the recognition of the right to secede in situations of gross injustice such as systematic violations of human rights, unjust military occupation or annexation of territories, and persistent violations of intrastate autonomy agreements by the host state.[50]

State-making, as discussed earlier, is a long-term dynamic process that is shaped by the relative capabilities of a variety of societal interests struggling to dominate the control of state power in a competitive 'field of power'. This process has also a socio-political aspect that entails transforming the political landscape through rewriting the rules of the political game. The institutional arrangements and policy choices made in relation to the exercise of political power (such as the adoption of electoral and constitutional systems, language policies and identity symbols) privilege particular outcomes over others. The way in which the formal rules of participation and contestation are made and institutionalised (e.g. the adoption of a parliamentary or presidential system, requirements for eligibility to run as an independent or party candidate in the elections, voting threshold, etc.) reflects particular constellations of power. In the case of zones of indeterminacy, the unifying factor for the groups struggling to dominate the uses of power becomes the achievement of statehood.

While offering new opportunities for previously oppressed political movements including territorial secession, the involvement of foreign actors in the institutional domain, operationalised on the basis of the 'exceptionalism' argument, may evolve into routines over time. Intervention may become the main constituent principle of the emerging political order, following Agamben's theory of 'exception-as-the-rule'.[51] What we are witnessing worldwide today, according to Agamben, is a permanent state of emergency in the face of what he terms a 'global civil war'.[52] This 'global civil war' manifests itself in the instrumentalisation of techniques and machinery of power without any consideration of legal rights (such as the denial of prisoners-of-war status to detainees in Guantánamo)[53] during the 'global war on terror' declared by the Bush administration in the aftermath of the September 11 attacks and the subsequent military interventions conducted against Afghanistan and Iraq in the name of destroying terrorist networks and other 'existential threats' associated with failed states. Western governments' increasing employment of exceptional security policies on both domestic and global levels (e.g. introduction of Guantánamo-like 'camps' and detention centres for asylum seekers, counter-terrorism legislation and the military action in Iraq without UN Security Council endorsement) reflects the emergence of a new form of regulation that presents security as the 'sole criterion of political legitimation'.[54]

On the other hand, security, according to 'securitisation' theorists, is not an objective condition but an act: a 'speech act', which means 'something is a security problem when the elites declare it to be so'.[55] The designation of an issue as a security matter is a self-referential practice of moving certain public issues out of the normal spectrum of politics placing them onto the agenda of panic politics. Through labelling something as an 'existential threat' to the survival of its referent object, political actors claim a right to eliminate it by taking extraordinary measures (e.g. secrecy, conscription, surveillance, etc.) that fall outside the bounds of normal political procedures.[56] The social construction of security issues, however, is not solely restricted to subjective definitions of state officials of certain issues as threats. It is an 'inter-subjective' process, as it requires the acceptance of their 'speech act' by the targeted 'audience'. By acceptance, it is not meant the issue in question is widely discussed and then verbally or symbolically agreed by society at large or by those aimed at being convinced. It rather denotes the creation of an enabling political environment that helps legitimise particular actions that would not be possible to apply, if the language of existential threats and necessity were not invoked in the first place.[57]

When it comes to the language of security that has 'permeate[d] every sphere of life ... from finance to the environment' in the post-September 11 era,[58] insecurity has become the main reference point for interventionist policies framed as a preventive strategy against terrorism and other dangers arguably posed by failed or potentially failing states. In this logic of prevention, exceptional security measures (such as unilateral intervention and pre-emptive strikes) are legitimised as a form of risk management.[59]

Risk management refers to a set of ongoing activities that seek to identify uncertainties and challenges in advance, and develop the necessary tools to avert their potential adverse consequences. As a policy tool, risk management, it is argued, does not achieve a 'perfect' security but helps prevent an unwanted scenario from becoming real.[60] A key feature of this precautionary modelling of security that has dominated the post-September 11 (in)security discourse has been the emphasis placed on the dangers of the sovereign incapacity of certain states and the need for rebuilding these 'risky' states in an attempt to eliminate the seeming 'symptoms' of state failure before they have fully emerged. As Jack Straw, the UK's Foreign Secretary at the time, remarked in his 'failed and failing states' speech delivered at the University of Birmingham in September 2002:[61]

> State failure can no longer be seen as a localised or regional issue to be managed simply on an ad hoc, case by case basis. We have to develop a more coherent and effective international response which utilises all of the tools at our disposal, ranging from aid and humanitarian assistance to support for institution building. And to reduce the costs of intervention, we need courage and foresight to bring our influence to bear at the point when a state begins to display the symptoms of failure, rather than when it is a lost cause.

From Straw's perspective, the prevention of risks emanating from failed states also requires a global division of responsibilities among Western countries:

> the EU, NATO or the OSCE [Organization for Security and Co-operation in Europe] taking the lead in dealing with problems around the margins of Europe; the French or ourselves (perhaps jointly) in parts of Africa; and countries like Canada or the USA under the OAS [Organization of American States] in the Americas.

The necessity of preventive intervention and 'exceptionalist readings of political power'[62] were also central to the Bush administration's 'speech act' to convince the domestic (and global) audience on the necessity of ongoing military engagement in the face of an existential threat to the security and values of democratic nations. For instance, during his state of the union address four months after the September 11 attacks, Bush narrates a dangerous and uncertain global environment that not only provokes fear but legitimises continuous intervention as a solution:

What we have found in Afghanistan confirms that, far from ending there, our war against terror is only beginning.... Thousands of dangerous killers, schooled in the methods of murder, often supported by outlaw regimes, are now spread throughout the world like ticking time bombs, set to go off without warning.[63]

As it was also emphasised in the 2002 National Security Strategy document, the uncertainties of terrorism can only be dealt with by 'proactive' intervention:[64]

Given the goals of rogue states and terrorists, the United States can no longer solely rely on a reactive posture as we have in the past. The inability to deter a potential attacker, the immediacy of today's threats, and the magnitude of potential harm that could be unleashed by our adversaries' choice of weapons, do not permit that option. We cannot let our enemies strike first.

Through declaring it as a 'global enterprise of uncertain duration' against a non-territorial threat, the Bush administration also set the operational parameters of the war on terror as a near permanent exercise in global policing:[65]

The struggle against global terrorism is different from any other war in our history. It will be fought on many fronts against a particularly elusive enemy over an extended period of time.... Thousands of trained terrorists remain at large with cells in North America, South America, Europe, Africa, the Middle East, and across Asia.

By way of securitising the governance capacity of non-Western states, the US and its Western allies, in other words, not only rationalised intervention as a necessary engagement with preventing 'existential threats' but also routinised the exception as an organising political principle. The constitution of the exception as the 'dominant paradigm of government', according to Agamben, who draws his theory of 'exceptionalism' from a critique of Carl Schmitt's analysis of the state of exception, has its origins in European liberal democracies. Exceptionalism, Agamben argues, began with the French Constituent Assembly's decree of 8 July 1791, which distinguished between a 'state of peace' and a 'state of siege', in which 'all the functions entrusted to the civil authority for maintaining order and internal policing pass to the military commander, who exercises them under his exclusive responsibility'.[66] Since then, the state of exception, which legitimises extraordinary security measures, has gradually been extended from wartime conditions to include those of peacetime 'to cope with internal sedition and disorder'.[67]

For Schmitt, however, the functioning of the state and the law is determined by the capacity to decide and respond to an 'exceptional' situation. What he means by the state of exception is not any event of irregularity or emergency decree but 'a general concept in the theory of the state', which originates from a 'gap' in the law that cannot be filled by jurists but by a competent sovereign power only.[68] That is, no matter how detailed the law describing the complexities of everyday life, there will always be 'unpredictable times' or circumstances that fall outside the scope of law because 'the power of real life breaks through the crust of a mechanism that has become torpid with repetition'.[69] The potential forms that life may take or the situations that are impossible to anticipate in the legal system, Schmitt argues, may pose 'a case of extreme peril, a danger to the existence of the state, or the like'.[70] What matters most at this 'critical moment' is the definition of who makes the decision on whether there is an 'emergency' and what needs to be done to eliminate it.[71] As he famously puts it, 'Sovereign is he who decides on the exception'. The 'exception' from a Schmittian perspective thus privileges the question of 'who decides' over 'how to decide'[72] on the suspension of law, in which 'the state remains, whereas law recedes'.[73]

Agamben, on the other hand, rejects Schmitt's claim that there is a normative 'gap' in the law which requires the sovereign power to complete it, because Schmitt's totalising definition of sovereignty in terms of the capacity to act in the face of unforeseen events 'by default and in effect' eliminates the possibility of such a gap to occur.[74] 'Far from being a response to a normative lacuna', the exception denotes the 'opening of a fictitious lacuna' in the juridical order, as it suspends the law in force and provides the conditions of the applicability of emergency powers to the normal situation.[75] It is fictitious because the lacuna is not in the law but in the relation between law and reality.[76] This is evidenced in the use of the concept of necessity, which is often argued to be the origin of the state of exception ('necessity has no law'). However, deciding on what makes a particular situation a necessity is entirely a subjective judgement, because 'the only circumstances that are necessary and objective are those that are declared to be so'.[77] Aside from the subjectivity of such decisions deemed necessary, it is almost impossible to put in place a system of institutional mechanisms that guarantee the temporary deployment of emergency powers and overcome the likelihood of dictatorship through the exercise of such powers on a permanent basis.[78]

Exceptions are thus likely to become the norm through a process of prolonged practices of exceptional measures and perpetuation of conditions which are declared to be an exceptional situation that demands new and more extraordinary responses. Expanded implementations of exceptional policy responses create a political environment in which the distinction between peace and war disappears, and the exception becomes the norm. Separation between what is normalcy and what is an exception erodes over time and the difference between the two realities becomes a matter of the degree of the shifting balance of power to the executive.[79] In other words, what used to be deemed emergency powers in the past are now viewed as normal, routine and ordinary practices in light of more recent and more extensive exercise of powers.[80]

In the case of 'zones of indeterminacy' created as a result of foreign intervention, the involvement of new actors in the conflict opens new windows of opportunity for self-determination and secession claims. The forced removal of the host state's military and civilian authorities enables the formerly oppressed groups to establish their identity through utilising the surrounding uncertainties in a relatively autonomous environment. On the other hand, their dependent existence on foreign patronage creates vulnerabilities and perpetuates the conditions of intervention. The institutions they create in pursuit of international legitimacy often suffer from weaknesses to respond to the needs of their populations such as law enforcement, social justice and economic security. While they emerge as new centres of power aspiring to attain their state-making objectives, intervention in the form of capacity-development becomes the 'dominant paradigm of government'.

Conclusion

International intervention in countries facing violent conflict and secessionist movements brings shifts in the dynamics of political and social power upon which state sovereignty is structured. The use of military force and the establishment of administrative frameworks result in a partial or complete removal of the political landscape in disputed territories from the jurisdiction of the central governments of intervened states. The political environment is characterised by fluidities. These fluidities, on the other hand, can be turned into new opportunities to clarify the status of these territories which empirically exist but are not recognised internationally.

The newly introduced governmental and institutional arrangements present a relatively favourable political space for previously excluded groups to operate and expand their movement's sphere of influence. Intervention, in other words, helps enlarge the scope of the conflict in question and facilitates its discussion in a policy space that is outside the physical and legal reach of the central governments of intervened states. While providing new political opportunities, intervention, at the same time, creates conditions of a long-term involvement of foreign agencies in the domestic policy space. In this way, external regulation and control becomes a near permanent practice. Through capacity-building programs, foreign agencies are indeed integrated into the state apparatus.

Notes

1 Parts of this chapter are drawn from Selver B. Sahin, 'How Exception Became the Norm: Normalizing Intervention as an Exercise in Risk Management in Kosovo', *Journal of Balkan and Near Eastern Studies*, 5, no. 1 (2013): 17–36. Reproduced with permission of the publisher, www.tandfonline.com.
2 Neal, 'Foucault in Guantánamo'.
3 Helman and Ratner, 'Saving Failed States'.
4 See, for example, The White House, 'The National Security Strategy of the United States of America', September 2002; Straw, 'Failed and Failing States'; Cooper, 'The New Liberal Imperialism'; 'From Chaos, Order: Rebuilding Failed States'; Fukuyama, *State-Building*; Rotberg, *When States Fail*; the 'Failed State Index' released annually by the Foreign Policy and Fund for Peace since 2005.
5 Torres and Anderson, 'Fragile States'; François and Sud, 'Promoting Stability and Development in Fragile and Failed States'.
6 See, for example, Fukuyama, *State-Building*; Rotberg, *When States Fail*.
7 See, for example, World Bank, *Building Effective States, Forging Engaged Societies*; DFID, *Governance, Development and Democratic Politics*.
8 Bickerton, 'Exporting State Failure'.
9 ICISS, 'The Responsibility to Protect', viii.
10 Ibid., 67.
11 Ibid., 19–24.
12 United Nations, *2005 World Summit Outcome*, 24 October 2005, paras. 138–9.
13 Ghani and Lockhart, *Fixing Failed States*.
14 Ibid.
15 Morgenthau, *Politics among Nations*, 314.
16 Hinsley, *Sovereignty*, 26.
17 Ghani *et al.*, 'Closing the Sovereignty Gap'.
18 Brown, 'Sovereignty vs. Human Rights in a Post-Western World'.
19 Annan, 'Two Concepts of Sovereignty'.
20 Krasner, 'Shared Sovereignty'.
21 Fearon and Laitin, 'Neotrusteeship and the Problem of Weak States'.
22 Cooley and Spruyt, *Contracting States*.

23 Lake, 'Delegating Divisible Sovereignty.
24 Morgenthau, *Politics among Nations*, 320.
25 Weber, *Simulating Sovereignty*.
26 Ibid.
27 Ibid.
28 ICISS, 'The Responsibility to Protect', 16.
29 Ibid., viii.
30 Ibid.
31 Migdal, *State in Society*.
32 Schattschneider, *The Semisovereign People*.
33 Ibid., 71.
34 Ibid., 2.
35 McAdam, *Political Process and the Development of Black Insurgency, 1930–1970*.
36 Williams, 'When Opportunity Structure Knocks', 445.
37 McAdam, *Political Process*; McAdam, 'Conceptual Origins, Current Problems, Future Directions'.
38 McAdam, 'Conceptual Origins'.
39 Ibid.
40 McAdam, *Political Process*, 41.
41 Tarrow, 'States and Opportunities', 54–6.
42 Rucht, 'The Impact of National Contexts on Social Movement Structures', 190.
43 Chen, *Social Protest and Contentious Authoritarianism in China*.
44 McAdam *et al.*, 'Opportunities, Mobilizing Structures, and Framing Processes', 8.
45 Agamben, *The State of Exception*.
46 Jones, *ASEAN, Sovereignty and Intervention in Southeast Asia*, 22.
47 Williams and Pecci, 'Earned Sovereignty', 4.
48 Ibid., 9.
49 Ibid.
50 Buchanan, *Justice, Legitimacy and Self-Determination*.
51 Agamben, *The State of Exception*.
52 Ibid.
53 Ibid.
54 Agamben, 'On Security and Terror'.
55 Wæver, 'Securitization and Desecuritization', 54.
56 Buzan *et al.*, *Security*.
57 Ibid.
58 Jayasuriya, '9/11 and the New "Anti-Politics" of "Security" '.
59 Jayasuriya, *Reconstituting the Global Liberal Order*.
60 Rasmussen, *The Risk Society at War*.
61 Straw, 'Failed and Failing States'.
62 Huysmans, 'The Jargon of Exception', 165–6.
63 George W. Bush, *The State of the Union Address*, 29 January 2002.
64 The White House, *The National Security Strategy of the United States of America*, 15.
65 Ibid., 5.

66   Agamben, *The State of Exception*, 5.
67   Ibid.
68   Schmitt, *Political Theology*.
69   Ibid., 12.
70   Ibid., 6.
71   Ibid., 7.
72   Huysmans, 'The Jargon of Exception'.
73   Schmitt, *Political Theology*, 12.
74   Neal, *Exceptionalism and the Politics of Counter-Terrorism*.
75   Agamben, *The State of Exception*, 31
76   Ibid.
77   Ibid., 30.
78   Ibid.
79   Gross and Ní Aoláin, *Law in Times of Crisis*.
80   Ibid.

3   Kosovo and conflicting sovereignty claims[1]

The Kosovo Assembly's unilateral declaration of independence on 17 February 2008 was instantly recognised by some of the most influential members of the international community, including the US, UK, France, Germany and Italy. The recognition of Kosovo's 'internationally supervised' statehood triggered mixed reactions in different corners of the world. While it raised hopes in other unrecognised or de-facto states such as Northern Cyprus, Palestine, Taiwan, Tibet, Republika Srpska, Abkhazia, South Ossetia, Transdniestra and Somaliland, fears of secession were also provoked in some other countries facing separatist tensions.

In response to these mixed reactions worldwide, representatives of leading Western governments declared that Kosovo was a *sui generis* case that could not be equated with other self-determination conflicts.[2] In their view, Kosovo would remain as an 'exceptional' case of state-building. Its exceptionality, it was argued, came from the territory's complicated recent history including its administration by the UN for almost a decade, implications of the resolution of its political status for regional security, as well as from the political and social conditions on the ground. The formal recognition of Kosovo's separation from Serbia was therefore presented as the only solution available. The alternatives such as continuing international administration of the territory, re-establishment of Belgrade's rule and territorial partition were ruled out due to their potential to provoke internal violence and regional instability.[3]

However, this was not the first time that Kosovo's 'unique' circumstances were emphasised. Since Kosovo came on the international policy agenda in the late 1990s, it was constantly portrayed as an 'exception' rather than the rule. This includes NATO's military intervention launched in the spring of 1999 without explicit authorisation of the UN Security Council. The operation was defended by the intervening governments as an 'exceptional' engagement that was necessitated by a humanitarian emergency in the making. Similarly, the subsequent conversion of the territory into a UN-administered entity was put forward as an 'exceptional' governance solution necessitated by the emerging 'state of economic and social chaos' following the NATO intervention.[4] UN Secretary-General's Special Envoy Martti Ahtisaari's proposal of 'supervised independence' as a 'compromise solution' was also described as a 'unique' peace-building plan.[5]

This chapter explores Kosovo's 'exceptionalism' against the background of an increasingly interventionist international policy-making. It is not concerned with whether or not the Kosovo case is 'exceptional', as the claim for Kosovo's 'uniqueness' is nothing more than an image constructed and enforced by the most powerful of the contemporary global order.[6] Indeed, any self-determination conflict or secessionist movement emerging out of a distinct political, social and historical context may well be argued to be 'unique', even though some parallels may also be drawn between cases. Neither does it deal with the forms of power exercised by international agencies in Kosovo, and how this has impacted on the everyday life of the local populations, who found themselves part of a quasi state authority.[7] It is rather focused on the specific role of contemporary intervention as an act of state-making that is rationalised and operationalised on the basis of the 'exceptionalism' argument. It does so by examining how the involvement of foreign actors in the conflict has, on one hand, created new 'opportunity structures' for the Kosovo Albanian independence movement in an 'enlarged' political landscape, while, at the same time, creating a repertoire of actions that has perpetuated the conditions of intervention as the 'dominant paradigm of government' in the emerging domestic political order, on the other.

Origins of the Kosovo conflict and its internationalisation

The Kosovo question was essentially a conflict over sovereignty. It was rooted in the competing claims of the Serbs and Albanians to rule over the territory of Kosovo. The Serbs based their claims to sovereignty on the historical role of the territory as the heartland of the medieval Serbian kingdom and the 'cradle' of Serbian national identity. The Albanian claims centred around the right to self-determination were premised on the territory's demographic structure, the unbroken continuity of the Albanian settlement in the region, and the view that Kosovo's independence would contribute to regional stability.[8]

Both Albanians and Serbs also considered themselves as the 'victims' of historical mistakes and 'inequalities' that should have been remedied. For the Kosovo Albanians, their exclusion from the state of Albania created at the end of the Balkan Wars of 1912/13 was itself 'unfair'. They never felt an integral part of the state into which they were incorporated: the Serb-dominated, centralised first Yugoslavia at the end of the First World War[9] and the second Yugoslavia, proclaimed by Marshall Tito during the Second World War. Under the 1974 Constitution, the territory was recognised as a constituent unit of Tito's socialist Yugoslavia consisting of six republics (Serbia, Bosnia-Herzegovina, Croatia, Macedonia, Montenegro and Slovenia) and two autonomous provinces (Vojvodina and Kosovo). The Kosovo Albanians were represented in the federal policy-making bodies with a veto power, and enjoyed complete autonomy over their administrative, legislative and judicial bodies. But they did not have the right to secede from the federation, which the republics had. The denial of the status of republic, which aimed to prevent irredentist claims, was reserved to 'nations' whose ethnic centres lay outside Yugoslavia. This situation remained a significant source of discontent and rising sense of unequal treatment among the Albanians against the Slav peoples.[10]

For the Serbs, the creation of two autonomous units within their republic was 'unfair' against the other republics, especially given the denial of a similar special ethno-territorial status to the Serbs living in Croatia and Bosnia-Herzegovina.[11] They were already frustrated with the recognition of extensive political and cultural rights including the establishment of educational and cultural contacts with Tirana in the 1970s and strongly opposed the granting of republican status to the Kosovo Albanians, whom they thought would use it to unite with Albania. The declining proportion of the Serbs and Montenegrins, resulting from their growing outward emigration from the province since the early 1970s and a high rate of birth among the Albanians, fuelled tension and mistrust between the Serbs and Albanians in the post-Tito period, especially following Slobodan Milošević's rise to power in Serbia.[12]

The adoption of a series of constitutional measures by the Serbian Parliament in March 1989 seriously undermined the province's legislative, executive and judicial powers and established Belgrade's direct control over Kosovo. Belgrade's action provoked a political crisis, which, coinciding with the collapse of the socialist regimes in Eastern Europe, accelerated the disintegration of Yugoslavia. Fearing that similar centralising measures could be extended to the republics, the Slovene and Croat political leaderships sided with the Kosovo Albanians against Serbia. The leaderships of the two most economically developed republics, who repeatedly complained about the 'exploitation' of their wealth by the least developed units,[13] had little incentive to maintain the federation with the demise of the Soviet threat, and were seeking foreign support for secession.[14] They, however, would later leave Kosovo to its own dynamics and focus on their own agendas once they achieved their goal.[15] The political leaderships of the two republics declared their 'disassociation' from the federation in June 1991, followed by Macedonia and Bosnia-Herzegovina shortly afterwards.

The secession of the Yugoslav republics led to a significant change in the Kosovo Albanian leadership's strategic orientation: from demanding a republican status to independent statehood. The political leadership's strategy, which was influenced by the Slovene and Croat experience, combined the elements of democratisation and the 'belonging to Europe' rhetoric[16] to secure international recognition and avoid armed confrontation with the Milošević regime.[17] The Slovene and Croat examples also made it clear that the international community's approach to the claims to self-determination can change if the sympathy of some of its influential members is won. When the Yugoslav conflict first came on the international agenda following the declarations of independence by the Slovene and Croat republican leaderships, it was referred to in the Western media as a secessionist conflict shaped by nationalist political and economic concerns,[18] much like similar references that would be made about Kosovo in ten years' time. The Western governments repeatedly stressed their support for the preservation of Yugoslavia's territorial integrity to avoid creating a precedent for other separatist movements in Europe and for the Soviet Union.[19] On the other hand, they later changed their position and endorsed the republics' right to self-determination as a result of the increasing German pressure.

The Kosovo Albanian resistance was organised under the leadership of Ibrahim Rugova's Democratic League of Kosovo (LDK) which was founded in 1989. Similar to the East Timorese resistance united under the umbrella of the CNRT (National Council of Timorese Resistance) against the brutality of the Indonesian military, the LDK was a broad-based movement involving different groups from former communist party members to intellectuals, students and liberals who were marginalised and oppressed by the Milošević regime. Rather than an armed struggle, the LDK adopted a strategy of nonviolence in response to the central government's human rights violations and discriminatory policies following the revocation of the province's autonomous status. The practice of nonviolence, according to Rugova, was 'not only a necessity but also a choice' because:[20]

> By means of this active resistance based on non-violence and solidarity, we 'found' ourselves.... [W]e have succeeded in touching this point of the spirit of the Albanian people.... Oppressed, but organized ... this is the first time [Kosovo Albanians] feel that they have a power ... that they feel citizens despite the occupation.

The language of democracy, pluralism and human rights was a key element of the resistance leaders' efforts to 'enlarge' the scope of the Kosovo conflict. 'Ours is the largest peace movement in Europe' was the claim they repeatedly raised in different platforms at the time.[21] These liberal democratic principles, according to Kosovo Albanian leaders, indeed represented the 'ultimate ideological signifiers of nations and societies from the prosperous, western Europe and of what generally connoted the "western world"'.[22] The impulse towards nonviolence was therefore closely linked to a vision of 'modernity' that reflected a desire to become or be accepted as European.[23] In this process of constructing a modern Albanian identity by reference to Europeanness, the practice of nonviolence also served to validate the self-perceptions of Kosovo Albanians 'in contrast to an "Other", in this case a rival and enemy nation'.[24] Through the nonviolent approach, the Rugova leadership sought to demonstrate to the outside world that Kosovo Albanians were different from the 'primitive and uncivilised' stereotype propagated by Serbs.[25] In 1990, for instance, they organised a petition 'For Democracy Against Violence', collecting 400,000 signatures (corresponding to around 40 per cent of the province's adult population). The petition was also presented at the UN in New York. In addition, as part of a community reconciliation process introduced to abolish the traditional practice of blood feuds, a series of public ceremonies of forgiveness were initiated the same year and some 2,000 families were reportedly reconciled within two years.[26]

The Kosovo Albanians declared independence in October 1991 but failed to attract international recognition. The arbitration commission of the Peace Conference for Yugoslavia (known as the Badinter Commission), which was established by the European Community and its member states in August 1991 to provide a legal opinion on the break up of Yugoslavia, rejected the Kosovo Albanian claims for self-determination, which sought a revision of the existing federal internal boundaries.[27] The Badinter Commission's decision did not lead the Kosovo Albanians to give up their secessionist claims. Instead, they sought to establish a public system of schooling, health care, communication, taxation and transportation as the basis of empirical statehood. The result was the emergence of a 'virtual state ... existing in a weird, parallel form to the Serbian authorities who were very much in charge'.[28]

Kosovo Albanians also boycotted the Serbian elections in 1992 and held their own presidential and parliamentary elections, with Ibrahim Rugova becoming the president and his LDK emerging as the dominant political organisation. Writing on the reasons why the Albanians boycotted elections, Shkelzen Maliqi, a respected human rights activist in Kosovo and abroad at the time, notes that 'diplomatic representatives of democratic countries exerted considerable pressure' on Albanian political parties to run in the Serbian elections. However, participation without restoration of the province's previous constitutional system would mean the 'legalisation of violence' and 'recognition of an illegal constitution and a system that was established without the consent' of the Kosovars.[29] It should be noted, on the other hand, that the votes of approximately 1 million Albanian voters for pro-Western Milan Panić, who promised to restore democratic and human rights if he had won the election, may have helped to remove Slobodan Milošević from power. Many Albanians believed that it would be more likely to achieve independence, which was the only preferred outcome, if Milošević remained in power.[30] Fehmi Agani, then Vice-President of the LDK, who was killed during the NATO campaign, elaborates on the Kosovo Albanian leadership's strategic approach at that time:[31]

> Frankly, it is better [for us] to continue with Milošević.... Milošević was very successful in destroying Yugoslavia and, in the same way, if he continues, he will destroy Serbia.... Panić is offering crumbs but it is not enough to resolve the crisis.... He thinks we will accept him because he is an opponent of Milošević. It is not enough. He may offer us to take part in the elections but without offering anything concrete. We are against Milošević but we also know that he must fall, with or without Panić.

While struggling to strengthen the governmental and societal basis of the de facto Kosovo state at home, the political leadership simultaneously sought its recognition abroad. Their international lobbying efforts were successful at the level of gaining resolutions condemning human rights violations[32] but failed to receive support for the establishment of a UN-administered protectorate to supervise the territory's transition to independence.[33] In the meantime, Kosovo's exclusion from the Dayton peace process and the sudden proliferation of weapons in 1997 smuggled from neighbouring Albania[34] deeply changed the Kosovo Albanian strategy. Rugova's passive resistance was considered ineffective by many who felt that an organised armed struggle was necessary to trigger an international military intervention. The following comments by Xhafer Shatri, Rugova's minister of information in exile, are a reflection of these growing frustrations with the failure of the nonviolent approach:[35]

> Albanians saw at Dayton that the international community only respects and reacts to the law of the jungle. This had a terrible impact, especially on the new generation that for six years has had little work, little schooling and lived under brutal Serb occupation. We have gone beyond frustration. We speak now of revolt.

The Kosovo Liberation Army (KLA), engaged in sporadic attacks on the Serb police in the province since 1993, increased its attacks in 1997.[36] Given the military imbalance against the Serbian security forces, the guerrillas did not hope for a victory but retaliation from Belgrade that would result in outside intervention on their behalf.[37] Serbian security forces responded to the KLA attacks by launching counter-offensive operations in February 1998 at villages thought to have harboured the rebels.[38] Resulting in civilian deaths, the Serbian reprisal prompted the US leadership to renew its position in relation to military intervention. Madeleine Albright, US Secretary of State, warned the Serbian leadership in the Contact Group meeting in March 1998: 'We are not going to stand by and watch the Serbian authorities do in Kosovo what they can no longer get away with doing in Bosnia.'[39]

These developments were also accompanied by a subtle change in the discourses of Kosovo Albanian leaders. Rather than insisting on the achievement of independence in the immediate future, they became more supportive of a phased approach; an approach that prioritised ending Serbia's rule over Kosovo and undertaking a democratic transformation on the way to statehood. For instance, in an interview with Voice of America (VOA) in May 1998 just after the Kosovo Albanian delegation's meeting with President Clinton, Veton Surroi, who participated in the Rambouillet talks as a member of the Pristina delegation, hinted at this change:[40]

VOA: You presented your stand on the future judicial order of Kosova, which should be independence in your view, to President Clinton. This gives the impression of something unrealistic at the moment, since the international community does not accept something like that. What compromise would have to be achieved for the status of Kosova in this aspect?

SURROI: I think that we should not deal with the status of Kosova. I repeated this publicly several times. It is important to determine the way to enlighten the democratic will of the people of Kosova for their future. Such a democratic process could lead to a solution that would be part of a new configuration in the Balkans and Europe, and part of a process that, I hope, at the same time would initiate the process of the democratisation of Serbia, as a last bastion of Europe's unreformed society along with Byelorussia.

VOA: ... Is it possible to reach the independence of Kosova by non-violent means, something that you are determined to do and why did you receive recognition by President Clinton today?

SURROI: The process of Kosova's independence is irreversible.

At the same time, differences of opinion among the various Kosovo Albanian factions, who were only united by the common goal of independence,[41] became more pronounced. According to Yakup Krasniqi, KLA's spokesperson, who gave an interview to BBC in June 1998, Rugova was an 'obstacle to independence'.[42] On the other hand, Krasniqi's remarks reflected the competing factions' commonly shared goal of independence. For instance, he demanded the fulfilment of three conditions for negotiating with Belgrade: the withdrawal of Serb forces, release of all political prisoners and the presence of the international community in the peace talks. Again, Krasniqi reiterated Pristina's commitment to internationally advocated government principles and organisations: 'We want Kosovo to be free, democratic, pluralist, we want Kosovo as its people want it, to fit into the modern world'.[43] Similarly, Adem Demaçi, who spent 28 years of life in Yugoslav prisons and is referred to as Kosovo's Mandela, also became a severe critic of Rugova and his passive resistance strategy. The Albanian movement in Kosovo, according to him, was 'inadequate for the circumstances' and Rugova was becoming a 'dictator and usurper of powers'.[44] Demaçi advocated 'active resistance of a Gandhian type' that entailed 'permanent pressure on the Serbian regime and readiness to sacrifice for achieving its goals'.[45]

By 1999, Rugova's LDK, which had led the passive resistance movement since the early 1990s, was sidelined by the KLA both in Kosovo and the international arena. This became abundantly clear during the peace talks held at Rambouillet (France) in February 1999. The Kosovo Albanian delegation, consisting of Rugova, KLA and civil society representatives, was headed by Hashim Thaci, who was appointed as the leader of the newly formed political directorate of the guerrilla organisation. Under increasing US pressure, Thaci agreed to the peace plan which proposed a three-year transitional period to be followed by an international meeting 'to determine a mechanism for a final settlement for Kosovo, on the basis of the will of the people, opinions of relevant authorities'. The Rambouillet Accords which also called for the stationing of some 28,000 NATO troops throughout the territory of Serbia and Montenegro were rejected by Milošević. Thaci's acceptance of the deal, according to some observers, was part of a tactful move to legitimise NATO's use of force. In their view, Rambouillet was designed to fail and provide a pretext for bombing.[46] Henry Kissinger, former US Secretary of State and National Security Adviser, for instance, claimed that 'the Rambouillet text ... was a provocation, and excuse to start bombing', and some reporters suggested that they were told by Madeleine Albright off the record during the talks that the US 'intentionally set the bar too high for the Serbs to comply. They need some bombing, and that's what they are going to get'.[47]

The political leadership's lessening emphasis on achieving independence in the immediate near future helped generate international intervention on their behalf. The involvement of powerful foreign actors in the conflict has created new 'opportunity structures' for the Kosovo Albanian independence movement, which clearly had almost no chance for success in the absence of international support. Serbia's military defeat by NATO forces was followed by the establishment of an international territorial administration under the auspices of the UN. This institutional arrangement placed the province out of reach of Serbian rule, paving the way for its eventual separation as the only but 'exceptional' solution.

Operation Allied Force and its 'exceptional' political consequences in Kosovo

NATO's 1999 military intervention in Kosovo, known as Operation Allied Force, was not based on an explicit UN Security Council resolution. The intervening powers rationalised the launching of the air strikes in a mixture of moral and political terms rather than offering a legal justification for the unauthorised use of force.[48] For instance, in a press statement issued by Javier Solana, then NATO Secretary-General, on the day the air campaign was launched, it was emphasised that NATO was acting to fulfil its 'moral duty' to avert a 'humanitarian catastrophe' and restore peace and political stability in the region.[49] It was only British Prime Minister Tony Blair who argued during the air campaign for an evolving 'doctrine of the international community' for humanitarian intervention that permitted the North Atlantic Alliance to act against Serbia.[50] However, the British leader never mentioned this 'doctrine' or its legal and operational specifics after the bombing ended. Instead, the Allied governments, except Belgium, defended the Kosovo intervention as a 'justifiable exception' to the non-intervention principle in the proceedings before the International Court of Justice in The Hague.[51] Moreover, the intervening powers reiterated the need for obtaining Security Council authorisation when responding to similar situations of humanitarian crisis. For instance, during his address to the UN General Assembly in September 1999, Lionel Jospin, then French Prime Minister, reaffirmed the 'primary responsibility' of the UN Security Council to 'resolve crisis situations' and stressed that NATO's approach to the Kosovo conflict 'must remain an exception'. The Kosovo intervention, in other words, was an ad hoc deviation from international law that would not be repeated in the future.[52]

The 'exceptionalism' argument, which provided a powerful justification for the unauthorised use of force, set the discursive and operational parameters of subsequent acts of intervention. Indeed, the 'exceptional' exercise of military powers produced new states of exception in Kosovo.

Resolution 1244, adopted by the UN Security Council on 10 June 1999 following Belgrade's acceptance of the Kumanovo Agreement at the end of eleven weeks of intensive air campaign, created a new state of institutional affairs in Kosovo. First, an international civilian mission, known as the United Nations Interim Administration Mission in Kosovo (UNMIK), was set up and vested with all sovereign powers to act as a temporary governing agency and construct democratic self-government institutions. Second, the Council authorised the deployment of a NATO-led multinational security presence (Kosovo Force, KFOR) to verify the withdrawal of Serbian military and police forces and provide a secure environment for all the people in Kosovo.

The conversion of the entire territory of Kosovo into an international protectorate, which was kept outside the legal jurisdiction and physical control of Serbia's central government through the presence of a large civilian and military mission, provided the Kosovo Albanian nationalist leaders with a significant 'political opportunity structure'. This administrative arrangement created a relatively favourable political environment, as it opened up an 'enlarged' political space which enabled Albanians to establish self-government institutions and campaign for the recognition of some form of independence as the only way forward. Kosovo's gradual transition to independent statehood was structured on a mixture of 'remedial secession' and 'earned sovereignty' claims, which was first pronounced as a conflict resolution strategy in a policy report jointly produced by the Public International Law and Policy Group (PILPG) and the International Crisis Group (ICG) in November 1998.[53] In this policy document it was stated that the past human rights abuses by the Milošević regime rendered Kosovo entitled to sovereignty and 'earn full sovereignty at the end of an interim period by demonstrating their commitment to democratic self-government, to the protection of human rights, and the promotion of regional security'.[54] It also called for an international intervention to supervise a three-to-five year transitional period.[55] Later in October 2000, the Independent International Commission on Kosovo proposed the idea of 'conditional independence', and recommended that the Serb government's rejection should not be allowed to derail the peace process.[56]

In a number of reports successively published following the release of the said report on Kosovo, the International Crisis Group[57] continuously promoted the recognition of externally guided independence as the only viable solution with no alternative regardless of opposition from Belgrade and Moscow. While advocating the secession of Kosovo from Serbia, the Brussels-based think-tank organisation, however, without suggesting any convincing argument, presented completely different solutions for two other very similar conflicts: re-uniting the divided island of Cyprus[58] and supporting the autonomous status of South Ossetia within Georgia.[59] In a similar fashion, in another report released in 2005, the International Commission on the Balkans, established to analyse the political, economic and social situation in the countries in the Balkan region, called for independence of Kosovo.[60] In fact, the key issue, according to the authors of this report, was not the recognition of independence but 'how [to] get there'.[61] In this respect, the EU was advised to adopt a 'member-state building strategy' with a view to facilitating Kosovo's integration into the EU and other Western organisations. In June 2006, while the UN-sponsored status talks were underway in Vienna, the fifth Special Representative of the UN Secretary-General in Kosovo, Soren Jessen-Petersen suggested that '[t]he destiny of Kosovo is clear, it is in the hands of the political leaders and the people of Kosovo'.[62]

The international administration of Kosovo, in other words, helped prepare the ground for its eventual secession from Serbia. The withdrawal of Serbian forces changed the balance of power, and the UN-run province practised de facto independence, even though Resolution 1244 reaffirmed respecting the 'sovereignty and territorial integrity of the Federal Republic of Yugoslavia' and left the final definition of Kosovo's political status subject to the conclusion of a diplomatic process. The erection of monuments for the KLA 'martyrs' and erasing or crossing of the Serbian names of municipalities from road signs by the majority Albanians since the early days of the UN mission exemplify the neglect of Serbia's sovereignty in practice.

Indeed, the establishment of the UN interim administration, which removed Serbia's authority over Kosovo, was in line with what the Rugova leadership campaigned for in the international arena throughout the 1990s – establishing an interim governance structure to supervise the territory's transition to independence.[63] By the time the UN administration was put in place, it was more or less clear on the ground that the Kosovo Albanians, who had been seeking international recognition since the early 1990s, would not agree to the restoration of Belgrade's governance after having accomplished the first step towards the ultimate goal of statehood. The prolonged status negotiations, during which it was frequently reiterated that the administration of the territory by the UN was unsustainable and that the old state of affairs prior to it could not be reinstated, served to prepare the other members of the community of states to the idea that Kosovo's secession is the only, albeit 'exceptional', solution to the conflict.

An important point that needs to be made in relation to the legitimising effect of the 'exceptionalism' argument is the use of a passive language to portray the international administration of Kosovo. It is reflected in the prevailing descriptions of UNMIK as an administrative structure 'the international community had to establish' in anticipation of a governmental vacuum in the post-armed conflict period.[64] However, such a technocratic representation of UNMIK as a necessary, temporary policy device to provide transitional administration and construct government institutions from scratch conceals the fundamentally political nature of the international activity,[65] which is closely related to the regulation of the way state power is exercised. It therefore presents the Kosovo conflict as a matter of governance failure of local actors rather than as a 'sovereignty problem'.[66] However, the Kosovo conflict, as discussed earlier, was essentially a sovereignty-related conflict centring on the question of who has the right to rule over the territory and its people. Following the establishment of UNMIK, sovereignty became 'no longer an applicable concept' in Kosovo because the UN's takeover of full international authority as a way of reconciling the law with the political realities on the ground created a 'temporary legal abnormal situation in anticipation of a final settlement'.[67] The international administration of the territory, on the other hand, paved the way for its eventual secession from Serbia.

Furthermore, presenting the international involvement in Kosovo as 'essentially [a] passive and reactive' response[68] to an emerging break-down in governance 'fails to acknowledge' that the pull-out of Serbian forces was actually part of the Kumanovo Agreement,[69] which was signed following the military defeat of Serbia by NATO forces. UNMIK, in other words, was not born out of an objective necessity to fill a gov-ernmental vacuum, which supposedly came into being on its own as a consequence of the armed conflict. It was rather enforced on the party who lost the war. It sought to 'replace' an already existing administrative authority deemed to be unable or unwilling to operate in a manner pro-moted by international agencies.[70] The democratic institution-building process that UNMIK was mandated to oversee following the NATO intervention can therefore be described as an example of the 'victor's peace' following Oliver Richmond's analysis of the contemporary liberal peace missions.

Moreover, the NATO intervention changed the balance of power and resulted in a realignment of interests in Kosovo. Similar to the situation in East Timor, at the time of the arrival of the international civilian and military staff from mid-June 1999 onwards, Kosovo was in no sense a *terra nullius* but a highly contentious site of power struggles. The emerg-ing social environment in the immediate aftermath of the NATO opera-tion can be best described as one in which a 'political war' already replaced the 'war with bombs', borrowing Kosovo Albanian politician and journalist Veton Surroi's description.[71] Within days following the entry of KFOR, the KLA-led 'provisional government' headed by Hashim Thaci swiftly sidelined the Rugova faction in most of the muni-cipalities and appointed mayors to provide public services, including tax collection and issuing vehicle licence plates that would fall under the jur-isdiction of UNMIK.[72] Aside from rivalries in local administration, violent attacks on the Serb and Roma populations as well as Albanians accused of having collaborated with Belgrade during the conflict led to the departure of approximately 200,000 Serbs and other non-Albanians to Serbia, Macedonia and other regional states.[73] Those who stayed in Kosovo clustered together in ethnically homogenous areas, mainly in northern municipalities, where they relied on the Belgrade-funded 'parallel structures' of administration, courts, health, education and security, leading to the emergence of alternative centres of power. On the other hand, the institutionalisation of inter-ethnic segregation, which was in place since the early-1990s when the Rugova leadership initiated a passive resistance in search for international recognition of statehood, perpetuated the political conditions of a permanent exercise of international intervention around the concept of 'multi-ethnicity'. Former UN Secretary-General Kofi Annan,[74] as well as his Special Representatives in Kosovo such as Hans Haekkerup,[75] Michael Steiner,[76] Harri Holkeri[77] and Soren Jessen-Petersen,[78] emphasised on different platforms that the creation of a multi-ethnic Kosovo, in which all the people, regardless of their ethnic background, can live and freely and safely exercise democratic rights and freedoms, constituted the basic objective of the international engagement in Kosovo. Similarly, UNMIK's 'standards before status' policy adopted in December 2003 to revitalise the stagnated relations between UNMIK and the local Albanian leadership prioritised the maintenance of a multi-ethnic society to initiate negotiations on the future status of the UN-run province.[79] The 'standards before status' approach contained the elements of 'earned sovereignty', as evidenced in its call for a measured devolution of sovereign authority and responsibilities to Kosovo's institutions in accordance with their demonstrated ability to function effectively and satisfy the criteria set.[80] However, it postponed the initiation of final status talks until after certain standards were met.[81]

On the other hand, the rhetorical and policy credence afforded to the principle of 'multi-ethnicity' and the 'standards before status' policy approach to address Kosovo's political status could not be substantiated, as evidenced by the eruption of violent riots in March 2004 and the limited progress in relation to the return of refugees and displaced persons who had left Kosovo in the post-1999 period. Indeed, the March 2004 violence, which was directed not only at minorities but UNMIK and KFOR, illustrates how the surrounding ambiguities over the status issue worked to break the status quo. In this respect, Norwegian diplomat Kai Eide, commissioned by the UN to undertake a political assessment of the situation in Kosovo, stated in his report dated July 2004:[82]

> Seen from an internal Kosovo perspective, the longer we wait, the more would the frustration in the Kosovo majority population increase. The economic situation would deteriorate further. The lack of a political perspective – clear future – would be felt even more intensely than today.

In a subsequent comprehensive review of whether the conditions were in place in Kosovo to initiate a political process towards the negotiation of its future status, Eide wrote that 'Regrettably, little has been achieved to create the foundation for a multi-ethnic society. The Kosovo leaders and the international community should take urgent steps to correct this grim picture.'[83] Notwithstanding a 'very mixed' progress in the implementation of the above governance benchmarks, the Norwegian diplomat recommended the opening of status talks, because further postponing this process was apparently 'unlikely' to yield better results in reaching the 'standards', unless 'the international community is ready and able to mobilize greater energy and pressure' in this regard.[84]

'Supervised independence' as an exceptional political solution

The status of 'conditional independence', on which the UN Secretary-General's special envoy, former Finnish President Martti Ahtisaari's 'Comprehensive Proposal for Kosovo Status Settlement' was conceptually based,[85] was first put forward by the Independent International Commission on Kosovo in 2000. Rather than granting full statehood, the Commission, which was set up in August 1999 to examine the aspects of the conflict and the subsequent NATO intervention, proposed a prolonged international security and civilian presence to monitor Kosovo's path to 'gradually acquire the rights of a state as it demonstrates that its peoples can live in peace with each other and with the neighboring states in the region'.[86]

Similarly, the status plan Ahtisaari presented as a 'compromise solution'[87] to the Secretary-General in March 2007 conditioned Kosovo's independence on the international supervision of its state structures. Supervised independence, Ahtisaari argued, was the 'only realistic option'[88] for two major reasons. One was that 'a history of enmity and mistrust' between the Serbs and Albanians, exacerbated under the repressive Milošević regime, made the re-institution of Belgrade's rule unviable. The other was the international administration of the territory in 'complete separation' from Serbia since 1999. Reversing this 'reality' on the ground was argued to be likely to trigger violent opposition from the majority Albanians, as they were clearly unwilling to live under Serb authority again.[89] The Ahtisaari plan also dismissed territorial partition due to its potential to destabilise Macedonia and Bosnia and Herzegovina. It rather reiterated the maintenance of Kosovo's multi-ethnic character as the foundation of its future development and proposed a highly decentralised state structure, with a number of new Serb-majority municipalities, such as North Mitrovica, granted 'enhanced competencies' in health care, higher education and the selection of their police station commanders. While describing independence as the only option because 'continued international administration is not sustainable', the independence package still envisaged a protectorate-like system, similar to the administrative system put in place in Bosnia and Herzegovina. Ahtisaari proposed the creation of an International Civilian Representative (ICR) to be appointed by an International Steering Group (ISG). This person would also act as the EU Special Representative (EUSR) and exercise 'the final authority' in Kosovo on interpretation of the civilian aspects of the plan proposed. Echoing the so-called 'Bonn powers' exercised by the Office of the High Representative (OHR) to neutralise the impact of nationalist politicians on the functioning of the ethnically divided Bosnian state, the ICR was recognised as the power to 'take corrective actions', including by annulling laws or decisions adopted by Kosovo institutions in violation of the status plan and removing public officials who failed to comply with the 'spirit' of the settlement. The ISG was set up on 28 February 2008 and appointed Pieter Feith from Holland as the ICR to support and advise the Kosovo government and institutions in the areas of rule of law, democratic development and multi-ethnicity as part of the implementation of the Ahtisaari plan and Kosovo's integration with the EU.

Kosovo's independence, on the other hand, the former Finnish President declared, would not set a precedent for other separatist movements, arguing 'Kosovo [was] a unique case that demand[ed] a unique solution' because:[90]

> In unanimously adopting resolution 1244 (1999), the Security Council responded to Milosevic's actions in Kosovo by denying Serbia a role in its governance, placing Kosovo under temporary United Nations administration and envisaging a political process designed to determine Kosovo's future. The combination of these factors makes Kosovo's circumstances extraordinary.

Serbia's acceptance of the establishment of the UN interim administration at the end of the NATO air bombing, in other words, was treated as if Belgrade had permanently relinquished its legal right to govern the province. In this respect, in response to the Serbian Parliament's adoption of a new constitution in October 2006, which declared Kosovo as an integral part of Serbia, the US Ambassador to the UN-mediated status talks, Frank Wisner, argued that the Kosovo issue was 'not a matter of Serbian sovereignty, which changed when the UN agreed on [Resolution] 1244'.[91] From this perspective, Belgrade had no choice but to accept the independence of Kosovo, especially given the growing impatience of the 90 per cent Albanian majority for the recognition of their statehood.

Similarly, the representatives of the leading Western governments such as then British Foreign Secretary David Milliband explained the recognition of the Kosovo Assembly's declaration of independence in February 2008 by reference to the territory's 'unique' circumstances: 'What makes it [Kosovo] unique is that for nine years there's been a UN protectorate within the independent country of Serbia'.[92] Therefore, the way in which the Kosovo conflict was addressed would arguably remain as an exceptional case of state-making. However, Milliband's justification does not fully reflect the prior experience in international administrations established after conflict, which did not always result in territorial secession. For instance, Eastern Slavonia was returned to Croatia in 1998 following two years of transitional administration.

As it becomes clear in the declaratory statements of the Kosovo Albanian leaders, Kosovo's 'uniqueness' appears to derive from their agreement to a 'shared sovereignty' arrangement in exchange for the recognition of its international identity as a separate territorial unit from Serbia. Prime Minister Hashim Thaci, for instance, stated before the Kosovo Assembly in January 2008 that his government would not declare independence without US and EU approval: 'Kosovo will do nothing without Washington and Brussels. No unilateral actions [will be taken]'.[93] The Kosovo Albanian leader was also quoted in the media during the mass demonstrations in December 2008, stating 'the EU mission was invited by the institutions of the Republic of Kosovo; it is therefore welcomed by us and all the citizens'.[94] The recognition of territorial separation conditioned on local actors' readiness to share sovereignty with external agencies, on the other hand, might be seen as setting a precedent in terms of establishing the institutional conditions of international state-making that make intervention a permanent exercise. The relevance of this situation is supported not only by the presence of NATO-led military forces and Kosovo's dependence on foreign aid,[95] but by the institutions' restricted exercise of political authority over territorial control and policy-making. The Kosovo government continues to share political authority not only with UNMIK but with EULEX (European Union Rule of Law Mission in Kosovo), although Kosovo was declared 'fully independent' following the end of the ICR's mandate in September 2012.[96]

EULEX as a crisis management mission

Resolution 1244 has become the main source of reference to rationalise the exercise of highly intrusive powers by international actors. The normalisation of intervention on the basis of a broad interpretation of the

Security Council mandate in Resolution 1244 is mirrored not only in the security role tailored for KFOR but in the deployment of an EU civilian mission following the declaration of independence. The Ahtisaari plan proposed the creation of a national security sector for Kosovo. The plan also recommended that the NATO-led security force stay for an unspecified period of time to provide internal security, protect the conditionally independent state from external threats, and facilitate its future integration in the North-Atlantic alliance.[97] Within this context, the KFOR commander was explicitly authorised to exercise 'the authority, without interference or permission, to do all that he/she judges necessary and proper, including the use of military power'. Similarly, while authorising the adoption of a constitution by the Kosovo Assembly to formalise the territory's secession from Serbia on the one hand, the Ahtisaari plan called for the deployment of a European Security and Defence Policy (ESDP) mission, known as EULEX, to replace UNMIK and assist with the capacity-development of the Kosovo institutions in the areas of rule of law, judiciary, police and customs[98] on the other.

However, due to marked Russian opposition, the status plan could not be endorsed by the Security Council. In the absence of a new resolution to authorise EULEX as a successor mission to UNMIK, the solution found to provide a legal basis for EULEX deployment was re-interpreting Resolution 1244 to reconfigure the international presence.[99] On 4 February 2008, two weeks before the Kosovo Assembly's unilateral declaration of independence, the EU Council adopted a 'joint action' establishing the EULEX mission by selective reference to Resolution 1244, such as the continued presence of the international civilian and military agencies in Kosovo until the Security Council decides otherwise, and the recognition of EU's support for the stabilisation and economic development of Kosovo under a Stability Pact for Southeastern Europe.[100] The joint action also partially refers to UNMIK's mandate. It reaffirms the oversight of the 'transfer of authority from Kosovo's provisional institutions to institutions established under a political settlement' and the maintenance of 'civil law and order, including establishing local police forces and meanwhile through the deployment of international police personnel to serve'. However, the provision of 'interim administration under which the people of Kosovo can enjoy substantial autonomy within the Federal Republic of Yugoslavia' is not mentioned in the joint action.

In addition to this, the definition of the EULEX mandate is a particular case in point to illustrate the prevailing representations of state incapacity or 'failure' as a security concern. The above-mentioned joint action describes the mission's mandate to 'monitor, mentor and advise'

Kosovo's institutions as a 'crisis management operation' undertaken as part of 'its readiness … to play a leading role in strengthening stability in the region'.[101] By way of monitoring the institutional capacity-development of Kosovo, the EU, in other words, seeks to address future emergencies in advance. While aiming to support Kosovo's institutional development as part of a regional crisis management exercise, the deployment of EULEX became a crisis itself. It not only met strong resistance from Belgrade and the Kosovo Serbs, who rejected the declaration of independence, but failed to win even the endorsement of all EU member states,[102] let alone broader international support.[103] The 'six-point plan', put forward by UN Secretary-General Ban Ki-moon as another 'compromise' solution to break the impasse, was endorsed by the Security Council in November 2008. It was proposed that international agencies would exercise control in six key areas, namely policing, customs, justice, transportation and infrastructure, boundaries and the Serbian cultural heritage. Additionally, the EU mission was placed under the general authority of UNMIK and its 'status neutrality' approach.[104] This new arrangement, according to Belgrade, meant EULEX would not 'supervise' Kosovo's independence as outlined in the Ahtisaari plan. Pristina initially opposed the plan because it was seen as undermining the already problematic exercise of sovereign authority of Kosovo institutions.[105] But the government later agreed to it following the US assurance that this would only be 'interim, not permanent' with no harm to Kosovo's sovereignty.[106] It was, in other words, another international attempt to reconcile the law with the political realities on the ground through another set of necessary but 'temporary arrangements'.[107]

EULEX began its deployment in December 2008 amidst mass demonstrations organised by the nationalist Vetevendosje (Self-Determination) movement campaigning for unconditional state sovereignty. EU officials tended to downplay the importance of protests, arguing it was an 'orderly demonstration' of a few thousand people who were protesting against the UN's six-point plan, not EULEX as such.[108] They therefore expressed their commitment to establishing the rule of law throughout Kosovo. For instance, then EU security chief Javier Solana declared in April 2009 that EULEX would 'do its utmost to make rule of law institutions work better and faster for the benefit of all the people in Kosovo'.[109] As discussed earlier, rule of law activities, aimed at supporting a stable and prosperous market economy, constitute a key pillar of state-building interventions. The creation of a secure environment through institutional capacity-development is thought to generate investment in the wealth of conflict-affected countries.

However, this policy credence attached to the international activity in Kosovo sits uneasily with the empirical evidence on the ground. As evidenced by the UNDP and World Bank statistics, Kosovo remains as one of the poorest countries in Europe. Approximately 30 per cent of its population of 1.8 million lives below the national poverty line and the youth unemployment rate stands at around 60 per cent.[110] In addition, rule of law weaknesses particularly in northern municipalities, where smuggling, fraudulent evasion of import duty, money laundering and political intimidation remain as a serious cause for concern. The 2010 EU Progress Report for Kosovo found that 'the weak rule of law, corruption, uncertainty over property rights and high interest rates continue to impact negatively on the business environment and prevent economic development'.[111] These challenges, according to the EU, are arising from deficiencies in the policy formulation and implementation capacity of Kosovo's institutions,[112] illustrating the prevalent technocratic understandings of state capacity. Regarding the rule of law weaknesses in northern municipalities, international agencies attribute this problem to the incapacity of the local authorities to take decisive measures against the criminal groups there.[113] According to Kosovo Albanian representatives, on the other hand, EULEX should be held 'co-responsible' for this policy failure, because its inclusion in the Kosovo constitution, they argue, makes the EU mission an integral part of the Kosovo rule of law agencies.[114]

This mutual finger pointing begs the question: who is the sovereign in Kosovo, particularly to the north of the Ibar River? According to the Brussels-based International Crisis Group, the political and social situation in northern Kosovo is one of 'dual sovereignty in practice', as the Serbs reject the jurisdiction of the Kosovo institutions and continue to rely on the Belgrade-funded government structures.[115] However, the events surrounding the 'border crisis' in northern municipalities in July 2011 tend to suggest that the NATO-led security force is the only sovereign there, if approached from Schmitt's definition of sovereign power as an expression of capacity to decide on the exception or emergency. The events that eventually resulted in the declaration of a state of emergency in the border area were sparked by Pristina's decision to ban the entry of all Serbian products in response to Belgrade's continued refusal to let in any products bearing a Kosovo customs mark. The local Serbs protested against the Kosovo government's decision and set up roadblocks along the border with Serbia. In response, the Thaci government sent special police units to remove the barricades and extend centralised authority in the north. Following the intensification of tensions over the control of the border, KFOR Commander Erhard Buhler declared the two checkpoints there as restricted military zones and authorised his troops to use deadly force in case of an armed attack. As an interesting point to note, the Serb leadership in Belgrade described the KFOR action as a move towards establishing Pristina's sovereignty.[116] However, the Serbian government's statement fails to capture the situation on the ground, as the KFOR Commander specifically cited the lack of rule of law as the main factor contributing to the border crisis.[117] Rather than supporting the Pristina government's sovereign control, the KFOR action in effect represents the foreign security agencies' capacity to control Kosovo. After all, what matters with respect to the declaration of a state of exception, if conceptualised as the ultimate expression of sovereignty, is 'who decides' rather than 'how it is decided'. In this particular case, it was not decided by the Kosovo President in consultation with the Prime Minister as outlined in the Kosovo constitution but by a foreign military commander who has been recognised as 'the final authority in theatre regarding interpretation of those aspects of the said [Status] Settlement that refer to the International Military Presence'.[118]

Conclusion

The Kosovo conflict, rooted in the competing sovereignty claims of the Serbs and Albanians over the territory and population of Kosovo, entered a new stage with the NATO military action in 1999. The air campaign, which was operationalised as an 'exceptional' military action necessitated by the humanitarian and security conditions on the ground, created a new state of political affairs in Kosovo. All Serbian military, security and paramilitary forces were removed from the territory and it was placed under the administration of the UN. A NATO-led security presence was also deployed to verify the withdrawal process and provide public security.

Although the issue of Kosovo's future status was left uncertain, the newly emerging institutional arrangement produced new 'opportunity structures' for the Kosovo Albanian independence movement. First, the conversion of the entire territory of Kosovo into an international protectorate, which was kept outside Belgrade's legal and physical control through the presence of a large international civilian and military mission, created a relatively freer political environment. Second, intervention helped open up the political space, in which the idea of the recognition of some form of independence was promoted as the only solution. Indeed, for the majority Albanians, who were in favour of nothing short of statehood, independence was already declared in 1991. They therefore were just waiting for the recognition of their status by the international community.[119] In this respect, surrounding ambiguities over Kosovo's status also worked to break the status quo. The proposal by Ahtisaari particularly underlined the unsustainability of Kosovo continuing to be governed by the UN.

While creating a new window of opportunity for the Kosovo independence movement, the NATO intervention produced new states of 'exception', including the establishment of UNMIK, recognition of 'supervised independence', and deployment of EULEX as part of the EU's regional crisis management engagement. All these institutional arrangements were introduced as necessary partnerships to improve the sovereign and functional capacity of the Kosovo institutions. However, the expanded practices of state capacity-building over time set the conditions of foreign intervention as a permanent exercise.

Notes

1 Parts of this chapter are drawn from Selver B. Sahin, 'The Use of the 'Exceptionalism' Argument in Kosovo: An Analysis of the Rationalization of External Interference in the Conflict', *Journal of Balkan and Near Eastern Studies*, 11, no. 3 (2009): 235–55; Selver B. Sahin, 'How Exception Became the Norm: Normalizing Intervention as an Exercise in Risk Management in Kosovo', *Journal of Balkan and Near Eastern Studies*, 5, no. 1 (2013): 17–36. Reproduced with permission of the publisher, www.tandfonline.com

2 Snyder, 'Kosovo Does Not Set Precedent, US Says'; 'Condoleezza Blasts South Ossetia's Independence'; Gamage, 'Independence of Kosovo Sets No Precedent Anywhere Else in This World'; 'Kosovo Case Unique, Says Miliband'; 'EU Splits on Kosovo Recognition'; European Parliament, 'Kosovo: A Special Case Say MEPs'; 'New Focus on the Western Balkans'.

3 Many of these points were discussed by two professors in the Spring 2006 issue of *NATO Review* with both supporting independence for Kosovo as the 'only feasible option' while disagreeing on whether such a move would affect the resolution of similar conflicts elsewhere in the world. For details, see 'Debate: Would Independence for Kosovo Contribute to or Undermine International Stability?'.

4 Matheson, 'United Nations Governance of Postconflict Societies'.

5 United Nations, *Letter Dated 26 March 2007 from the Secretary-General Addressed to the President of the Security Council (Report of the Special Envoy of the Secretary-General on Kosovo's Future Status)*.

6 Sahin, 'The Use of the "Exceptionalism" Argument in Kosovo'.

7 For a discussion of this point, see Pula, 'The Permanent State of Exception International Administration in Kosovo'.

8 Pavkovic, 'Kosovo/Kosova'; Batakovic, *Kosovo-Metohija*; Malcolm, *Kosovo*; Vickers, *Between Serb and Albanian*; Mertus, *Kosovo*.

9 The term 'first Yugoslavia' is used here to refer to the Kingdom of Serbs, Croats and Slovenes, which was established in 1918. The monarchy was renamed Yugoslavia in 1929 and ceased to exist following its occupation by the Axis powers in 1941.

10 Vickers, *Between Serb and Albanian*; Malcolm, *Kosovo*; Mertus, *Kosovo*.

11 Magas, *The Destruction of Yugoslavia*.

12 Artisien, 'A Note on Kosovo and the Future of Yugoslav–Albanian Relations'; Malcolm, *Kosovo*; Vickers, *Between Serb and Albanian*; Mertus, *Kosovo*.

13 Bojicic, 'The Disintegration of Yugoslavia'.

14 Woodward, 'The West and the International Organisations'.

15 Vickers, *Between Serb and Albanian*, 242.

16 For a discussion of the use of the 'return to Europe' rhetoric by the Croat and Slovene political leaderships with a view to securing international recognition and distinguishing themselves from 'Balkan' identities, see Lindstrom, 'Between Europe and the Balkans'.

17 Clark, *Civil Resistance in Kosovo*.

18 See, for example, Harden, 'Yugoslav Regions Assert Independence'.

19 Sudetic, 'Yugoslav Army Threatens Truce, 2 Republics Say'; Riding, 'Separatists in Europe Indirectly Reinforce Unity in Yugoslavia'. For a detailed discussion of the international community's response, see Weller, 'The International Response to the Dissolution of the Socialist Federal Republic of Yugoslavia'.

20 Clark, 'The Limits of Prudence', 281.

21 Clark, *Civil Resistance in Kosovo*, 2.

22 Gorani, *Orientalist Ethnonationalism*, 9.

23 Clark, *Civil Resistance in Kosovo*, 67–8.

24 Ibid.

25 Independent International Commission on Kosovo, *The Kosovo Report*.

26 Ibid; Clark, *Civil Resistance in Kosovo*.

27 The Badinter Commission maintained that the existing borders among the Yugoslav republics would be accepted as international boundaries because 'the right to self-determination must not involve changes to existing boundaries at the time of independence (uti possidetis juris) except where the States concerned agree[d] otherwise'. For further information, see Pellet, 'The Opinions of the Badinter Arbitration Committee'.

28 Judah, *Kosovo: What Everyone Needs to Know*, 69.

29 Maliqi, 'The Albanian Movement in Kosovo', 150–1.

30 Vickers, *Between Serb and Albanian*, 268.

31 Quoted in Judah, *Kosovo: War and Revenge*, 79–80.

32 Clark, *Civil Resistance in Kosovo*, 120.

33 'Rugova Calls for Kosovo "Protectorate"'.

34 The collapse of the pyramid investment schemes in Albania in early 1997 ignited social unrest that led to the collapse of the Albanian law enforcement and security institutions in a short span of time. Many military and police arms depots were looted by the rioters and most of these arms ended up on the black market. Judah, *Kosovo: War and Revenge*, 127–8.

35 Hedges, 'Notes from the Underground on Another Balkan Rift'.
36 Judah, *Kosovo: War and Revenge*, 129–34.
37 Loza, 'Kosovo Albanians'; Hedges, 'Both Sides in the Kosovo Conflict Seem Determined to Ignore Reality'.
38 Independent International Commission on Kosovo, *The Kosovo Report*.
39 Quoted in Erlanger, 'Albright Warns Serbs on Kosovo Violence'.
40 'Interview with Veton Surroi'.
41 ICG, *Unifying the Kosovar Factions*.
42 'Kosovo is Ours'.
43 Ibid.
44 Maliqi, 'Why Peaceful Resistance Movement in Kosova Failed'.
45 Ibid.
46 See, for example, Hammond, ' "Good Versus Evil" after the Cold War', 22.
47 Quoted in Herring, 'From Rambouillet to the Kosovo Accords', 227–8.
48 See, for example, Independent International Commission on Kosovo, *The Kosovo Report*; House of Commons Foreign Affairs Committee, '4th Report of the House of Commons Foreign Affairs Committee'; Danish Institute of International Affairs (DUPI), *Humanitarian Intervention*; Simma, 'NATO, the UN and the Use of Force'; Cassese, 'Ex Iniuria Ius Oritur'; Bellamy, *Kosovo and International Society*.
49 'Press Statement by Dr Javier Solana, Secretary General of NATO'.
50 Blair, 'Doctrine of the International Community'.
51 O'Connell, 'The UN, NATO, and International Law after Kosovo'.
52 Guicherd, 'International Law and the War in Kosovo'; O'Connell, 'The UN, NATO, and International Law after Kosovo'; Roberts, 'NATO's "Humanitarian War" over Kosovo'; Bring, 'Should NATO Take the Lead in Formulating a Doctrine on Humanitarian Intervention?'.
53 Bolton and Visoka, 'Recognising Kosovo's Independence'.
54 Ibid., 6.
55 Ibid.
56 Independent International Commission on Kosovo, *The Kosovo Report*.
57 ICG, *After Milosevic*; ICG, *Collapse in Kosovo*; ICG, *Kosovo: The Challenge of Transition*; ICG, *Kosovo Status: Delay is Risky*; ICG, *Kosovo's Status: Difficult Months Ahead*; ICG, *Kosovo: No Good Alternatives to the Ahtisaari Plan*.
58 ICG, *Cyprus: Reversing the Drift to Partition*.
59 ICG, *Georgia's South Ossetia Conflict: Make Haste Slowly*.
60 International Commission on the Balkans, 'The Balkans in Europe's Future'.
61 Ibid., 17.
62 'UN Preparing to Leave Kosovo, Jessen-Petersen Says'.
63 Maliqi, 'Is Rugova Going to be Arrested?'.
64 Matheson, 'United Nations Governance of Postconflict Societies', 78.
65 Wilde, 'Representing International Territorial Administration'.
66 Wilde, 'From Danzig to East Timor and Beyond'.
67 Yannis, 'The Concept of Suspended Sovereignty in International Law and Its Implications in International Politics', 1049.
68 Wilde, 'Representing International Territorial Administration', 87.

69 Ibid., 85.
70 Ibid.
71 Surroi, 'Kosovo: An Unfinished Political War'.
72 ICG, *Waiting for UNMIK: Local Administration in Kosovo*.
73 OSCE, 'Human Rights in Kosovo'.
74 United Nations, 'Transcript of Press Conference by Secretary-General Kofi Annan and Deputy-Secretary-General Louise Frechette at Headquarters'.
75 UNMIK, 'SRSG Hans Haekkerup Addresses North Atlantic Council'.
76 UNMIK, 'SRSG Michael Steiner Addresses Permanent Council of the OSCE'.
77 UNMIK, 'Harri Holkeri's Address to the UN Security Council'.
78 UN News Centre, 'Foes of Multi-Ethnic Democracy still Threaten Kosovo's Progress – UN Envoy'.
79 UNMIK, 'Standards for Kosovo'.
80 Williams and Pecci, 'Earned Sovereignty'.
81 Ibid.
82 Eide, 'The Situation in Kosovo: Report to the Secretary General of the United Nations'.
83 United Nations, *Letter Dated 7 October 2005 from the Secretary-General Addressed to the President of the Security Council*, para. 44.
84 Ibid., para. 64.
85 United Nations, *Letter Dated 26 March 2007 from the Secretary-General Addressed to the President of the Security Council*.
86 Independent International Commission on Kosovo, *The Kosovo Report*.
87 UNOSEK, Press Conference by UN Special Envoy for the Future Status Process for Kosovo Martti Ahtisaari, in Pristina.
88 United Nations, *Letter Dated 26 March 2007 from the Secretary-General Addressed to the President of the Security Council*, para. 11.
89 Ibid., paras. 6–7.
90 United Nations, *Letter Dated 26 March 2007 from the Secretary-General Addressed to the President of the Security Council*.
91 'Wisner: Kosovo Status Agreement is Close'.
92 'Kosovo Case Unique Says Miliband'.
93 'Ex-Rebel Becomes Kosovo's Prime Minister'.
94 'Thaci Says Kosovo Backs EU Mission, Not Six-Point Plan'.
95 Although Kosovo is often described as the biggest recipient of EU assistance in the world, as manifested in the allocation of approximately €2 billion since 1999, with a GDP per capita of US$3,579, the country remains one of the poorest parts of Europe. Approximately 30 per cent of the population lives below the national poverty line and the youth unemployment rate stands at around 60 per cent. Data is compiled from the European Union Office in Kosovo/European Union Special Representative in Kosovo, 'Political and Economic Issues'; UNDP, 'About Kosovo'.
96 'Kosovo Declared "Fully Independent"'.
97 United Nations, *Letter Dated 26 March 2007 from the Secretary-General Addressed to the President of the Security Council (Comprehensive Proposal for the Kosovo Status Settlement)*, *Addendum 1*, Annex XI.
98 Ibid., Annexes IX and X.

99 For a discussion of debates on the legality of EULEX, see, for example, de Wet, 'The Governance of Kosovo'.

100 'Council Joint Action 2008/124/CFSP of 4 February 2008, on the European Union Rule of Law Mission in Kosovo, EULEX Kosovo'.

101 Ibid.

102 Five EU member states, namely Spain, Greece, Cyprus, Slovakia and Romania, have refused to recognise Kosovo.

103 de Wet, 'The Governance of Kosovo'.

104 United Nations, 'Report of the Secretary-General on the United Nations Interim Administration Mission in Kosovo', 24 November 2008.

105 Foniqi-Kabashi, 'International Community Urges Kosovo Leaders to Accept UN Chief's EULEX Plan'.

106 The full transcript of US Assistant Secretary Dan Fried's two press conferences with the Kosovo President Fatmir Sejdiu and Prime Minister Hashim Thachi on 17 and 18 November 2008 can be accessed online at http://pristina.usembassy.gov.

107 See, for example, United Nations, 'Report of the Secretary-General on the United Nations Interim Administration Mission in Kosovo', 12 June 2008.

108 'Ethnic Albanians Now Oppose EU Kosovo Mission'.

109 Beqiri, 'EULEX Becomes Fully Operational'.

110 UNDP, 'About Kosovo'.

111 European Commission, 'Key Findings of the 2010 Progress Report on Kosovo'.

112 Ibid.

113 EULEX, *EULEX Programme Report 2011*; US State Department, *Trafficking in Persons Report 2011*.

114 Derks and Price, *The EU and Rule of Law Reform in Kosovo*.

115 ICG, *North Kosovo: Dual Sovereignty in Practice*.

116 'KFOR Declares Gates 1 and 31 Military Zones, Angers Serbia'.

117 Brajshori, 'Mitrovica: Temporary Fix, Long Term Problem'.

118 Article 153 of the Kosovo constitution also states that 'No Republic of Kosovo authority shall have jurisdiction to review, diminish or otherwise restrict the mandate, powers and obligations referred to in this Article'.

119 ICG, *Collapse in Kosovo*, 2.

4 The Kurdish Regional Government and the question of increasing autonomy

The formation of an independent state has long been a dream of Kurds. With a population of some 30 million people living in the Middle East, the Kurds are often referred to as the 'largest stateless nation in the contemporary world'.[1] According to common estimates, about half of the Kurds live in Turkey, while they constitute around 10 per cent of the population in Iran, approximately 10 per cent in Syria and about 20 per cent in Iraq.[2]

Divided by geography as well as by political, linguistic, religious and tribal differences, the Kurds, compared to Arab and other subjects of the Ottoman Empire, were late to develop a nationalist movement as a political project.[3] The Kurdish hopes for an independent state were high during the redrawing of boundaries by the victor powers of the First World War during the 1920s. However, the creation of Turkey and Arab states in the formerly Ottoman-ruled lands in the Middle East shortly buried the Kurdish expectations.

Rather than as a single movement, Kurdish nationalism therefore developed in distinct forms determined by different political settings and state-building policies in Iran, Turkey, Iraq and Syria.[4] In Iran, a relatively inclusive political space for Kurdish and Shi'a communities enabled the emergence of a secular, leftist-oriented nationalist movement and the establishment of a short-lived Kurdish government in Mahabad in the immediate post-Second World War era.[5] However, the movement was suppressed by the nationalist Iranian government, and it was only after the Islamic revolution of 1979 that the Kurds were once again able to articulate their demands for political autonomy.[6] The highly restrictive policies of early republican Turkey, including the prohibition of the terms Kurds and Kurdistan, and the use of Kurdish in schools and social life prevented the expression of a Kurdish ethnic identity in the public space.[7] This situation, Natali suggests, gave rise to a highly ethnicised, urbanised and diversified national movement in which tribal leaders played no significant role compared to the emerging Kurdish nationalist movement in Iraq.[8] Turkey's revitalised EU bid with the opening of accession negotiations in 2005 and the ruling Justice and Development Party (AKP) government's subsequent initiation of a democratic opening program in 2009, on the other hand, provided Kurds with expanding political and cultural rights. In Iraq, Kurdish nationalism emerged as a semi-legitimate, influential movement that involved tribal leaders as a significant actor and took an ethnicised form particularly following the central government's attempts to create an Arabised identity of the Iraqi state after the nationalist revolution in 1958.[9] The Gulf War of 1991 and the forced regime change in 2003 significantly altered the political status of the Iraqi Kurds. While they have been able to exercise territorial control and political power in an emerging de facto state, dependency on foreign assistance in the form of democratic capacity development has also become a key feature of the administrative structures they have created. The changes in the political and institutional sphere, in other words, have defined the parameters of Kurdish nationalism as an organising force in Iraq and the region.

This chapter investigates the major aspects of the Kurdish state-making movement in Iraq in light of the changes in the political sphere that were brought about by domestic and external developments. It begins with a brief overview of the historical background of the Kurdish question. It then continues with the effects of the 1991 Gulf War and the US-led intervention in 2003 on the dynamics of the conditions of political power in Iraq.

Historical background of the Kurdish question and emergence of a *de facto* Kurdish State

The Treaty of Sèvres signed in 1920 at the end of the First World War established the states of Iraq, Syria and Kuwait from the formerly Ottoman-ruled lands. It also promised the possibility of an independent Kurdish state in the region. Articles 62 provided that:[10]

> a Commission sitting at Constantinople and composed of three members appointed by the British, French and Italian Governments respectively shall draft within six months from the coming into force of the present Treaty a scheme of local autonomy for the predominantly Kurdish areas.

Article 64 which provided the Kurds of the Mosul *vilayet* (province) with the option to join a future Kurdish state specified the conditions of independence in the following way:[11]

> If within one year from the coming into force of the present Treaty the Kurdish peoples within the areas defined in Article 62 shall address themselves to the Council of the League of Nations in such a manner as to show that a majority of the population of these areas desires independence from Turkey, and if the Council then considers that these peoples are capable of such independence and recommends that it should be granted to them, Turkey hereby agrees to execute such a recommendation, and to renounce all rights and title over these areas.

However, the terms of the Treaty were never implemented. It became void with the victory of the Turkish independence movement led by Mustafa Kemal Atatürk, founder of modern Turkey, and was replaced by the Treaty of Lausanne in 1923, which contained no reference to the status of the Kurds. Unable to exercise the opportunity created by the Treaty of Sèvres due to changing dynamics of international balance of power, the Kurds have lived under Turkish, Iranian, Syrian and Iraqi sovereignty since then. In addition to a strong opposition from the newly created states in the region, Britain's shifting position for a single Iraq including Mosul following discovery of rich oil fields in Mosul and Kirkuk prevented the realisation of the Kurdish dream of statehood.[12]

The Kurds of Iraq, and Kurds in general, received little interest from international scholarship that was largely focused on the processes of post-colonial state-building in the region until the 1960s.[13] The dynamics of the Kurdish movement in Iraq and the neighbouring countries were also closely linked to the power struggles between the US and the Soviet Union, whose objective was to defend their respective interests in their own spheres of influence.[14] It is important to note that the Soviets, who, along with the British, occupied Iran in 1941, supported the short-lived Kurdish Mahabad Republic proclaimed by Mustafa Barzani in western Iran in 1946. The Soviet troops withdrew from Iran and left it under the British sphere of influence in 1946, leading to the defeat of the Kurds by Reza Shah.[15] The Soviet interest in the Kurds, as can be anticipated, derived from its intention to use them as a disruptive element against the pro-Western governments of Turkey, Iran and Iraq.[16] Mustafa Barzani who was granted refuge by the Soviets following the collapse of the Mahabad Republic enjoyed Soviet support until 1972 when the Baath

Party signed a treaty of friendship with Moscow.[17] Having Iranian support, Barzani then turned to the US. However, he failed to garner Washington's support for the Kurdish uprising against the Baathist regime due to the conclusion of the Algiers Accord between the Shah and Iraq's Vice President Saddam Hussein in 1975[18] and due to the US concerns about the possibility of a Soviet intervention in Iran and Turkey, which were both US allies with substantial Kurdish populations.[19]

In addition to these external factors, the Kurdish nationalist movement in Iraq was weakened by internal rivalries and clashes between political groupings; the Kurdistan Democratic Party (KDP) founded by Mustafa Barzani in 1946 and the Patriotic Union of Kurdistan (PUK) formed by Jalal Talabani in 1975. The PUK was an urban-based and left-oriented party as opposed to the tribally organised KDP, whose *peshmerga* (meaning 'those ready to die') forces were fighting the Iraqi security forces through guerrilla warfare following the collapse of negotiations for an autonomy proposal offered by Saddam Hussein in 1970.[20]

The Kurds of Iraq were also affected by the renewed tensions between Baghdad and Teheran following the overthrow of the Shah in 1979. The Iran–Iraq war, on the other hand, created new opportunities for the Kurdish groups to internationalise their struggle. During the war, they fought Saddam Hussein's forces.[21] Saddam, however, responded with intensive chemical attacks on Kurdish villages between February and September 1988, known as the Anfal (Spoils of War) campaign,[22] which led to the death of at least 50,000 and as many as 100,000 civilians.[23] It is important to note that the Reagan administration, whose priority was to contain Iran and maintain the best possible relations with Turkey, was unwilling to investigate the attacks through a congressional process, as evidenced by the House of Representative's refusal to support the Senate-endorsed Genocide Prevention Bill which envisioned imposing sanctions on Iraq.[24]

Similar to the situation in East Timor, the end of superpower rivalries in the post-Cold War era and other political developments including the Gulf War of 1991 and the growing efforts of the diaspora to unify the Kurdish struggle and attract international attention to the Kurdish demands of political recognition and representation helped change the international community's approach to the Kurds in Iraq.[25] Saddam Hussein's invasion of neighbouring Kuwait in August 1990 and displacement of many Kurdish civilians as a result of his offensive against the Kurds, along with the Shi'ites in the south, who revolted against the Baathist regime in 1991, prompted the US-led international coalition forces to launch a military intervention and impose a no-fly zone in northern Iraq, north of the 36th parallel, to create a 'safe haven' for the Iraqi Kurds.

The military action against Iraq, according to the intervening powers, was an exceptional operation that arguably symbolised the beginning of a 'new world order'; a world in which the principles of human rights, democracy and rule of law rather than the 'law of the jungle' would prevail.[26] The Gulf War, it was argued, was exceptional in several other ways as well. First, as described in the Security Council documents, Saddam Hussein's policy of repression and population displacements in northern Iraq were viewed as an 'exceptionally serious situation' threatening regional peace and security.[27] Second, the military intervention against Iraq was claimed to have been a 'unique' coalition supported by thirty-four countries to ensure the withdrawal of Iraqi forces from Kuwait.[28] Third, the US and Soviet leaderships developed cooperative action in defence of Kuwait's sovereignty which was essential for the success of Operation Desert Storm launched in January 1991.[29] Fourth, the Gulf War was exceptional in terms of demonstrating the 'dissolution of the Arab unity', as the coalition forces included Israel and a number of Arab countries (such as Saudi Arabia, United Arab Emirates, Bahrain and Oman) providing military assistance in a war waged against a central Arab state.[30]

Through enforcing a no-fly zone in northern Iraq, the US and UK governments sought not only to secure and stabilise the region bordering Iran and Turkey, where hundreds of thousands of Kurds took refuge fearing gas attacks, but to 'contain' the Saddam Hussein regime.[31] Throughout the 1990s, British and US fighter planes flying from the Incirlik military base in southern Turkey patrolled over the Iraqi airspace in the north as well as in the south.[32] Foreign military intervention enabled the Kurds to reinforce their ethnic identity and develop new forms of political organisation in an emerging state-like entity protected by coalition forces.[33] Operating in an enlarged political and institutional sphere that came into existence as a result of foreign interference, the Kurds enjoyed the opportunity to utilise the institutional underpinnings of self-rule. This is evidenced by the organisation of elections in May 1992 and the formation of the Kurdistan Regional Government (KRG) to gain legitimacy and fill the power vacuum created by the forced withdrawal of the Iraqi central authorities. A report dated 1992, for instance, describes the situation in northern Iraq as a site of uncertainties where 'the remnants of Iraqi civil authority in this region, deprived of leadership and money from Baghdad but lacking direction from any central Kurdish authority, are nearly paralysed'.[34] The elections, proposed to solve the authority and legitimacy problems, resulted in a power-sharing arrangement between the KDP and PUK, each of which gained 50 seats in a 105-member Assembly.[35] However, similar to the intensifying rivalries between the East Timorese and Kosovo Albanian groups struggling to control uses of political power and economic resources in a zone of uncertainties following the withdrawal of a shared enemy, the two Kurdish groups were shortly involved in a civil war. The war was initiated by the PUK to change the balance of power, which was at that time in the KDP's favour by virtue of the greater income derived from the latter's control of the border trade with Turkey.[36] The parties sought to create their own administrative authority in their respective territories: the KDP in Erbil and Dohuk and the PUK in Sulaymaniyah.[37]

The war ended in September 1998 with mediation from the US. The agreement the Kurdish parties signed in Washington was based on the Ankara Peace Process which the US, British and Turkish governments initiated in October 1996 to conclude a sustainable peace settlement through a series of diplomatic talks.[38] During this diplomatic process, the Turkish government also formed an alliance with Massoud Barzani's KDP and sought to destroy the Kurdish Workers' Party (PKK) units based in northern Iraq.[39] The PUK and KDP also strengthened their economic and operational capacity as result of receipt of 13 per cent of Iraq's oil revenues under the UN's Oil-for-Food Programme (OFFP) since 1996 and agreed to unify the two administrations later in 2002.[40] The OFFP remained in operation until November 2003 and provided the KRG with the necessary external patronage and financial resources to develop infrastructure projects such as rehabilitation of the agricultural sector, water and sanitation facilities and electricity supplies to encourage political and social stability.[41] During this period, the Kurdish region was allocated nearly US$10 billion, while it received only US$1 billion in goods and services between 1991 and 1996.[42] Through utilising the emergent conditions and fruits of reconstruction assistance channelled by foreign agencies, the KRG constructed its existence as an autonomous unit, even though preserving the territorial integrity of Iraq was prioritised by the OFFP.[43] It should be also noted that the OFFP was used by Saddam Hussein to consolidate the formal patronage capacity of his regime domestically through exercise of discretionary control over oil pricing, selection of purchasers of oil exports and humanitarian imports, and generation of illicit revenues from surcharges on oil sales and commissions for humanitarian purchases (which ranged between $268 million and $7.5 billion according to different estimates).[44] The programme was, at the same time, politically manipulated by international actors including some

UN Security Council members following the Iraqi leadership's extension of its reward system overseas in the form of oil vouchers provided as gifts or in payment for goods to foreign companies.[45]

The overthrow of the Saddam Hussein regime by the US invasion of Iraq in 2003 profoundly changed the dynamics of the political sphere in the country and created new opportunity structures for the Kurds including the formal recognition of the autonomous status of the KRG within Iraq restructured as a federal state. While the surrounding uncertainties and emergencies arising from changing political dynamics enabled the KRG to consolidate its existence and administrative qualities as a state-like entity in a relatively secure and stable region compared to the rest of Iraq, the same uncertainties and emergencies have increased its vulnerability and dependency on foreign capacity-development assistance. Following Caspersen' analysis of unrecognised states, the KRG appears to 'insist on [its] right to self-determination' and 'exist in the shadows of international relations, in a kind of limbo, and the renewed outbreak of war is an ever-present risk and defining feature of [its] existence'.[46]

Democratic capacity-building experience of the KRG since 2003

The contemporary debate on state capacity, as noted earlier, revolves around a perceived disconnect between states' legal recognition as independent polities with the right to exercise ultimate authority over their own affairs (or 'negative sovereignty' in Jackson's words) and their actual ability to demonstrate the empirical attributes of sovereign statehood ('positive sovereignty'), such as the exercise of territorial control and provision of security and other public goods to their populations. Those states that are unable or unwilling to fulfil the requirements of positive sovereignty are now referred to as fragile or failing states in need of long-term capacity-development. Because sovereignty is now treated as synonymous with a demonstrated capacity of good governance, the long-term involvement of foreign agencies in their domestic policy-making and institutional processes is argued to be a necessary engagement to fill this 'sovereignty gap'[47] rather than as a violation of sovereignty.

In this context, the KRG's existence as a non-recognised entity with empirical attributes of statehood including an elected parliament, a president, a prime minister, a cabinet, overseas diplomatic representations, a military (peshmerga), intelligence services, a flag and a growing economy provides an interesting case in the above sovereignty debate.[48] That is, the KRG, which has empirically established itself as an influential actor through capitalising on the changing dynamics of political power and sovereignty in Iraq brought about by the military interventions in 1991 and 2003, is now seeking formal recognition through a process of 'earned sovereignty'.[49] Referring to a conditional, gradual handover of administrative authorities, as discussed in the previous chapters, 'earned sovereignty' has become the main strategic approach of the political leaderships of many unrecognised states seeking to attain international support and legitimacy. A key aspect of this strategy has been a coordinated action towards demonstrating a governmental capacity and willingness to exercise territorial control and domestic security and commitment to internationally advocated democratic ideals and practices. In their quest for formal recognition, the leaderships of these entities have also often highlighted systematic human rights violations inflicted by the previous authoritarian regimes or unlawful annexation of their territories and demanded secession as a way of remedying these past wrong doings and governmental deficiencies.[50] This is exemplified by the East Timorese nationalists' emphasis on the disruption of decolonisation due to Indonesia's invasion and civilian atrocities under Suharto, and the Kosovo Albanians' reference to Milošević's ethnic cleansing in Bosnia and Kosovo to uphold their claim that their parent states had no legitimacy to exercise territorial rule. In the case of Iraqi Kurdish nationalists the suffering they endured under Saddam Hussein, particularly the Anfal campaign, has occupied a central place in their discourses and actions to win international support for secession.[51]

The KRG's aspiration to consolidate its claimed sovereign capacity over the region and demonstrate this sovereignty to the outside world in pursuit of international recognition is further evidenced by: (1) Kurdish leaders' rhetorical emphasis on the democratic credentials of their governmental structures such as the organisation of regular multi-party elections and adoption of liberal practices in the fields of civil society activism, freedom of expression, minority rights and gender equality; (2) their efforts to promote economic viability through exploitation of oil reserves in the autonomous region and securing control of the disputed areas of Kirkuk, Ninevah (Mosul) and Diyala;[52] as well as (3) Barzani's occasional threats to declare independence whenever the federal government has attempted to exert greater authority over regional units.[53] Moreover, the birth of new exceptional states such as Kosovo's achievement of conditional independence in 2008 at the end of a nine-year international administration and South Sudan's separation following an internationally negotiated referendum in 2011 has provided a particular source of encouragement for the pro-independence factions.[54]

Clearly, whether or not the KRG will be able to succeed in exceptional state-making depends on the specific preferences and decisions of a variety of foreign actors motivated by a mixture of pragmatism and considerations of stability in Iraq and the broader region. On the other hand, the KRG is actively pursuing foreign support, while striving to consolidate the key pillars of viable statehood, including a functioning market economy. In this regard, the positions of the regional powers and the leading members of the international actors, primarily the US and other influential Western countries, will determine the prospects of its exceptional state-making experience, if Kurdish leaders happen to materialise their statehood aspirations through a formal declaration of independence.

One of these key regional actors is Turkey. While Ankara has long been known as the most ardent opponent of an independent Kurdish state due to its spillover potential into its south-eastern region, it has developed stronger commercial and political ties with the KRG over the past few years. The ruling AKP government's growing engagement with the KRG has been motivated by a convergence of strategic interests between the two such as Turkey's discomfort with former Prime Minister Maliki's Shi'ite-dominated government, satisfaction of its pressing energy needs and the KRG's wish to find a way to export its oil and gas to Western markets independently of Baghdad's control.[55] It should be however noted that Turkey's interest in the Kurdish region was driven not only by its trade potential but also by its concerns that instability in the north will necessarily spread to other already problematic parts of the country and impede the consolidation of a unified Iraq and improvement of Turkish–Iraqi ties.[56] Moreover, Ankara's shifting policy towards Erbil since 2008, as will be discussed further below, was also rooted in the increasing power of the KRG as a dependable ally of the US advised to 'continue improving its relationship and coordination with Turkey' for maintaining stability in the region, while the south of the country was engulfed in violence.[57] A special analysis written by Richard Holbrooke for the *Washington Post* in February 2007 highlights the parameters of the US interest in bringing Turkey and the KRG closer:[58]

Despite their history, Turkey and Iraqi Kurdistan need each other. Kurdistan could become a buffer between Turkey and the chaos to the south, while Turkey could become the protector of a Kurdistan, though still technically part of Iraq that is effectively cut loose from a Baghdad that may no longer function.

Turkey still would not prefer an independent Kurdish state in its neigh-
bourhood. Yet, the AKP government does not appear to consider the
current autonomous Kurdish government as the biggest threat to its
security. Indeed, the Turkish leadership has adopted a 'less security-
focused' approach to solve its own Kurdish question under the so-called
Kurdish Opening (later renamed Democratic Opening) process launched
in 2009 to introduce legal and political reforms on minority rights.[59] The
AKP also initiated state-level negotiations with the PKK for its disarma-
ment and withdrawal from the country.[60] Moreover, the changing regional
balance of power brought about by the overthrow of the authoritarian
regimes in Tunisia, Egypt and Libya, outbreak of the Syrian conflict, and
rising sectarian tensions in the broader region particularly following the
recent rise of the Islamic State of Iraq and Levant (now calling itself the
Islamic State) have necessitated an alliance between Turkey and the KRG
in the field of security. The remarks of AKP leaders on the territorial
integrity of Iraq illustrate Turkey's foreign policy dilemmas. In June
2014, Huseyin Celik, spokesperson for the AKP, was quoted in the
Kurdish and Turkish media stating that 'The Kurds of Iraq can decide for
themselves the name and type of the entity they are living in'.[61] However,
during Barzani's visit to Ankara a month later in search of Turkish
support, Turkey's Erdoğan, Prime Minister at the time, reportedly urged
the Kurdish leader to 'avoid incidents that could inflame ethnic and sectarian strife in Iraq and that the political efforts to preserve the integrity
of the country should be supported'.[62]

When it comes to the US, whose position will surely determine the
prospects of Kurdish political aspirations, Washington has been opposed
to Erbil's export of oil extracted from the disputed territories through a
pipeline to Turkey amidst tensions with Baghdad.[63] The Obama administration's policy is driven by concerns that allowing KRG's oil deals
would precipitate the territory's secession which, in turn, could provoke
Turkey and Iran.[64] However, it would be misguided to view the current
US position as unchangeable, considering the initial international emphasis on the maintenance of Serbia's territorial integrity and sovereignty
over Kosovo and the latter's eventual recognition argued to have been
conditioned by the realities on the ground.

In terms of the prospects for shifting US foreign policy anchored in
security and economic interests, the changing balance of power in Iraq
and the broader region with the rise of the Islamic State is seen by some
as a 'golden opportunity' for Kurds to make a stronger case for independence.[65] The peshmerga forces took control of Kirkuk in June 2014 following the withdrawal of the Iraqi army from the region in the face of a

rapid incursion of the Islamic State militants and advances with seizure of a number of cities including Mosul, Iraq's second largest city. The control of the oil-rich city provided the Kurds with the opportunity to implement Article 140 of the Iraqi Constitution.[66] Barzani ordered the Kurdish Regional Parliament in July to begin preparations for an independence referendum.[67] However, the renewed Islamic State attacks in northern Iraq resulting in population displacements postponed the referendum plans. The Islamic State advances shifted the US reluctance to militarily involve in Iraq following the departure of its troops in 2011. It is important to note that the Obama administration's decision to launch air strikes followed Barzani's telephone conversation with Vice-President Joe Biden, telling him the militants were only 25 miles away from the capital Erbil.[68] Seemingly, Obama's policy shift came after the KRG's agreement to suspend referendum plans and to stay part of Iraq based on an expanding autonomy framework that allows Iraqi Kurds the right to sell their own oil, purchase their own arms and conduct a referendum on the resolution of the status of the disputed territories.[69] In addition to coming to the help of its ally in a volatile region, Obama's decision was also motivated by the protection of US personnel in the oil rich area where billions of dollars have been invested by American companies.[70]

This makes it clear that the KRG's formal separation is dependent on Kurdish leaders' ability to adapt to the shifts in the US policy-orientation triggered by emerging economic and security developments as well as to convince the regional actors that they have no irredentist claims in pursuit of foreign endorsement for statehood. However, formal recognition of statehood is not the only area of foreign intervention on which the process of Kurdish state-making is dependent. Indeed, the KRG's diplomatic strategy of presenting itself as an actor that is capable of exercising territorial control and running its own administrative affairs[71] is complicated by its increasing dependence on foreign assistance with the resolution of the ownership of the disputed oil rich territories and strengthening the functional capacity of its democratic state institutions. Whereas the southern and central parts of Iraq have become mired in insecurity and sectarian violence following the externally imposed regime change in 2003, the Kurdish autonomous region has experienced stability and certain levels of prosperity as a result of foreign aid, lucrative contracts with international companies and increasing commercial relations with regional states.[72] The Kurdish region has experienced few serious bombings in the last decade, while the death toll in Shi'ite-majority areas of Baghdad rose up to 1,000 a month as of mid-2013.[73] Turkey, as noted earlier, has become one of the KRG's biggest business partners, with trade between the two amounting to US$12 billion at the end of 2012.[74] The KRG is also acting like a foreign policy actor as manifested in the opening of diplomatic representations in more than 20 countries, including the US, UK, France, Germany, Iran, Russia and Australia.[75]

The KRG's rise as a state-like entity with leverage in domestic and regional politics was enabled through the greater external support Iraqi Kurds received following the 2003 US-led intervention. First, the KDP and PUK, as noted earlier, agreed to form unity as a single administration in 2002 in an attempt to take advantage of the interventionist tide in US foreign policy following the September 11 attacks. As detailed in the *9/11 Commission Report*, President Bush ordered his staff as early as 12 September 2001 to 'explore possible Iraqi links' to the attacks and began preparing for a military operation against Saddam Hussein following the overthrow of the Taliban in Afghanistan, even though 'no "compelling case" that Iraq had either planned or perpetrated the attacks' was found.[76] Second, Kurdish leaders' opposition to the Saddam Hussein regime and portrayal of their involvement in the planned US-led operation as a struggle to liberate the country from tyranny rather than as an effort to secede from Iraq helped attract sympathy in Western countries committed to regime change.[77] Third, when the Turkish Parliament rejected a resolution permitting the deployment of US troops through Turkey in March 2003, the Kurdish administration presented itself as a reliable ally ready to facilitate the military operation from the lands they controlled in the north of Iraq.[78] The images of peshmerga forces fighting side-by-side with US troops were often circulated in the American media throughout the war. Their entry in April 2003 into Kirkuk, which Ankara regards as a historic Turkmen centre, on the other hand, led the Turkish government to threaten the Kurdish groups with a military intervention if they refused to leave the city.[79] Fourth, taking advantage of the strained relations between Turkey and the US since the rejection of the above-noted parliamentary motion and the 'Suleymaniyah incident',[80] the Kurdish administration solidified its existence as an 'indispensible US ally' for implementation of the regime change in Iraq.[81] President Bush's meeting with Barzani as the President of the KRG at the Oval Office in October 2005, for instance, was politically important in terms of the reaffirmation of the Kurds' enhanced status in the newly constructed Iraq.[82] Fifth, the political stability and democratic governance institutions Kurdish-controlled northern Iraq has enjoyed in the post-Saddam era helped solidify the Kurdish claims as a political community capable of governing itself.[83]

One of the key factors that has contributed to political stability in the Kurdish region was the Kurdistan Alliance Barzani's KDP and Talabani's PUK formed in an attempt to reinforce their position as a unified front in the reconstructed Iraqi state. Their candidates ran in a joint list during the national and regional parliamentary elections held respectively in January and December 2005. Kurds occupied significant positions in the newly formed federal government, with Talabani becoming the President of Iraq, Hoshyar Zebari being appointed as foreign minister, and Barham Salih as deputy prime minister in the cabinet headed by the Shi'ite Ibrahim Al Ja'afri.[84] In the regional elections, the Kurdistan Alliance won 104 of the 111 seats in the Regional Parliament, with the KDP holding a majority of votes in Dohuk and Erbil, and the PUK dominating the polls in Suleymaniyah.[85]

The Kurds' shifting fortunes in self-governance in the post-Saddam environment are also reflected in the 2005 Constitution, which was drafted in consideration of Kurdish interests as a reflection of their alliance with the US during the war. This is evidenced in a specific provision (Article 117) that describes the KRG's status as an autonomous entity and designates Arabic and Kurdish as the two official languages of a federal Iraq.[86] The new Iraqi Constitution reiterates the 'unity, integrity, independence, and sovereignty of Iraq'[87] and creates three levels of government made up of the federal government in Baghdad, regional governments (such as the KRG) and governorates (currently eighteen).[88] However, it leaves the question of how the relations between these levels of government are organised in ambiguity.

Of the major uncertainties surrounding the exercise of governmental authority, the ownership of oil and gas resources has become a particular source of tension between Baghdad and Erbil. For instance, Article 111's stipulation that '[o]il and gas are owned by all of the people of Iraq' is interpreted by the KRG to mean that the management of these resources within its territory falls under its sovereignty, as the wording leaves the meaning of ownership wide open – whether they are jointly or equally owned by the Iraqi people.[89] Article 110, on the other hand, sets out a list of exclusive powers vested with the federal government including the formulation of foreign economic and trade policy, and negotiation and ratification of international agreements, while Article 114 addresses shared competencies between the federal and regional constituencies in a range of areas that are also relevant to oil and gas management such as the formulation of development and general planning policies, generation of electric energy, environmental policies and internal water resources policy.[90] Moreover, Article 112's establishment of the federal government as responsible for the management of 'present' oil and gas fields remains as another matter of contention, as it is unclear whether this means fields that are known to exist or includes fields that are in the development stage or in full production.[91] For the Kurds, who were more interested in the question of 'what role was left for the national government' rather than that of 'what control regions should have' during the drafting of the constitution,[92] the word 'present' suggests that the management of future oil fields, meaning those around Kirkuk, is reserved for the KRG.[93]

Oil is the main export of Iraq, which has the world's second largest oil reserves, albeit vulnerable to corruptive practices of elites as well as to security challenges posed by insurgents particularly during the presence of US troops.[94] The fragility of the Kurds' financial circumstances was clear during Iraq's 2008 budget negotiations, when there was a coordinated attempt by Sunni and Shi'ite Arab members of the Federal Parliament to reduce the KRG's transfer of annual capital investment fund from 17 per cent of the federal budget (around 90 per cent of which is financed from oil money) to 13 per cent.[95] The Kurds managed to sustain their annual budget share thanks to a threat of veto of the proposed 2008 budget law by President Talabani.[96]

Seeking to create a funding mechanism operating independently from the federal government, the Iraqi Kurds aspire to take over control of oil rich Kirkuk,[97] which they view as their traditional capital city oppressed by Saddam Hussein.[98] Regarding the future status of Kirkuk, the Iraqi Constitution stipulates that a referendum would be held no later than 31 December 2007. However, the delays arising from the Maliki government's attempts to reassert Baghdad's authority over regional units and opposition to addressing the ownership of the disputed territories led the Kurdish leaders to speak more openly about independence.[99] This situation, on the other hand, triggered threats of military intervention from Turkey, which, as noted earlier, is concerned with the PKK activities in northern Iraq and considers Kirkuk historically a Turkmen city.[100]

Amidst boiling tensions with Turkey and the federal government, the KRG invoked Article 115 of the Iraqi Constitution which, in the event of a conflict among the federal, regional and provincial governments, gives 'priority' to regional authorities and governorates in matters that are not specified as those falling under the sole authority of the federal government, even though the applicability of this principle to the oil and gas sector was challenged by the federal government.[101] Notwithstanding the surrounding controversies, the Kurdistan Regional Parliament passed a new hydrocarbon law in August 2007, which authorised the KRG to independently sign contracts with foreign oil companies. Based on the new law, the Kurdish government concluded twenty-five oil exploration and production-sharing contracts with international companies by early 2008.[102] The year 2008, at the same time, witnessed a rapprochement in Turkish–Kurdish relations, as illustrated by the organisation of the first direct high-level meeting in Baghdad where KRG's Prime Minister Nechirvan Barzani and Ahmet Davutoglu, Erdogan's chief foreign advisor at the time, came together to discuss potential areas of economic and political cooperation, including the prevention of the PKK activities in the region.[103] This was followed by the KRG's signing of production sharing agreements with Exxon Mobil (the world's largest oil company) in 2011 on six blocks, three of which are in the disputed territories, and subsequent conclusion of an agreement with the Turkish government to construct a pipeline that would directly connect the Kurdish oil to Western European markets via Turkey.[104]

The KRG's moves met a strong objection from the US, which has been concerned with the destabilising effects of potential Kurdish independence in the region, as noted earlier. For KRG's Natural Resources Minister Ashti Hawrami, however, his government was acting in accordance with the Constitution, arguing 'local oilfield managers are answerable to the local authorities' as per Article 115 which establishes the 'supremacy of regional laws over federal laws' and Article 112 which authorises the federal government to regulate the extraction and marketing of oil from existing producing fields only.[105] The KRG is hoping to sell 300,000 barrels per day once the planned pipeline starts functioning and export over one million per day by December 2015 and two million by 2019 with the construction of new pumping stations.[106]

However, the KRG's actions that have been driven by a desire to create a viable economy and develop self-sustaining democratic state institutions as a foundation of successful state-making have yet to yield the expected results of 'good governance', as evidenced by the region's continuing dependence on external assistance and patronage to sustain its existence.[107] The problems facing the Kurdish region, as elsewhere in other fragile or post-conflict environments, are not limited to but include *inter alia* the lack of accountability and transparency, corruption, human rights violations and gender inequalities.

To start with the problems of governmental accountability and transparency, a power-sharing agreement Barzani and Talabani concluded in January 2006 gave rise to a highly politicised institutional setting dominated by the KDP and the PUK, with little room for genuine political opposition. Based on this agreement following the 2005 regional elections, Massoud Barzani was voted as the President of the Kurdistan region and his nephew Nechirvan became the Prime Minister of the KRG. The Ministries of Finance, Peshmerga Affairs, Agriculture, Natural Resources were assigned to the KDP, while the Ministries of Security, Justice, Education, Health and Water Resources were left to the PUK.[108] In an environment where 'there has been no culture of accountability', the KRG has operated in a 'similar way to other Middle Eastern countries', with MPs voting on issues based on their party leaders' position rather than on deliberation and individual judgement.[109] In the absence of checks and balances, the ministerial portfolios were divided according to tribal affiliations. For instance, Barzani assigned the Foreign Ministry portfolio to his uncle and gave his son the responsibility to run the intelligence service, while Talabani appointed one of his brothers-in-law as the Ministry of Water Resources and his wife's brother-in-law as the ambassador to China.[110] Many of the region's investment and infrastructure projects for social services such as communications, transportation, hospitals and schools financed through a flow of over $30 billion between 2006 and 2013[111] have also reportedly been awarded to those close to the dominant political parties.[112] In the telecommunication sector, for instance, Korek Telecom is chaired by one of Barzani's nephews, while Asiacell is widely associated with the PUK.[113] In this environment where economy becomes a frontline of power struggles (between Baghdad and Erbil, and between and within Kurdish and other groups), different communities have become 'increasingly focused on narrow group interests' as a means of securing aid from foreign agencies and the central government in Baghdad, while the 'unified Kurdish voice' has sought to 'lobby for Kurdish nationalist interests' rather than striving to create a sense of trust through shared cultural mechanisms and issues of common concern such as human insecurity, dubious property ownership practices and lack of health, education and other public services and employment opportunities in rural areas.[114]

This 'unified Kurdish voice' promoted by the KDP and the PUK in the post-Saddam period, on the other hand, has been seriously challenged with the intensification of cleavages between Kurdish groups and the emergence of Gorran (Change Party) as a new political actor. As elsewhere, the policy space in Northern Iraq has been a contentious 'field of power'. Gorran was founded in 2009 out of a major split within the PUK by Nawshirwan Mustafa, who was Talabani's deputy until 2006. The party structured its political campaign during the 2009 elections on the basis of a commitment to fight against corruption, address inequalities in distribution of wealth, and repossess the ownership of Kirkuk and other disputed territories.[115] The Gorran List won 25 of the 111 seats in the Regional Parliament (11 of which are reserved for minorities), while the KDP-PUK alliance gained 59 seats.[116] During the 2013 elections, the KDP and the PUK ran on separate lists and won 38 and 18 seats respectively, while Gorran received the second biggest share in the Regional Parliament by holding 24 seats. The election results, which changed the Kurdish political landscape, led the PUK to search for the causes of the defeat including in Suleymaniyah, a PUK stronghold. However, the explanations they came up with (such as mismanagement of key ministries, and 'preoccupation ... with business deals and maintaining their personal interests') have had almost no impact on the party's internal dynamics, as party officials are mired in a power struggle over who will lead the party, in the absence of Jalal Talabani who has been receiving medical treatment abroad since a stroke he suffered in 2012.[117]

In the meantime, Suleymaniyah witnessed increasing tensions between Kurdish parties, which centred around a dispute that arose out of a Gorran demand that the PUK-appointed governor of Suleymaniyah be replaced by one of its own members. PUK, which had control over Peshmerga forces in the area, responded to the Gorran demand by warning that it would 'take legal measures against any attempts to cause trouble'.[118] The conflict, however, according to one observer, was rooted in the opposing views of the parties about the future of the Kurdish region including the formation of a Suleymaniyah region operating independently from Erbil where Turkish influence is strongly felt.[119] It is, on the other hand, important to note that Gorran also appears to be internally divided. Rivalries between its 'young' and 'old' cadres resulted in the resignation or ouster of many reformist party members between 2011 and 2013.[120]

In addition to power struggles, rule of law weaknesses and declining press freedom also pose a serious challenge to the Kurdish region's development as a self-sustaining democratic polity, as documented in the reports of international NGOs such as Amnesty International. Reported cases of arbitrary detentions by members of the Asayish (local security agency of the KRG) without an arrest warrant, denial of access to legal representation, allegations of torture and forced disappearances under detention, and intimidation against judges criticising Asayish interference in judicial processes illustrate human rights abuses and the pressure the judiciary is facing in northern Iraq.[121] Journalists covering allegations of corruption, nepotism and mismanagement by the government and dominant parties have increasingly been targeted by the Kurdish authorities. The detention of Kamal Said Qadir, an Iraqi-born Kurdish journalist with Austrian citizenship, during his visit to the region in October 2005 is a particularly illustrative case in point to highlight the government-imposed restrictions on press freedom in the region. Qadir was charged with defamation of public institutions and threatening the security of Iraqi Kurdistan in his coverage of allegations of corruption by the Barzani family and sentenced to 30 years of imprisonment in December 2005. As a result of worldwide protests and international pressure from international press associations, he was released later in April 2006 following a special amnesty granted by Massoud Barzani.[122]

Regarding declining press freedom in northern Iraq, Michael Rubin who had worked as a lecturer at the universities of Salahuddin and Suleymaniyah writes the following in January 2008:[123]

> Although there are two independent newspapers in Iraqi Kurdistan – Awene and Hawlati – they are increasingly constrained. Both parties [KDP and PUK] use their control over law courts to intimidate, bankrupt, and even imprison journalists who criticize ruling parties and officials. The PUK, for example, prosecuted Hawlati editors after the paper accused the PUK prime minister of abuse of power. Nechervan Barzani's office has even threatened frivolous lawsuits against foreign writers and analysts who fail to adhere to his party's line.

Jalal Talabani, then Iraqi President, however, sued Hawlati for defamation and spreading false information following its publication of a translated version of Rubin's article. Charges were laid against the newspaper under Article 433 of the Iraqi Penal Code, which criminalises defamation and has often been invoked to restrict freedom of expression in the Kurdish region.[124]

Last but not least, as in many other internationally 'reconstructed' territories, there has been minimal progress in northern Iraq with improving the social status of women through formal institutional reforms, as it requires a daunting task of changing long-established attitudes and practices. By law, Kurdish women who are over 25 years old are entitled to run for the 30 per cent of the seats reserved for female representation in the Regional Parliament.[125] However, instances of violence and discrimination against women such as polygamy, domestic violence, 'honour killings' and self-immolation are extensively covered in a range of reports produced by domestic and international agencies. A more recent example is an assessment published by *The Economist* in March 2014 shortly after International Women's Day. The piece reports that 'self-burning has claimed the lives of as many as 10,000 women, including girls as young as 13, since the region gained autonomy in 1991' and honour killings by male relatives are still common, despite the adoption of laws by the Parliament to protect women.[126] According to the official data provided by the KRG's Ministry of Human Rights, the number of women and girls killed increased from 778 in 2005 to 812 in 2006.[127] The figures compiled by Amnesty International indicate that at least 102 women and girls were killed between July 2007 and June 2008 in Iraqi Kurdish region in addition to a further 262 women and children who died or were severely injured in the same period due to intentional burning and suicides.[128] Indeed, the Kurdish region's 'patriarchal political system', borrowing the description of Bahar Munzir, a local women's rights activist,[129] makes even a symbolic implementation of women's rights and their visibility in the public sphere extremely difficult, as evidenced by the presence of only one female minister in the previous cabinet and total exclusion of women from the current council of ministers sworn in on 18 June 2014,[130] even though they constitute half of the Iraqi Kurdish population.

Conclusion

Commenting on the degree of autonomy the KRG has exercised over time, Henry Kissinger concludes in 2004 that 'Kurds define self government as only microscopically distinguishable from independence'.[131] With its constitutionally recognised status as an autonomous region, self-government institutions (including a parliament, a military and overseas diplomatic representations), growing commercial ties with regional states and political leverage against the central government, the KRG has established itself as a de facto state seeking formal recognition. The realisation of its political aspirations is dependent on the shifts in the position of key foreign actors that are beyond its control. Nonetheless, the KRG is working towards consolidating its empirical attributes of statehood in an attempt to 'earn' sovereignty.

The KRG's emergence as an increasingly autonomous entity has been enabled by the changes in the Iraqi political space rendered through the foreign military interventions in 1991 and 2003. The enforcement of a no-fly zone during the Gulf War created a zone of exception characterised by uncertainties and vulnerabilities. These uncertainties provided the Iraqi Kurds with significant opportunity structures to develop a new political order as the basis of their statehood aspirations. However, the same uncertainties, at the same time, produced and perpetuated the conditions of its dependence on foreign assistance and patronage to sustain its existence and shape its future.

Notes

1 Vali, 'The Kurds and Their "Others"', 83.
2 McDowall, *A Modern History of the Kurds*.
3 Özoğlu, *Kurdish Notables and the Ottoman State*.
4 Halliday, 'Can We Write a Modernist History of Kurdish Nationalism?'; Natali, *The Kurds and the State*; Romano, *The Kurdish Nationalist Movement*; Vali, 'The Kurds and Their "Others"'.
5 Natali, *The Kurds and the State*.
6 Olson, 'Turkish and Syrian Relations since the Gulf War'.
7 Vali, 'The Kurds and Their "Others"'; Natali, *The Kurds and the State*.
8 Natali, *The Kurds and the State*.
9 Ibid.
10 The Treaty of Peace between the Allied and Associated Powers and Turkey, Signed at Sèvres, August 10, 1920.
11 Ibid.
12 Romano, *The Kurdish Nationalist Movement*.
13 Bengio, *The Kurds of Iraq*. See also, Shareef, *USA, Iraq and the Kurds*.
14 Bengio, *The Kurds of Iraq*.
15 O'Leary and Salih, 'The Denial, Resurrection, and Affirmation of Kurdistan'.
16 Jwaideh, *The Kurdish National Movement*.
17 Shareef, *USA, Iraq and the Kurds*.
18 In exchange for Iraq's acceptance of a contested border demarcation in the Shatt al-Arab waterway, Iran dropped its support for Kurdish rebels in Iraq. For details, see Romano, *The Kurdish Nationalist Movement*.
19 Shareef, *USA, Iraq and the Kurds*.
20 Metz, 'Iraq', 163.
21 Gunter, 'Turkey's New Neighbor, Kurdistan'.
22 The operation was named after the eighth sura in the Quran which specifies the rules governing booty in battle. Through naming the operation Anfal, Saddam sought to provide a religious justification for the killing of the Kurds. Gunter, 'A De Facto Kurdish State in Northern Iraq', 296.
23 According to the Kurdish authorities' estimates, as many as 182,000 civilians lost their lives during the Anfal campaign. For details, see Human Rights Watch, *Genocide in Iraq*.
24 Shareef, *USA, Iraq and the Kurds*.
25 Romano, *The Kurdish Nationalist Movement*.
26 George H. Bush, *New World Order Speech*, 11 September 1990.
27 United Nations, *Repertoire of the Practice of the Security Council 1989–1992*, Chapter 8, No. 22.
28 Ibid.
29 Rakisits, 'The Gulf Crisis'.
30 Kober, *Coalition Defection*.
31 'Containment: Iraqi No-Fly Zones'; US Department of Defense, 'Cohen Declares Iraq No-Fly Zones "Successful"'.
32 US, British and French forces imposed a second no-fly zone in the south of Iraq in April 1991.

33 Natali, *The Kurdish Quasi-State*; Gunter, 'Kurdish Future in a Post-Saddam Iraq'.
34 Gunter, 'A De Facto Kurdish State in Northern Iraq', 296.
35 Romano, *The Kurdish Nationalist Movement*.
36 Ibid.
37 Aziz, 'Kurdistan', 51.
38 Meho, *The Kurdish Question in U.S. Foreign Policy*.
39 Ibid.
40 Aziz, 'Kurdistan'.
41 Natali, *The Kurdish Quasi-State*.
42 Natali notes that when the programme ended in 2003, nearly US$4 billion of the KRG's funds remained unspent. Ibid.
43 Ibid.
44 Le Billon, 'Corruption, Reconstruction and Oil Governance in Iraq'.
45 Ibid.
46 Caspersen, *Unrecognized States*, 1–2.
47 Ghani *et al.*, 'Closing the Sovereignty Gap'.
48 I am grateful to Nevzat Soguk for bringing this point to my attention.
49 Hadji, 'The Case for Kurdish Statehood in Iraq'.
50 Buchanan, *Justice, Legitimacy and Self-Determination*.
51 See, for example, Hadji, 'The Case for Kurdish Statehood in Iraq'.
52 Voller, 'Kurdish Oil Politics in Iraq'; Stansfield, 'The Unravelling of the Post-First World War State System?'.
53 See, for example, Jakes, 'AP Interview: Iraqi Kurd Leader Hints at Secession'; Ben Solomon, 'Iraqi Kurds Close to Declaring Independence'; 'Barzani Asks MPs to Organize Independence Vote'.
54 'Iraqi Kurds Inspired by Secession of South Sudan'.
55 Stansfield, 'The Unravelling of the Post-First World War State System?'.
56 Barkey, *Preventing Conflict Over Kurdistan*.
57 Charountaki, 'Turkish Foreign Policy and the Kurdistan Regional Government', 200.
58 Holbrooke, 'Opportunity for Turks and Kurds?'.
59 For Turkey's shifting approach to KRG, see, for example, Tol, 'Untangling the Turkey-KRG Energy Partnership'.
60 Ibid.
61 'Turkey's AKP Spokesman: Iraq's Kurds Have Right to Decide Their Future'.
62 'Will Turkey Midwife an Independent Iraqi Kurdish State?'.
63 Stansfield, 'The Unravelling of the Post-First World War State System?'.
64 Rubin, 'Why Won't Washington Support Kurdish Independence?'.
65 Kaijo, 'The Rise of ISIS, A Golden Opportunity for Iraq's Kurds'.
66 Ibid.
67 Filkins, 'The Fight of Their Lives'.
68 Parkinson and Entous, 'How Kurds Came to Play Key Role in U.S. Plans to Combat Islamic State'.
69 Ibid; Hélène Cooper and Gordon, 'Iraqi Kurds Expand Autonomy as ISIS Reorders the Landscape'.
70 Cooper and Gordon, 'Iraqi Kurds Expand Autonomy as ISIS Reorders the Landscape'.

71 Voller, 'Kurdish Oil Politics in Iraq'.
72 Natali, *Kurdish Quasi-State.*
73 Cook, 'Kurdistan – Just Being Independent'.
74 'Turkish Companies Dominate Northern Iraq'.
75 Ahmed, *Iraqi Kurds and Nation-Building.*
76 National Commission on Terrorist Attacks upon the United States, 'Phase Two and the Question of Iraq', 3 October 2004.
77 Romano, *The Kurdish Nationalist Movement*; Stansfield, 'The Unravelling of the Post-First World War State System?'.
78 Romano, *The Kurdish Nationalist Movement.*
79 Ibid.
80 The 'Suleymaniyah incident' refers to the detention of a group of Turkish special operations personnel by US forces in July 2003 which caused the 'worst crisis of confidence' between Turkey and the US. For details, see Charountaki, 'Turkish Foreign Policy and the Kurdistan Regional Government', citing 'The US Had Substantial Intelligence that the Turks were in Activity against the Local Leadership', *Washington Times*, 8 July 2008.
81 Charountaki, 'Turkish Foreign Policy and the Kurdistan Regional Government'.
82 'President Bush Meets with President Barzani of Kurdistan Regional Government of Iraq'.
83 Olson, *The Goat and the Butcher.*
84 Voller, *The Kurdish Liberation Movement in Iraq.*
85 Aziz, 'Kurdistan'.
86 Barkey, *Preventing Conflict over Kurdistan.*
87 Article 109.
88 Article 116.
89 Mahdi, 'Iraq's Oil Law', 16.
90 Zedalis, *Oil and Gas in the Disputed Kurdish Territories*, 55–6.
91 Mahdi, 'Iraq's Oil Law'.
92 Kane, 'Iraq's Oil Politics'.
93 Atesoğlu Guney, *Contentious Issues of Security and the Future of Turkey.*
94 Le Billon, 'Corruption, Reconstruction and Oil Governance in Iraq'.
95 Kane, 'Iraq's Oil Politics'.
96 Ibid.
97 Alkadiri, 'Oil and the Question of Federalism in Iraq', 1318–19.
98 Romano, *The Kurdish Nationalist Movement.*
99 Stansfield, 'The Unravelling of the Post-First World War State System?'; see also ICG, *Iraq and the Kurds.*
100 Atesoğlu Guney, *Contentious Issues of Security and the Future of Turkey.*
101 For details of the KRG's position, visit http://mnr.krg.org/index.php/en/the-ministry/legal-framework/laws (accessed 8 July 2014).
102 Alkadiri, 'Oil and the Question of Federalism in Iraq'.
103 Charountaki, 'Turkish Foreign Policy and the Kurdistan Regional Government'.
104 Stansfield, 'The Unravelling of the Post-First World War State System?'.
105 Gunter, *The Kurds Ascending*, 146.
106 Idiz, 'Turkey Adds Fuel to Fight of Iraqi Kurds for Independence'.

107 Natali, *The Kurdish Quasi-State*.
108 Aziz, 'Kurdistan'.
109 Ibid.
110 Rubin, 'Is Iraqi Kurdistan a Good Ally?'.
111 'Economy Overview: Kurdistan Region of Iraq – Determined to Grow'.
112 Abdulla, *The Kurds*.
113 Hamid, 'Corruption and Cronyism Hinder Kurdistan'.
114 Natali, *The Kurdish Quasi-State*, 141.
115 ICG, *Iraq's Uncertain Future*.
116 Ibid.
117 National Democratic Institute, 'Iraq Election Watch: KRG Parliamentary Elections'.
118 Ibid.
119 Abbas, 'Sulaimaniyah Scene of Power Struggle among Iraqi Kurdish Parties'.
120 Watts, 'Democracy and Self-Determination in the Kurdistan Region of Iraq', 161.
121 Amnesty International, *Hope and Fear*.
122 Ibid; Natali, *The Kurdish Quasi-State*.
123 Rubin, 'Is Iraqi Kurdistan a Good Ally?'.
124 Amnesty International, *Hope and Fear*.
125 For further information, see KRG, 'The Kurdistan Parliament'.
126 'Why are So Many Kurdish Women Setting Themselves on Fire?'.
127 Aziz, 'Kurdistan'.
128 Amnesty International, *Hope and Fear*.
129 'Women Demand Greater Role in New Kurdistan Government'.
130 KRG, 'Ministries and Departments'.
131 Kissinger, 'Reflections on a Sovereign Iraq'.

5 Timor-Leste as an 'exceptional' state

Timor-Leste's[1] arduous path to independent statehood illustrates the centrality of international factors to the emergence and success of social movements including national self-determination and secessionist struggles. Indeed, a short overview of the country's turbulent history reveals how the territory's political fate was essentially shaped by external forces and their actions. This includes the division of the island of Timor into two halves as a result of intensifying rivalries between two European colonial powers in the eighteenth century: Portugal and the Netherlands. While the eastern half of the island was controlled by the Portuguese, West Timor was ruled by the Dutch and eventually became part of the newly created Indonesian state in 1949.

Indonesia's invasion of East Timor in 1975, following the departure of the Portuguese in the face of a civil war between rival Timorese groups, was also closely linked to the events in the external political environment. The Indonesian intervention came shortly after a visit by US President Gerald Ford and Secretary of State Henry Kissinger to Jakarta.[2] As it becomes clear in the now declassified documents from the US, United Kingdom, Australia and New Zealand, President Suharto received the necessary international political support for Indonesia's military involvement amidst prevailing geopolitical considerations at the end of the Vietnam War.[3] The Indonesian case for intervention was based on the claim that the creation of an independent, 'weak' East Timorese state ruled by a leftist government led by Fretilin (Revolutionary Front for an Independent East Timor) would be a threat to Indonesia's own security[4] and regional stability.[5] East Timor's right to self-determination and the brutal oppression of its people by the Indonesian military were sacrificed to Cold War politics, as evidenced by the disappearance of East Timor from the agenda of the Security Council between 1976 and 1999.[6]

The changes in the structure of global balance of power with the end of the Cold War, on the other hand, created new 'opportunity structures' for the East Timorese resistance movement, and helped them 'enlarge' the scope of the conflict in their favour. The demise of the ideological contest between the US and Soviet Union following the latter's disintegration deprived Jakarta of the use of the communist threat as a significant source of rationalisation for its continued occupation of the territory. In addition to this, the Portuguese government's growing support for the exercise of self-determination particularly following its entry into the European Community, and the rise of a human rights-based policy agenda within the UN and other international policy circles helped the East Timorese nationalists win international sympathy with their struggle. The global media's coverage of the Indonesian military's killing of more than 200 civilians at Santa Cruz cemetery in November 1991[7] and the awarding in 1996 of the Nobel peace prize to two leading East Timorese resistance figures, José Ramos-Horta and Bishop Belo, illustrate the sea change in the international community's treatment of the question of East Timor. The mounting domestic and international pressure by civil society groups and declining support of its Western allies precipitated a significant change in the Indonesian leadership's position over East Timor's status.

In January 1999, President Habibie, who had succeeded Suharto in the previous year following mass demonstrations triggered by the collapse of the Indonesian economy during the Asian financial crisis of 1997/8, offered the East Timorese people the choice between independence and autonomy within Indonesia. The operational details of the referendum were outlined in a UN-mediated agreement concluded in May 1999 by the foreign ministers of Indonesia and Portugal without participation of East Timorese representatives. While the UN authorised the establishment of a small mission (United Nations Assistance Mission in East Timor, UNAMET) to assist with the registration of eligible voters and organisation of the 'popular consultation', the responsibility for security was left to the Indonesian authorities. Despite violence and intimidation by militia groups, 98 per cent of the people registered went to the polls on 30 August 1999 and a great majority of them (78.5 per cent) rejected the autonomy proposal.[8] The UN's subsequent announcement of the voting results was followed by a scorched-earth campaign orchestrated by the Indonesian military-backed pro-autonomy militias. The escalating violence prompted the deployment of the Australian-led International Security Force for East Timor (INTERFET) in September to restore law and order. INTERFET, according to the Australian authorities, was an

'exceptional' military engagement not because it was a 'unique necessity' conditioned by the deteriorating security situation on the ground but
because of its potential to become a 'model for the future'.[9] INTERFET
was replaced later in February 2000 by a larger UN mission (United
Nations Transitional Administration in East Timor, UNTAET) entrusted
with exceptional powers to govern the territory and facilitate its transition
to independence through establishing the institutional foundations of sustainable liberal peace. While international intervention facilitated East
Timor's separation from Indonesia, it also altered the power dynamics of
its organisational structures complicated by the resurfacing of old rivalries between Timorese groups and the country's continuing dependence
on foreign assistance.

This chapter examines the major aspects of the political process
leading to the making of Timor-Leste as an exceptional state. It is organised on the basis of two sections. An overview of the historical background of the conflict is provided in the first section. It is followed by a
discussion of the emerging conditions of East Timor's dependency in the
post-military intervention period.

Historical background of the East Timor conflict

The East Timor conflict began with the territory's invasion and subsequent occupation by Indonesia in 1975. While the East Timorese
claimed that they were denied the right to determine their political status
following Portugal's departure as the colonising power, for Jakarta the
issue of self-determination was already resolved in July 1976, when the
Popular Assembly of East Timor formally requested the territory's incor-
poration into Indonesia.[10]

Similar to the situation in Kosovo and Northern Iraq, East Timor's
domestic circumstances were determined by changing external power
dynamics over time. As documented in a variety of historical sources, the
island of Timor was renowned for its rich quality sandalwood, and it was
already part of the regional trading networks dominated by Chinese
traders long before the arrival of Portuguese merchants and missionaries
in the early sixteenth century.[11] With the coming of the Dutch in the following century, the Portuguese shifted their administrative seat from
Lifau (Oecussi) to Dili in the east. Following the official partition of the
island after the signing of a series of treaties between the Dutch and the
Portuguese in the late nineteenth and early twentieth centuries, the Portuguese sought to transform their territory's economic, political and social
structures through a mixture of coercive measures including forced

labour and overthrow of traditional local administrative systems based on kinship and exchange. Portugal's colonial rule was interrupted during the Second World War as a result of the Japanese occupation of the entire island in response to the landing of Dutch and Australian commandos in 1942 to pre-empt the territory's takeover by the Japanese. It is estimated that between 40,000 and 60,000 East Timorese lost their lives during the Japanese occupation.[12] Lisbon's administrative authority was restored at the end of the war.

In 1960, the UN added East Timor to its list of non-self-governing territories and recognising Portugal as an administrative power responsible for promoting the well-being of the territory's inhabitants and 'develop[ing] self-government and tak[ing] due account of the political aspirations' of its people according to Article 73 of the UN Charter. Portugal, however, claimed that East Timor and the other Portuguese-ruled territories were its *províncias ultramarinas* (overseas provinces), and thus they had no obligations for these territories demanded in the Charter. Contrary to Lisbon's claims, East Timor remained the least developed part of the Portuguese state throughout the post-war era. Outside Dili, the capital, public services and transport and communication infrastructure were either grossly inadequate or absent.[13] Even in the capital, it was not until the 1960s that electricity was installed and only a few of the main streets were paved by 1974.[14]

According to the Lusotropicalist argument, through which the Salazar regime sought to justify the Portuguese presence in Africa and South-East Asia in the post-Second World War era, the relations between the Portuguese state and the indigenous peoples in its overseas provinces were not based on racial superiority, oppression and exploitation, but tolerance and multiracialism.[15] For instance, in a state document published in the mid-1960s, East Timor is portrayed not only as an integral part of Portugal, but also as a showcase for the supposedly harmonious and multiracial character of the Portuguese state.[16] This line of thinking maintained that the East Timorese were not colonised, but were 'as Portuguese as the whiter ones living in Lisbon', as José Ramos-Horta pointed out with some irony during the resistance years.[17] UN documents, on the other hand, described the relationship between Lisbon and Dili as a 'colonial one' and noted that the former did little to improve 'very limited participation' in governmental processes in the latter.[18]

The political changes in Lisbon brought about by the overthrow of the Salazar regime through the 'carnation revolution' of 1974 strongly affected the course of political and social developments in East Timor, as mirrored in the formation of the country's first political parties in Dili.

These parties were created by members of a small community of educated *mestiço* (mixed race) and *assimilado* ('assimilated' natives) who were recruited by the colonial military or the civilian administration (for example José Ramos-Horta, Xanana Gusmão, Mari Alkatiri, Mario Carrascalão and Xavier do Amaral who would assume leading roles during the post-Indonesian era).

However, the emerging rivalries between political parties gave rise to the recruitment of armed groups, leading to a coup attempt by the Timorese Democratic Union (UDT) in August 1975. Initially, the UDT had the support of the police and some sections of the military, which led to the arrest of several high profile members of Fretilin. In response to the crisis, Portugal sent a small force which joined Fretilin's newly established armed wing (Armed Forces of National Liberation of East Timor, Falintil).

The escalation of the factionalised political movements prompted Indonesia to assert that an independent Timorese state ruled by the leftist Fretilin party would become a 'Cuba' or a hub for communist elements in the region.[19] Fretilin's staging of a counter-coup and the ensuing brief but bloody civil war in August 1975 led to the departure of the colonial governor, the death of at least 1,500 people and the flight of most of the UDT supporters to Indonesia.[20] Fretilin unilaterally declared independence on 28 November 1975. In the meantime, a group of Fretilin members, including Ramos-Horta, left the territory to attract legal recognition of East Timorese independence. However, the Indonesian military started its anticipated invasion shortly afterwards.

The Timorese resistance movement: origins and organisation

The Indonesian occupation of East Timor was brutal, resulting in up to 180,000 deaths from military operations, famine, disease and forced migration.[21] The Fretilin-led resistance movement was almost crushed completely by 1979 following the killing or capture of most of the guerrillas by the Indonesian military. The resistance then underwent significant changes in the 1980s. With a view to revitalising the struggle against Indonesian rule around the idea of national unity, the newly elected Falintil Commander, Xanana Gusmão, first brokered a cease-fire with the Indonesian military in 1981, then denounced Marxism-Leninism as Fretilin's ideology in 1984, and finally announced his resignation from Fretilin and the separation of the guerrilla force from the party in 1987. Gusmão's strategic moves encouraged the Catholic Church to join the resistance and bring together rival political groups under a single cause, illustrated by the establishment of the National Council of Maubere Resistance (Conselho Nacional de Resistência Maubere, CNRM) as an umbrella organisation for all East Timorese nationalist groups in 1988.[22]

In addition to a newly structured armed wing, the CNRM had two other components: the clandestine front and the diplomatic front. The clandestine front was made up of underground youth cells operating at high school and university levels in East Timor and Indonesia.[23] Infiltrating the government-approved student bodies and public departments, members of the clandestine network played a crucial role in intelligence gathering and provision of logistical assistance whenever the armed front needed.[24] They also organised public protests in East Timorese and Indonesian cities and operated in coordination with solidarity groups in Portugal, Australia and the US to generate international public opinion.[25]

The diplomatic front was led by José Ramos-Horta, who had left East Timor in 1975 in search of international recognition for Fretilin's unilaterally declared independence to prevent the Indonesian invasion. He resigned from Fretilin and was appointed as Gusmão's personal envoy and the special representative of the CRNM abroad in 1989. Ramos-Horta's leading position in the diplomatic wing reflected a changing tone in the political discourse the resistance leadership employed to attract international support for the East Timorese struggle. The new discourse adopted towards the end of the Cold War was marked by a strong emphasis on democratic values and principles and sought to change 'the entrenched international perception that the independence movement was an extreme left-wing project and a threat to Indonesia and regional stability'.[26] Ramos-Horta was known for his criticism of Marxism for being irrelevant to East Timor where there was no 'private enterprise ... to nationalize'. Commenting on the role of Marxism during the early days of the resistance, Ramos-Horta writes the following:[27]

We were all clear about the ultimate goal, and were aware of the complexities of the decolonization process; however, none of us had any coherent ideological vision beyond independence. Marxism was far from our minds. None of us, except Nicolau Lobato and I suppose Alkatiri, had read a single word of Marx or Lenin ... I was one of the least disposed to what I usually called 'the abstract extravaganzas' of Marx and Lenin. Social democracy to us, and to me particularly, seemed closest to the ideal. It stood for social justice, equitable distribution of the wealth of the country, a mixed economy and a democratic political system.

Regarding his appointment as the head of the diplomatic front, it is noted in the CAVR (Timor-Leste Reception, Truth and Reconciliation Commission) Report that the selection of Ramos-Horta, 'whose social democrat and human rights credentials were more acceptable internationally than the Marxist image of Abilio Araújo, demonstrated the extent of the reforms'.[28] The leadership's shift towards a language of human rights is also illustrated by Gusmão's declaration that CNRT was:[29]

> committed to building a free and democratic nation, based on respect for the freedoms of thought, association and expression, as well as complete respect of Universal Human Rights. A multi-party system and a market economy will be foundations of an independent Timor-Leste.... It will be a free and non-aligned state with the firm purpose of becoming a member of ASEAN, in order to contribute to regional stability.

As part of their efforts to reframe the resistance movement and its objectives in terms of democracy and universal human rights such as the right to self-determination, East Timorese leaders, from the mid-1980s onwards, also began establishing contacts with major human rights organisations such as Amnesty International and Human Rights Watch, and prepared reports for international dissemination, including the lists of civilians killed, tortured and detained by the Indonesian military.[30] This new strategic approach was stimulated by their realisation that the 'language of militant anticolonialism had failed to win the sympathy of the wider international community, and may have even undermined it'.[31] Drawing upon the rising international awareness of the East Timor conflict following the broadcasting of the Santa Cruz massacre by a British TV channel in 1992, Ramos-Horta also presented a revised version of Xanana Gusmão's three-phase self-determination plan to international agencies, including the European Parliament where they capitalised on the Portuguese support. The plan called for the demilitarisation of the territory, restoration of basic human rights, release of prisoners and access by UN bodies in the first stage (lasting two–three years) to be followed by a transitional period of autonomy within Indonesia (up to five years). The final phase of the plan envisioned the exercise of self-determination through a referendum within a year following its commencement.[32] The plan, as noted in the CAVR report, sought to put the Suharto government 'under pressure by offering an honourable way out and to present the Resistance as the more constructive of the two protagonists'.[33] The East

Timorese diplomatic capacity to widen the scope of the conflict was also enabled by Portugal's growing support following its EEC (European Economic Community) membership in 1986. As an important point to note, Lisbon showed little interest in the East Timor conflict following its withdrawal in 1975 due to its own preoccupation with consolidating democracy in the post-Salazar period as well as the European Community member states' wish to develop stronger economic ties with Indonesia, when the Portuguese government was negotiating membership.[34] Following its accession, which entailed the exercise of a veto power, however, the Portuguese government successfully campaigned for the East Timorese claim to self-determination and lobbied to prevent the recognition of Indonesian sovereignty over the territory by European states.[35] For instance, in a resolution adopted in 1986, the European Parliament criticised the Indonesian annexation and called for an act of self-determination.[36] Portugal also vetoed the upgrading of the EEC representation in Jakarta to embassy level a year later. In September 1988, the EEC states issued a common call that supported the talks between the Indonesian and Portuguese government under the auspices of the UN.[37] In addition to these diplomatic moves, as the administering power of East Timor, Portugal brought the 1989 Timor Sea Treaty between Jakarta and Canberra to the International Court of Justice which ruled in 1995 that 'the territory of East Timor remains a non-self governing territory and its people has the right to self-determination'.[38]

The Timorese nationalist leadership's efforts to internationalise the conflict as a matter of democracy and human rights helped change pro-Indonesian attitudes in Western capitals, illustrated by an increasing visibility of Timorese nationalist leaders in the global arena during the second half of the 1990s, such as the awarding of the Nobel Peace Prize to Ramos-Horta and Bishop Belo. This included a CNN interview with Ramos-Horta in January 1997 during which he remarked on the changing tide in the international arena in favour of East Timor:[39]

> To the people of East Timor, it has been a blessing from God because the worst problem for East Timor has been silence, neglect, ignorance, by the international community. And these in turn have forced many governments to rethink their policies and I am quite optimistic that many European countries, the West, US, in the next few months and two, three years to come, they will be more forceful in dealing with Indonesia in terms of at least the human rights situation in East Timor, but also in addressing the root of the problem – the ceasing of military occupation, and the need for their self-determination to take place.

In April 1998, shortly before Suharto's fall from power following the collapse of the Indonesian economy, CNRM was transformed into the National Council of Timorese Resistance (Conselho Nacional Resistência Timorense, CNRT) at a conference held in Peniche, near Lisbon. Due to its association with Fretilin and its Marxist implications, the word 'Maubere' was replaced with 'Timorese' to strengthen the policy of national unity both at home and abroad.[40] In addition, a charter of freedoms, rights, duties and guarantees for the people of East Timor, known as the Magna Carta, was also unanimously adopted at the Peniche convention. The Magna Carta sets out the political and institutional foundations of the future East Timorese state along liberal democratic principles such as upholding human rights, creating a pluralist and demo-cratic society and respecting the environment.[41] Unifying East Timorese political groups and emphasising their commitment to liberal democratic governance constituted a core pillar of the resistance leadership's diplomatic strategy in the international arena. In doing so, they sought to achieve two key interrelated objectives: to undermine Jakarta's claim that the Indonesian military's involvement was a necessary action in response to the escalating violence between FRETILIN and UDT sup-porters in 1975, and to demonstrate the East Timorese people's capacity to govern themselves. Ramos-Horta's remarks in the *Guardian Weekly* in 1998 illustrates Timorese leaders' efforts to discredit the Indonesian claims:[42]

> As for the civil war it should be remembered it was Jakarta that encouraged the Timorese to fight among themselves. Indonesia can't teach us anything – historically, it has been a much less stable country than East Timor.

The nationalist leadership's new strategy is also reflected in a speech delivered by former student leader Constâncio Pinto on behalf of RENETIL (National Resistance of East Timorese Students) before the UN Committee on Decolonization a month before: 'The formation of the CNRT and the adoption of the Magna Carta have shown the international community that the Timorese are capable of solving our [sic] differences and are ready to govern an independent East-Timor'.[43]

While the reorganisation of the resistance along bipartisan lines helped unify formerly competing East Timorese groups in a struggle against a common enemy (that is, the Indonesian military), the changing political dynamics outside East Timor facilitated the exercise of self-determination. Among these developments, three played a particularly decisive role in the creation of new opportunity structures for the East Timorese movement. These were Suharto's resignation in May 1998, the process of *reformasi* his successor Habibie initiated to alleviate the surrounding economic and social crisis, and the increasing pressure international actors exerted on the Habibie administration. As noted earlier, the monetary crisis that began in Southeast Asia in 1997 hit the Indonesian economy particularly heavily, as evidenced by a 15 per cent decline in GDP, a sharp depreciation of the rupiah from 6,000 to 16,000 against the US dollar, an 80 per cent inflation rate, and food shortages in 1998.[44] Suharto was forced to step down and transferred presidency to his Vice President B. J. Habibie as a result of the growing public disturbance across the country. Concerned with delays in the release of much-needed IMF loans, conditioned on political stability,[45] as well as in consideration of his own political legitimacy, Habibie introduced a reform process in an attempt to win domestic and international support for his interim administration.[46] He announced removal of restrictions on press freedom and formation of political parties and associations, release of political prisoners, devolution of fiscal authority to local administrations, and the organisation of the first free elections since 1955.[47] Habibie also presented a special autonomy proposal for East Timor. While the UN-mediated negotiations with Portugal on the specifics of the autonomy proposal were underway in New York, Habibie surprised Indonesians, East Timorese and the international community by announcing in January 1999 that his administration was prepared to allow the people of East Timor to choose between autonomy and independence through a 'popular consultation'. Habibie's decision was precipitated by the changing position of Indonesia's two key Western allies, including Australia. In a letter dated December 1998, Australian Prime Minister John Howard proposed an autonomy model (similar to the one France had agreed with New Caledonia in 1988) resulting in an eventual self-determination process for East Timor.[48] Habibie rejected Howard's proposal and brought the independence option to the table partly as a result of his conviction that the resistance was almost crushed and partly as a reflection of his wish to 'distinguish himself from Suharto' and 'make his mark' through solving the long-standing East Timor issue once and for all.[49]

The UN-sponsored ballot was held on 30 August 1999 and the announcement of the voting results was followed by the eruption of widespread committed by anti-independence militias supported by the Indonesian military. The militia violence resulted in the deaths of at least 1,000 people,[50] destruction of the territory's already limited physical infrastructure and displacement of two-thirds of the population, including

250,000 refugees in West Timor.[51] Habibie was forced to agree to the deployment of the Australian-led international military force (INTER-FET) under intense international pressure including the IMF's threat to suspend loans and the Clinton administration's decision to cut off military assistance.[52] The military intervention ended Jakarta's 24 years of territorial control and enabled the East Timorese nationalists to exercise self-determination.

Timor-Leste's exceptionality

Suharto's fall and lessening of government control, which paved the way for East Timor's separation, encouraged the secessionist rebels in Aceh and Irian Jaya (West Papua).[53] The outbreak of conflicts and emerging demands for a referendum to exercise their right of self-determination in other parts of the country after East Timor raised both domestic and international concerns about the future stability and territorial integrity of Indonesia.[54] The fear of Indonesia's disintegration arising from the resurgence of other separatist movements underpinned the discursive conditions of East Timor's exceptionality through a strong emphasis on its 'unique' circumstances. The following analysis provided in a report prepared for the Asia 2000 Foundation in September 1998 illustrates the rising concerns about the risk that East Timor's separation might pose as a precedent for other regions:[55]

> The chances that Aceh will be used as a counterweight to East Timor for domestic political reasons are high.... It has a history of separatism since Dutch colonial times and is called a 'special region'.... Unlike East Timor and Irian Jaya, it never had any special status in the eyes of the international community.... Failure to acknowledge the special circumstances of East Timor, on the other hand, could lead to renewed violence there.

The 'sui generis' nature of East Timor's separation, Chesterman describes in his analysis of post-Cold War international interventions, comes from the denial of a decolonisation process by the Indonesian invasion and the refusal of the majority international community, with the exception of Australia, to legally recognise its annexation.[56] The military intervention that Australia led in 1999 was also defended by the Australian authorities as an exceptional operation necessitated by the conditions on the ground in attempt of allaying Jakarta's fears that Canberra might provide refuge for similar movements in the future:[57]

[O]nce the eyes of the world were focused on East Timor and these constraints [i.e. Canberra's concerns with maintaining bilateral relationships with Jakarta and inflaming civil-military tensions in Indonesia] shifted, Australia's diplomatic efforts achieved rapid and remarkable successes. Australia's ability to marshal diplomatic pressure on Indonesia and coordinate military contributions for a PKF [peacekeeping force] ensured that East Timor was able to separate from Indonesia in a reasonably straightforward manner.... The unique circumstances that led to East Timor's independence are very unlikely to recur.

Even though Indonesia's acceptance of East Timor's independence encouraged other separatist movements in the country, the Timorese case was persistently argued to be an exceptional situation rather than as setting a regional precedent in several other respects as well. This includes East Timor's 'different colonial context' and its people's relentless struggle for independent statehood.[58] It was, for instance, emphasised that 'Indonesia's founding founders' viewed the former Portuguese colony as an integral part of their country; however, this was strongly rejected by the majority of the East Timorese who wanted to create their own state. The degree of opposition to Indonesian rule among the East Timorese was therefore claimed to have been much higher than in Aceh and Irian Jaya.[59] Moreover, it was argued that for Jakarta's economic fortunes East Timor possessed little to offer, despite the oil and gas reserves in the Timor Sea.[60] The recognition of statehood was also exceptional according to some East Timorese nationalists, who claimed that the 1999 referendum indicated the restoration of their independence, which had already been declared in November 1975. Last but not least, East Timor's exceptionality, it was argued, derived from its international status in terms of the support and moral legitimacy it garnered from civil society organisations and solidarity groups across the world, even though some Western states explicitly or implicitly recognised Indonesia's rule over the territory.[61] These factors altogether, in other words, helped East Timor to qualify as an 'exceptional state'.

The post-ballot militia violence in East Timor, as noted above, created an emergency that led to the Australian-led military intervention which was rationalised on the basis of the exceptionalism argument. The military intervention that facilitated the territory's separation and recognition as an exceptional state created new conditions of exception in East Timor. This includes the UN's deployment of another large mission entrusted with exceptional powers to govern another conflict-affected country modelled on the mission set up in Kosovo in June 1999. Like Kosovo, East Timor was turned into a site for experimenting with a liberal democratic transformation. The UN continued its presence in the country through successor missions until December 2012, responding to new circumstances of emergency or exception such as the security crises in 2006 and 2008.

Timor-Leste's state capacity-building experience under exceptional conditions

With the destruction of public infrastructure and the departure of around 7,000 (mostly Indonesian) civil servants in the wake of intense post-ballot violence, formal government functions virtually ceased in East Timor in late 1999.[62] This led international authorities to perceive the territory as a political and institutional *terra nullius*. In a report to the UN Security Council in February 2000, the late Sergio Vieira de Mello, UN Transitional Administrator at the time, described it as a place where there was 'nearly nothing'.[63] According to Jarat Chopra, UNTAET's former Head of District Administration, however, this description based on 'perceptions of a power vacuum' was far from reflecting the reality on the ground, as the 'social structures of indigenous communities invariably generate sources of political legitimacy according to their own paradigm', despite the collapse of formal forms of authority.[64] Instead of a 'blank slate', what international state-builders found when they arrived in Dili was rather a highly contentious 'field of power' where different local groups were competing for the distribution of aid, employment opportunities and ownership of properties left by refugees.[65]

The challenge for UNTAET was therefore political rather than technical – to use its wide-ranging powers to set up the institutional foundations of democratic statehood while developing a relationship with factionalised elites representing diverging societal interests such as guerrillas, returned diaspora, Indonesian-educated youth etc. Dealing with the factionalised elites and securing the commitment of powerful interests to the transitional process were among the greatest challenges the mission faced in respect to 'the peculiarities of politics in an incomplete state' from the early stages of its deployment, as former UNTAET official Anthony Goldstone puts it:[66]

> [B]y April 2000, six months into the mission, voices in the East Timorese leadership were calling for the UN's prompt withdrawal, and by early 2001 a consensus seemed to be forming that the

relationship was not a healthy one and should be terminated as soon as possible.

UNTAET was seriously challenged by its limited ability to respond to local frustrations due to delays with the restoration and delivery of essential services (such as food, shelter, access to running water, electricity, etc), as well as by Timorese leaders and its own staff criticising the mission for its slow pace of 'Timorisation' of the governance.[67] Through concentrating power, the UN, on the other hand, sought to establish the foundations of a functioning state, reduce the risk of conflict among Timorese groups and create a 'neutral' political environment for democratic elections.[68] This technocratic understanding of the political space, however, was in sharp contrast with the reality on the ground, as Timorese groups were involved in a fierce power struggle for utilising the 'opportunity structures' created by an internationally driven democratic state-building agenda. Through using the institutional trappings of self-rule in the post-Indonesian era, they also sought to strengthen their interests in a highly competitive 'field of power'.

When it comes to the other drivers of this fragmentation and competition, the unity Timorese groups formed under the umbrella of CNRT quickly crumbled with the disappearance of their common enemy – the Indonesian military. The resurfacing of old political, ideological and personal differences within the nationalist leadership shaped the definition of the nature of the Timorese state and nation. The adoption of a semi-presidential system, with a largely ceremonial president and a powerful prime minister, for instance, reflects the transfusion of rivalries between Xanana Gusmão and Mari Alkatiri into the institutional processes. The intensifying rivalries in the political landscape also resulted in an institutional entrenchment of power struggles in the newly created defence forces and the police service, and led to a competitive development of the two institutions.

It is important to note that Gusmaõ's proposal for the formation of a defence force shortly after the UN-sponsored independence referendum was a significant departure from his earlier assertion during the resistance that the future Timorese state would not have an army.[69] The emerging threat of mutiny among Falintil ranks during their cantonment and the danger of instability former guerrillas posed if their material expectations were not satisfied led to a shift in his position. In implementing a comprehensive study undertaken by King's College London in 2000, UNTAET proceeded to create a small force of 3,000 soldiers, half being regulars drawn from the guerrillas and half reservists. The recruitment of

650 ex-fighters into the newly formed defence force named F-FDTL (Falintil-Armed Forces of Timor-Leste) was done by Falintil high command which was dominated by 'Gusmão loyalists'[70] mostly coming from the eastern part of the country. In addition to the exclusion of some veterans from the recruitment process, the absorption of some 300 former Polri (Indonesian National Police) officers into the newly created police service (National Police of Timor-Leste, PNTL) further exacerbated grievances over scarce jobs and resources.[71] The politicisation of these grievances by some political figures further undermined the capacity of the newly created security institutions. While the F-FDTL was perceived to have been dominated mainly by former guerrillas from eastern districts, the PNTL was associated with the western part of the country due to Rogerio Lobato's (Minister of Interior at the time) establishment of paramilitary police units drawn mostly from western districts.[72]

When Timor-Leste's formal recognition of independence was greeted at an internationally attended public ceremony on 20 May 2002, the country was facing serious structural problems and dependencies. One of the major areas of institutional development for which the country was heavily dependent on foreign assistance was transitional justice and reconciliation. The process of transitional justice and reconciliation, however, was hampered by extremely limited progress being made towards establishing responsibility for the past human rights abuses. The national leadership, constrained by poverty and security problems at home and Indonesia's lack of co-operation abroad, held on to the idea that focusing on the past was likely to destabilise Timorese society and threaten the post-Suharto democratisation process in Indonesia. The recommendations made in the CAVR report such as seeking reparations and campaigning for an international tribunal, according to Xanana Gusmão, represented 'grandiose idealism'.[73] Instead, he advocated the idea that given the international recognition of their independence and the provision of generous development assistance by the donor community the country should take the lead in building a functioning democracy rather than asking for compensation. The Timorese leadership's pragmatic, 'forward-looking' approach is based on the understanding that in the absence of a genuine international will to push Indonesia, their small, poor country had no option other than concentrating on improving domestic governance and development conditions, and having good working relations with its powerful neighbour, on which it is fully dependent, from basic food and fuel imports to membership of the Association of Southeast Asian Nations (ASEAN).

It should, however, be acknowledged that international support for the delivery of transitional justice in Timor-Leste was very limited from the beginning and it almost disappeared following an emerging global 'war on terror' in the post-September 11 era that required the Indonesian military's cooperation to confront radicalised terrorist networks in the region. Despite its own experts' recommendations on the establishment of an international tribunal,[74] the UN, whose capacity is determined by the political will of the Permanent Five, endorsed a serious crimes regime, whose mandate was limited to investigating and prosecuting cases of war crimes, crimes against humanity, murder, torture and sexual offences perpetrated only in 1999. In addition to the Indonesian government's lack of cooperation, inadequate funding and time constraints severely undermined the unit's operational capacity, leading to the prioritisation of cases of murder. The UN budget for the serious crimes regime in 2001, for instance, was only US$6.3 million, which was far lower than what was spent on international tribunals established in Rwanda (US$178 million) and the former Yugoslavia (US$223 million) in 2002–3.[75] By the time of its closure in May 2005, the unit had indicted 391 persons in relation to 684 murders. Most of the indictees, some of whom are high-ranking military officers, however, remained in Indonesia. Almost half of the 1,339 reported murder cases went unaddressed, while other serious crimes, including rape and torture, could not be investigated at all.[76]

Despite a reportedly 'calm and stable' environment,[77] the boiling tensions came to the surface in 2006. On the other hand, a draft UNDP capacity-development project document produced early that year, having identified a shortage of qualified human resources as one of the biggest problems undermining the Parliament's operational capacity, portrays the country's development prospect as a unified national community in the following terms:[78]

> Several factors favor the new country's development prospects. The territory and population are relatively modest; there is no sectarianism, tribalism, secessionism, or external threats; the population is, relatively speaking, ethnically and religiously homogenous; and there is still a nation-building spirit.

While Timor-Leste was hailed as a successful democratic state in the making, including by then World Bank President Paul Wolfowitz,[79] the eruption of violence in Dili exposed how deeply rooted Timor-Leste's problems were indeed. The security crisis which revolved around regional differences was triggered in mid-March 2006 by the dismissal of approximately 600 soldiers, who were mostly from western districts. The dismissed soldiers, who came to be known as 'the petitioners', had claimed in a petition they filed with the then President Gusmão in January 2006 that they were being discriminated in promotion in favour of officers from the eastern part of the country. The outbreak of violent riots in the streets of Dili, including deadly clashes between the military and the police in May 2006, exposed how political rivalries and social tensions were entrenched in the institutional aspects of the state-making process developing in the context of dependencies. The riots cost the lives of at least thiry-seven people and led to the displacement of approximately 150,000 people in the capital.[80] The UN responded to the crisis by deploying another emergency mission (United Nations Integrated Mission in Timor-Leste, UNMIT) mandated to provide public safety and 'assist' the Timorese government to reconstruct and reform the PNTL and conduct a comprehensive review of the needs and responsibilities of the security sector.[81]

However, the reconstruction and reforming of the East Timorese armed forces and the police, which were part of the security problem in 2006, shortly turned into a messy process. The UN's approach to the reforming of the Timorese security sector was informed by a mechanistic perspective of policy implementation. However, security sector development is essentially a politically sensitive project, as security and defence issues fall under the realm of sovereignty. The surrounding confusions over who was doing what (which reflects an avoidance for responsibility for anything that may go wrong) further complicated the process. While UNMIT officials emphasised the 'assistance' rather than 'executive' nature of their mandate, Timorese leaders tended to disregard the UN mission's advice on clearly delineating the role of the military and the police, and establishing accountability for the crimes committed during the 2006 violence.[82] The military, where the unrest originated, was excluded from the UN-'assisted' security sector reform because neither the UN nor the Timorese government was willing to engage with the army. It was left to its own dynamics and the reform process was carried out on a bilateral basis. No vetting process was initiated and the key military figures identified in the report of the UN's Commission of Inquiry (CoI) as having responsibility for the crisis and violent events enjoyed immunity from prosecution.

The focus of the security sector reform was rather on the police formally operating under the authority of the UN police (UNPOL) since August 2006. The transfer of policing responsibilities from the UN police to the national police dominated the course of the restructuring of the

PNTL throughout the UN-assisted reform process. Although it was frequently emphasised by UNMIT that the handover of executive policing authority was not guided by a 'fixed timeline' but a phased-approach, it was largely driven by the growing dissatisfaction of the Timorese police with the vetting and mentoring processes and the government's increasing pressure for the transfer of executive policing authority to the national police.[83]

UNMIT's pursuit of a country-wide screening process for the PNTL rather than focusing on the Dili police only, which largely disintegrated during the 2006 crisis, was one of the key factors fuelled discontent among the Timorese police officers, who continued to work during the violent events. The provision of less than successful mentoring and training by UNPOL members coming from more than forty countries with differing policing approaches and training skills exacerbated the already strained relations. The Timorese government's lack of political will to dismiss the police officers involved in serious crimes during the 2006 violence also affected the process, undermining UNMIT's efforts to curb political interference in the police service. For instance, the Timorese-led Evaluation Panel, established by the government in August 2006 to make recommendations to the Secretary of State for Security on the suitability of PNTL members for service, failed to convene between January and September 2009. By September, UNMIT completed the final certification of 92 per cent of approximately 3,200 Timorese police officers, while some 250 officers were facing pending criminal and disciplinary charges. In addition to this, 71 PNTL members facing human rights and integrity issues were still unregistered and 63 of them were still on the payroll.[84] This posed a significant challenge to depoliticising the national police, which was one of the factors that sparked the 2006 crisis, as emphasised in the UN's CoI report.

The already flawed security sector reform process, focusing on the handover of policing responsibilities, was further complicated by increasingly strained relations between the Timorese government and UNMIT. The compounding tensions between the national and international authorities manifested itself in February 2008, when President Ramos-Horta was near fatally attacked by rebels led by the former head of the military police of F-FDTL, Alfredo Reinado, who had been at large since August 2006. Reinado was shot dead by presidential guards on the site. Following mutual accusations by the Timorese and international security forces revolving around the question of 'who is in charge [of security] around here', the Timorese Government declared a state of siege on 17 February 2008, which created a joint command structure.[85] The joint command, which was established without prior consultation with UNMIT, removed the national police from UNPOL's command and subordinated it to the command of the military. The joint security operations led to an increase in the allegations of human rights violations and ill treatment (such as armed threat) received by UNMIT.[86] However, the security operations were largely considered by the Timorese leadership as successful in achieving the objectives of preventing a relapse of violence and apprehending rebels without shooting a bullet. Timorese leaders believe that the joint command structure helped the two security institutions reconcile their differences and restored public confidence.[87] Whether the conduct of joint operations represented the healing of the deep-rooted rifts between the two organisations or was a public display of unity motivated by pragmatic and institutional concerns remains unclear. It is, however, abundantly clear that the operations brought together the two institutions against the rebels and provided a significant test case to show their administrative and operational capacity to the government and society as well as to their *malae* (Tetum word for 'foreigner')[88] supervisors and capacity builders.

The joint command was officially disbanded in late June 2008. However, Timor-Leste's newly drafted national security law in 2009 was modelled on the joined command structure which, as noted earlier, gave the military an internal security role during the operations conducted in 2008. This becomes clear in the 'integrated national security' architecture contained in the law. The law approaches security from a crisis management perspective rather than identifying an overall framework to regulate actual and potential forms of insecurity that may challenge the safety and well-being of society and the state. In addition, despite recognising the need to clearly delineate inter-institutional responsibilities to avoid future conflict, it remains unclear who will be in command in crisis and peacetime conditions.

The Timorese police, on the other hand, took over all policing responsibilities from UNPOL at a public ceremony held on 27 March 2011. PNTL's resumption of the executive policing responsibility for a second time since its creation in 2000 was significant in terms of the organisation's operational and institutional development. The UN mission maintained its police presence of around 1,200 personnel and provided monitoring activities until the completion of the presidential and parliamentary elections held respectively in April and July 2012, and withdrew from the country in December that year.

Timor-Leste currently enjoys relative security and stability compared to the period between 2006 and 2008. A key source of this stability has been the Gusmão-led government's 'buying peace' policy.[89] This includes the introduction of a retirement payout for the 'petitioners' and of benefit programmes for those displaced during the 2006 crisis and disgruntled veterans of the resistance, expansion of civil service and conclusion of lucrative construction projects contracts with 'potential spoilers'.[90] This strategy may work as long as the government is able to continue with high public spending financed through large transfers from the nation's Petroleum Fund, currently standing at around $16.5 billion. However, according to some estimates, the country's oil and gas reserves may run dry in less than ten years.[91] Around 95 per cent of Timor-Leste's revenues and 78 per cent of its GDP come from oil and gas exports,[92] making the young nation the world's second most resource-dependent country after South Sudan. In addition to the threat of the 'resource curse', Timor-Leste's vulnerabilities include poverty, youth unemployment and social inequalities that may endanger current conditions of stability. As highlighted in UNDP's 2011 Human Development Report, around 40 per cent of the population live on less than $1.25 a day and every year approximately 15,000 young people enter the labour market competing for only 400 new jobs.[93] Feeling excluded, many young East Timorese end up in martial arts groups and gangs. It is important to note that the 2006 unrest which originated within the army quickly escalated with the spread of violence between rival youth gangs.[94] A September 2006 study reports that there are 15 to 20 martial arts groups in Dili, with approximately 20,000 registered members and an estimated number of more than 90,000 non-registered members.[95] These figures are of particular concern in a country where almost one-third of the population (around a million) is between 15 and 29 years old, constrained by a high unemployment rate (43 per cent in urban areas).[96] Incidents of clashes between rival martial arts groups are frequently reported in the local media. This worrying situation is further complicated by the penetration of martial arts groups into the PNTL, as indicated by the killing of a police officer (reportedly a member of a martial arts group) during a fight between martial arts groups in August 2011.[97] Many of the country's approximately 3,000 police officers are thought to be members of these groups,[98] and they are argued to have a higher allegiance to their groups than their profession. Some of these groups are affiliated with particular political factions and used by them as leverage, as evidenced by their involvement in political intimidation and displacement of people from disputed properties during the 2006 crisis.

It is also important to note that while a significant portion of its population live in poverty, Timor-Leste has a generous income package and retirement benefits for politicians. Parliamentarians and ministers are entitled to a life-time pension ranging between $2,500 and $4,500 for ministers and full health benefits (including treatment in Singapore) paid by the government.[99] Despite some promises to review the benefits, neither the government nor the opposition has yet been willing to address this situation, which constitutes a particularly serious problem in achieving equitable development and stability.

Conclusion

After four centuries of Portuguese colonial administration, 24 years of Indonesian occupation and two-and-half years of UN transitional rule Timor-Leste finally 'earned' its sovereignty in May 2002 when it formally became independent. The country was largely viewed as a successful showcase for international state-building interventions until 2006, even though it was facing serious problems including poverty and institutional weaknesses. Its vulnerabilities came to light in April that year when the violent riots in Dili appeared in the global media. The UN responded to the crisis by deploying its fifth mission since 1999. This time it was an 'integrated' mission mandated to 'assist' the Timorese government with the reform of its security institutions. However, the UN mission found itself in an environment of tensions revolving around power struggles and sovereign sensitivities. This became more apparent during the Timorese government's formation of a joint command structure in 2008 without consulting UNMIT.

As a result of a bourgeoning oil wealth used by the government to purchase peace, Timor-Leste has exercised peace and stability since then. However, considering the limits of this policy complicated by the 'resource course' threat and social inequalities, it becomes difficult to foresee how long the government can rely on it to sustain stability in relative autonomy from foreign agencies.

Notes

1 Depending on the time period of the events discussed in this chapter, the terms 'Timor-Leste' and 'East Timor' are both used to refer to the eastern half of the island of Timor along with the islands of Atauro, off the northern coast, and Jaco, to the northeast, which together constitute the territory of what is now officially known as the República Democrática de Timor-Leste. 'East Timor' is used when events preceding independence are addressed, and Timor-Leste for the period following the formal achievement of independence in May 2002.

2 Ramos-Horta, *The Funu*.
3 Simpson, 'Illegally and Beautifully'.
4 Ibid; Rolls, 'Indonesia's East Timor Experience'.
5 Taylor, *Indonesia's Forgotten War*.
6 Regarding Australia's position during that time, it is noted in the 2005 report of the Timor-Leste Reception, Truth and Reconciliation Commission (CAVR) that after Prime Minister Gough Whitlam left office in 1975 he

> campaigned privately on behalf of Indonesia. Following a visit to Timor-Leste in 1982, on which he reported directly to President Suharto, he was instrumental in having Dom Martinho da Costa Lopes removed as the head of the Catholic Church in Timor and later that year he appeared before the UN Special Committee on Decolonization and petitioned it to have the question of Timor-Leste removed from the UN agenda.
> (CAVR, *Chega!*, 'Chapter 7.1 Self-Determination', para. 125)

7 'In Cold Blood'; 'The Tiananmen in East Timor'.
8 United Nations, *Secretary-General Informs Security Council People of East Timor Rejected Special Autonomy Proposed by Indonesia*.
9 Huntley and Hayes, 'East Timor and Asian Security'.
10 Alatas, *East Timor*.
11 Taylor, *Indonesia's Forgotten War*.
12 Dunn, *Timor*.
13 Weatherbee, 'Portuguese Timor'.
14 Ramos-Horta, *The Funu*.
15 Freyre, *The Portuguese and the Tropics*.
16 Agencia-Geral do Ultramar, *Timor*.
17 Ramos-Horta, *The Funu*, 25.
18 Weatherbee, 'Portuguese Timor'.
19 Anderson, 'East Timor and Indonesia'.
20 CAVR, 'Chapter 3 The History of the Conflict'.
21 CAVR, 'Chapter 4 Regime of Occupation'.
22 CAVR, 'Chapter 5 Resistance: Structure and Strategy'.
23 Ibid.
24 Braithwaite *et al.*, *Networked Governance of Freedom and Tyranny*.
25 Ibid; Fernandes, *The Independence of East Timor*; Braithwaite *et al.*, *Networked Governance*.
26 CAVR, 'Chapter 7.1 Self Determination', para. 397.
27 Ramos-Horta, *The Funu*, 35.
28 CAVR, 'Chapter 7.1 Self Determination', para. 398.
29 Ibid., para. 397.
30 Robinson, 'Human Rights History from the Ground Up', 41–3.
31 Ibid., 40.
32 *East Timor Peace Plan*.
33 CAVR, 'Chapter 7.1', para. 400.
34 Weldemichael, *Third World Colonialism and Strategies of Liberation*, 208.
35 Ibid.
36 Ortuoste, 'Internal and External Institutional Dynamics in Member-states and ASEAN', 348.

37 Ibid., 349.
38 International Court of Justice, 'Case Concerning East Timor (Portugal v. Australia)', para. 37.
39 'East Timor: An Interview with Prof. Jose Ramos Horta'.
40 CAVR, 'Chapter 5 Resistance'.
41 Walsh, 'From Opposition to Proposition'.
42 'E Timor "Will be Free Within Three Years"'.
43 Pinto, 'Statement before the United Nations Committee on Decolonization On Behalf of National Resistance of East Timorese Students'.
44 Weldemichael, *Third World Colonialism and Strategies of Liberation*.
45 Lloyd, 'The Diplomacy on East Timor'.
46 Gorjão, 'Regime Change and Foreign Policy'.
47 Hellwig and Tagliacozzo, *The Indonesia Reader*.
48 Fernandes, *The Independence of East Timor*.
49 Gorjão, 'Regime Change and Foreign Policy'.
50 Dunn, *Crimes against Humanity in East Timor, January to October 1999*.
51 Joint Assessment Mission, 'East Timor, Building a Nation'; United Nations, *Report of the Secretary-General on the Situation in East Timor*.
52 Wheeler and Dunne, 'East Timor and the New Humanitarianism', 818–19.
53 Anwar, 'Challenges to Indonesia's Democratic Consolidation'.
54 Ibid.
55 Jones, 'Political Dynamics of the East Timor Issue in Post-Soeharto Indonesia'.
56 Chesterman, *Just War or Just Peace?*.
57 Henry, 'Playing Second Fiddle on the Road to INTERFET', 109.
58 Huxley, *Disintegrating Indonesia?*, 33–4.
59 Ibid.
60 Ibid.
61 Ibid.
62 Joint Assessment Mission, *East Timor, Building a Nation*.
63 Shurke, 'Peacekeepers as Nation-Builders'.
64 Chopra, 'Building State Failure in East Timor', 979–80.
65 Jones, '(Post-)Colonial State-Building and State Failure in East Timor'.
66 Goldstone, 'UNTAET with Hindsight', 88.
67 Chopra, 'The UN's Kingdom of East Timor'; Beauvais, 'Benevolent Despotism'.
68 Ibid., 1113.
69 'Xanana Gusmão's Paper to NZ Conference'; Wainwright, *New Neighbor, New Challenge*.
70 See, King's College London, *A Review of Peace Operations*; Rees, *Under Pressure Falintil – Forças de Defesa de Timor-Leste*.
71 Amnesty International, *The Democratic Republic of Timor-Leste*; Rees, *Under Pressure Falintil – Forças de Defesa de Timor-Leste*.
72 Rees, *Under Pressure Falintil – Forças de Defesa de Timor-Leste*.
73 Gusmão, 'Speech of His Excellency President Kay Rala Xanana Gusmão on the Occasion of the Handing over of the Final Report of the CAVR to the National Parliament'.
74 United Nations, *Report of the International Commission of Inquiry on East Timor to the Secretary-General*.

75 Katzenstein, 'Hybrid Tribunals'.
76 United Nations, *Report of the Secretary-General on Justice and Reconciliation for Timor-Leste*.
77 United Nations, *Progress Report of the Secretary-General on the United Nations Office in Timor-Leste*, para. 53.
78 UNDP, 'Strengthening Parliamentary Democracy in Timor-Leste', 4.
79 During his visit to the country only a few weeks before the outbreak of violence, Wolfowitz remarked:

> Most post-conflict countries relapse into violence within five years. Though you have had difficult moments and times of tension, you have opted for peace. You have come together as a nation where so many other countries fall apart in factions.
>
> ('Timor-Leste: The Challenge of Keeping Peace for Development')

80 United Nations, Report of the United Nations Independent Special Commission of Inquiry for Timor-Leste.
81 United Nations, *Resolution 1704*.
82 ICG, *Timor-Leste: Time for the UN to Step Back*; Rees, 'Time for the UN to Withdraw from East Timor?'.
83 ICG, *Timor-Leste: No Time for Complacency*.
84 United Nations, *Report of the Secretary-General on the United Nations Integrated Mission in Timor-Leste*.
85 Wilson, *The Exception Becomes the Norm in Timor-Leste*.
86 OHCHR/UNMIT, *Report on Human Rights Developments: 1 July 2008 to 30 June 2009*; Wilson, *The Exception Becomes the Norm in Timor-Leste*; ICG, *Timor-Leste: No Time for Complacency*.
87 ICG, *Timor-Leste: No Time for Complacency*.
88 The concept of *malae* has historically been a 'deeply embedded' component of the Timorese identity, specifically the notion of unification against a foreign enemy. Jolliffe, *East Timor*.
89 ICG, *Timor-Leste: Stability at What Cost?*.
90 Ibid.
91 Lao Hamutuk, 'Can the Petroleum Fund Exorcise the Resource Curse from Timor-Leste?'.
92 IMF, *Democratic Republic of Timor-Leste: 2013 Article IV Consultation*.
93 UNDP, *Managing Natural Resources for Human Development*.
94 United Nations, *Report of the United Nations Independent Special Commission of Inquiry for Timor-Leste*.
95 Scambary, *A Survey of Gangs and Youth Groups in Dili*.
96 ILO, 'Timor-Leste National Youth Employment Action Plan (NYEAP)'.
97 'East Timor PM Mulls Closing Down Violent Martial Arts Groups'.
98 Roughneen, 'Potent Mix Brewing for Timorese'.
99 ICG, *Timor-Leste: Stability at What Cost?*.

6   Conclusion

Exceptionalism has become a constituent element of the discourse and act of contemporary interventions. This is evidenced in the employment of the language of 'exceptional' dangers (such as terrorism, breakdown of governmental authority, refugee flows, pandemics, human trafficking, etc) and the assumption of 'exceptional' forms of power (such as territorial trusteeships and shared sovereignty arrangements) by international agencies in the name of regulating conflict in fragile or war-torn countries. The act of intervention rationalised on the basis of the exceptionalism argument has become the main strategic approach to the management of global security challenges associated with state failure or fragility.

The analysis of the long-term involvement of foreign agencies in Kosovo, Timor-Leste and Northern Iraq illustrates how intervention has now become an act of exceptional state-making. The imposition of a no-fly-zone in northern Iraq and the establishment of international territorial administrations in Kosovo and Timor-Leste in the aftermath of military interventions operationalised as unique and necessary arrangements created the conditions of the making of exceptional states. This process was characterised by uncertainties and vulnerabilities that have both provided new political opportunity structures and created risks. These opportunities included the expansion of the political space within which the formerly oppressed groups, the Iraqi Kurds, Kosovo Albanians and East Timorese, have operated in autonomy from their parent states. The forced withdrawal of the security and civilian agencies of the host states as a result of military intervention facilitated these groups' exercise of relative autonomy and the continuing presence of foreign troops ensured its maintenance.

The political space enlarged through intervention in Kosovo, Timor-Leste and northern Iraq, in other words, was kept outside the physical and legal reach of the host states through continuing foreign military and civilian presence. This in turn enabled the challenging political groups to establish a new political order and express their identity as a political actor. The elements of these emerging orders and identities included the creation of democratic institutions (such as parliaments, militaries, etc) and adoption of policy reforms. The institutions and administrative structures capacity-built by international agencies have become the basis of the formerly oppressed groups' aspiration to demonstrate empirical attributes of governmental functionality in pursuit of 'earned sovereignty'.

Indeed, the policy sphere in Kosovo, Timor-Leste and northern Iraq turned into a site of mutually reinforcing agendas where international and local political groups have been involved in symbiotic relationships. In the case of Kosovo, for Albanians, the realisation of their long-sought-after independence was dependent on foreign intervention. The NATO operation in March 1999 created the conditions of their path to supervised independence in 2008. Similarly, Timor-Leste invaded and occupied by Indonesia in 1975 exercised self-determination as a result of the Australian-led military intervention in September 1999. Both Kosovo and Timor-Leste, where international territorial administrations with exceptional powers were put in place, became the sites of liberal democratic transformation experimentation by international agencies testing their policy frameworks and operational capacity to investigate whether conflict-affected territories can be turned into well functioning, peaceful polities. The problems with multi-ethnic society creation in Kosovo and the flawed security sector development process, undertaken twice, in Timor-Leste, on the other hand, highlighted the limits of external agencies' capacity and contradictions of their prescribed policy interventions as an objective solution to the problems of intervened states. The KRG, on the other hand, has enhanced its status as a growingly autonomous actor with significant leverage against Baghdad since 2003 as a result of the alliance Iraqi Kurds formed with the US during its military intervention. Following the rejection of the March 2003 parliamentary motion by the Turkish parliament, the Kurds successfully presented themselves as a strategic US ally. The constitutional rights and political privileges, including a recently agreed expanded autonomy framework, make it clear that the Iraqi Kurds have benefitted from the institutional and political trappings of this alliance.

When it comes to the priorities of international agencies, they have been concerned with the implementation of their prescribed capacity-development programmes, which required an alignment of powerful interests in favour of these programmes. Wolfowitz's description of Timor-Leste as the 'leader among post-war countries' due to its 'remarkable achievements' in establishing 'a functioning economy and vibrant democracy' in a short span of time[1] (even though 40 per cent of its population were living on less a $1 day according to World Bank statistics at the time) illustrates the centrality of positive speech to the processes of importing internationally advocated governance models. When the problems emerged, the management of institutional projects was left to the responsibility of local governments, as reflected in the 'assistance' role UNMIT was assigned in Timor-Leste following the 2006 security crisis. The case of KRG, which presented itself as a dependable US ally for consolidation of the Bush administration's imposed regime change exemplifies the importance of finding reliable local partners for policy implementation. The relative stability and security the region enjoyed helped raise its institutional profile. However, stopping the emerging Islamic State threat and protecting the local communities were left to the responsibility of the Peshmerga forces, while the involvement of US-led coalition was restricted to air strikes. In the case of Kosovo, the surrounding rule-of-law weaknesses and development problems were attributed to the local institutions' policy implementation incapacity.

While creating opportunities for domestic political groups, the political uncertainties created by intervention simultaneously produced certain risks that conditioned extended practices of foreign involvement in institutional and policy processes of these territories. UNMIK, for instance, still maintains its presence as a small mission due to Russia's objection to terminating Resolution 1244 and the EU has recently extended the mandate of its rule of law mission until 2016. The UN deployed five missions to Timor-Leste since 1999 and eventually withdrew in December 2012 amidst compounding tensions with local authorities. The KRG remains heavily dependent on foreign assistance and patronage to consolidate its existence amidst tensions with Baghdad, rise of jihadist terror, and sectarian violence and instability in the broader region.

A key feature of the contemporary policy and practice of international state-building has been the emphasis on its centrality to conflict regulation. Conceptualised from a perspective of cause and effect relationship, contemporary conflict has come to be regarded as a problem of weak governmental and institutional performance. The following summary of the 'underlying or triggering causes' of conflict in an OECD policy document provides an illustration of this widely shared consensus among international agencies:[2]

illegitimate or weak institutions, corruption, insufficient respect for human rights, lack of good governance, and the perception that the administrative and political channels are not adequate or that they are inaccessible.

Because conflict is defined by reference to the state's governance features and democratic credentials, in this approach strengthening the 'ability of states to plan and execute policies and to enforce laws cleanly and transparently'[3] becomes a priority to protect the state from predatory interests and promote a more effective use of its development resources.[4] As manifested in the language of 'building', 'construction', 'reconstitution' or 'fixing' employed to describe the policy measures and operational activities undertaken, state capacity is treated as an objective, mechanistic condition that is 'missing' or 'broken' in some states.[5]

In this definition of capacity as a matter of institutional performance, capacity becomes 'depoliticized'[6] and is presented as a product of 'good' or 'rational' policies.[7] This is not to suggest that donors are unaware of the power politics dimensions of policy-making.[8] Rather it is to point out that mainstream accounts of international state-building tend to treat the processes of institutional structuring and capacity development in rather technical and organisational terms. From the perspective of international agencies, this means that the policy sphere within which the capacity of institutions develops needs to be neutralised to be able to prevent the recurrence of violent conflict.

However, the policy space becomes a contentious 'field of power' where different groups of actors pursue their particular interests and seek to enjoy the opportunities provided through international intervention. In the case of Kosovo, this situation is exemplified by rising factional rivalries in the post-NATO military intervention period, eruption of violence in March 2004, and the increasing pressure local groups exerted to prompt the resolution of the status problem in their favour. In northern Iraq, the KDP–PUK coalition which has dominated the political and institutional domain since the 2005 elections has seriously been challenged by the Gorran party during the last elections, with instances of tensions and clashes between local party supporters in Suleymaniyah reported in the media. In the case of Timor-Leste, the resurfacing of rivalries within the elite resulted in a serious security crisis in 2006. The deadly clashes between the police and the military in May 2006 and the assassination attempts against the President and the Prime Minister in February 2008 indicated how deeply personal and political divisions were entrenched in the country's newly created security institutions.

The technocratic framing of contemporary interventions is also evidenced in the stabilisation of the meaning of sovereignty as capacity or 'responsibility' and of military action in terms of 'exceptional circumstances' of human risk and security.[9] Additionally, because intervention is prescribed as an objective solution to what is seen as a 'good governance' problem, the stated goal of intervention becomes creating a governmental model that supposedly helps strengthen sovereignty rather than undermine it.

However, intervention changes the conditions of political power upon which sovereignty is structured. The UN's engagement in Kosovo's reconstruction during the post-NATO military intervention period was informed by a technical perspective of creating democratic governance capabilities as a foundation of sustainable peace. However, the Kosovo conflict was essentially a sovereignty issue rooted in the opposing claims of the Serbs and Albanians to rule over the territory by reference to its history and demography. The establishment of UNMIK, for many Albanians, symbolised the end of Belgrade's sovereignty and the emergence of an enabling condition for the recognition of their claims. This was achieved with the granting of statehood status conditioned on a continuing international supervision to improve the sovereign and functional capacity of its institutions. However, the continuing isolation of the Serb-dominated northern municipalities and their reluctance to recognise Pristina's authority have had an undermining effect on the sovereign capacity-development of Kosovo. Similarly, Timor-Leste remained dependent on the UN and other agencies for the capacity-development of its security and other institutions, even though its sovereign status was recognised with the handover of authorities from UNTAET to the democratically elected Timorese government in May 2002. The weaknesses the Timorese institutions were facing came to the fore in 2006. The subsequent security sector reform process 'assisted' by UNMIT was constrained by surrounding tensions over sovereignty. The government's creation of the joint command structure in 2008 through removing the national police from UNPOL's authority and placing it under the command of the military (without prior consultation with the UN mission) reflected a desire to demonstrate sovereign capacity and identity.[10] Security and defence-related issues, after all, fall under the realm of state sovereignty. When it comes to the KRG, the Kurdish region's exercise of extensive autonomy has fuelled tensions with the federal government in Baghdad. This is evidenced in the Kurdish leadership's efforts to take ownership of the disputed territories and create an independent funding mechanism as a way of paving the way for the region's transition to statehood. In search for international support to achieve their political aspirations, Kurdish leaders have strived to 'earn' sovereignty through consolidating territorial control and strengthening the capacity of the institutional structures as a way of demonstrating the region's capacity to act as a sovereign power.

These developments make it fair to conclude that international state-building interventions are neither exceptional nor technically informed sovereignty supporting undertakings. They rather denote an act of state-making that develops in a context of exceptionalism. It remains unclear whether this will become a consistent practice in the future, but this is how states are now created: facilitating achievement of statehood aspirations through acquisition of the support of the most powerful (Western) states, while conditions of dependence on foreign supervision are perpetrated due to institutional weaknesses.

The questions of sovereignty, nationalism and self-determination continue to attract significant attention worldwide. The UN-sponsored-referendum in 2011 led to the separation of the South Sudanese and sparked speculations over the future status of other non-recognised states. The September 2014 referendum in Scotland was also followed closely in different parts of the world, with scenarios of its potential effects on other secessionist movements. The debate on sovereignty has indeed turned a new corner following the Scottish referendum results, with speculations over the appeal of territorial separation to minority communities. It will be seen whether other self-determination/secession movements will follow the pathway towards exceptional state-making or the Scottish way (staying within parent states) becomes a subject for another study that could be carried out on a comparison of the findings of this current one.

Notes

1 Wolfowitz, 'Timor-Leste: The Challenge of Keeping Peace for Development'.
2 OECD, *Preventing Conflict and Building Peace*.
3 Fukuyama, *State-Building*, 5.
4 World Bank, *The State in a Changing World*; World Bank, *Capacity Building in Africa*.
5 Rotberg, *When States Fail*; Fukuyama, *State-Building*; Ghani and Lockhart, *Fixing Failed States*; Ghani et al., *Closing the Sovereignty Gap*.
6 Hameiri, 'Failed States or a Failed Paradigm?', 131, 139.
7 Hadiz, 'Decentralization and Democracy in Indonesia', 698.
8 Ibid.
9 See ICISS, *The Responsibility to Protect*.
10 ICG, 'Handing Back Responsibility to Timor-Leste's Police'; Wilson, 'Smoke and Mirrors'.

References

Abbas, Mushreq. 'Sulaimaniyah Scene of Power Struggle among Iraqi Kurdish Parties'. *Al-Monitor*, 27 November 2013.

Abdulla, Jamal Jalal. *The Kurds: A Nation On the Way to Statehood*. Bloomington: Author House, 2012.

Agamben, Giorgio. 'On Security and Terror'. Trans. Soenke Zehle, *Frankfurter Allgemeine Zeitung*, 20 September 2001.

Agamben, Giorgio. *The State of Exception*. Trans. Kevin Attell. Chicago, London: University of Chicago Press, 2005.

Agencia-Geral do Ultramar. *Timor: Pequeña Monografia*. Lisboa: Agencia Geral do Ultramar, 1965.

Ahmed, Mohammed M. A. *Iraqi Kurds and Nation-Building*. New York: Palgrave Macmillan, 2012.

Alatas, Ali. *East Timor: De-bunking the Myths around a Process of Decolonization*. Remarks before the Members of the National Press Club. Washington, DC, 20 February 1992.

Alkadiri, Raad. 'Oil and the Question of Federalism in Iraq'. *International Affairs* 86, no. 6 (2010): 1315–28.

Amnesty International. *The Democratic Republic of Timor-Leste: A New Police Service – A New Beginning*. London: Amnesty International, ASA 57/002/03, 2003.

Amnesty International. *Hope and Fear: Human Rights in the Kurdistan Region of Iraq*. London: Amnesty International Publications, 2009.

Anderson, Benedict. *Imagined Communities: Reflections on the Origin and Spread of Nationalism*. London: Verso, 1991.

Anderson, Benedict. 'East Timor and Indonesia: Some Implications'. In *East Timor at the Crossroads: The Forging of a Nation*, ed. Peter Carey and G. Carter Bentley, 137–47. London: Cassell, 1995.

Annan, Kofi. *Support by the United Nations System of the Efforts of Governments to Promote and Consolidate New or Restored Democracies*. Report of the Secretary General to the Security Council, UN Document A/53/554, 29 October 1998.

Annan, Kofi. *The Causes of Conflict and the Promotion of Durable Peace and Sustainable Peace in Africa.* Report of the Secretary-General to the Security Council, UN Document S/1998/318, 16 April 1998.

Annan, Kofi. 'Two Concepts of Sovereignty'. *The Economist*, 18 September 1999.

Anwar, Dewi Fortuna. 'Challenges to Indonesia's Democratic Consolidation'. *PacNet 34*, 3 September 1999.

Artisien, Patrick F. R. 'A Note on Kosovo and the Future of Yugoslav–Albanian Relations: A Balkan Perspective'. *Soviet Studies* 36 (1984): 267–76.

Atesoğlu Guney, Nursin. *Contentious Issues of Security and the Future of Turkey.* Hampshire; Burlington, VT: Ashgate, 2007.

Atwood, Brian. 'Suddenly Chaos'. *Washington Post*, 31 July 1994.

AusAID (Australian Agency for International Development). *Australian Aid: Promoting Growth and Stability.* White Paper on the Australian Government Overseas Aid Program, Canberra, 2006, accessed 5 July 2011, www.ausaid. gov.au/publications/pubout.cfm?Id=6184_6346_7334_4045_8043.

Aziz, Salah. 'Kurdistan: Democracy and the Future of Iraq'. In *Iraq, Democracy and the Future of the Muslim World*, ed. Ali Paya and John Esposito. Abingdon, UK: Routledge, 2011.

Barkawi, Tarak and Mark Laffey. 'The Imperial Peace: Democracy, Force and Globalization', *European Journal of International Relations* 5, no. 4 (1999): 403–34.

Barkey, Henri. *Preventing Conflict over Kurdistan.* Washington, DC: Carnegie Endowment for International Peace, 2009.

'Barzani Asks MPs to Organize Independence Vote'. *Agence France Presse*, 3 July 2014.

Batakovic, Dusan T. *Kosovo-Metohija: The Serbo-Albanian Conflict.* Belgrade: Institute of Balkan Studies, 1998.

Beauvais, Joel C. 'Benevolent Despotism: A Critique of UN State-Building in East Timor'. *New York University Journal of International Law and Politics* 33, no. 4 (2001): 1101–78.

Bellamy, Alex J. *Kosovo and International Society.* Basingstoke: Palgrave Macmillan, 2002.

Bellamy, Alex J. 'Humanitarian Responsibilities and Interventionist Claims in International Society'. *Review of International Studies* 29, no. 3 (2003): 321–40.

Bellamy, Alex J. 'The "Next Stage" in Peace Operations Theory?'. *International Peacekeeping* 11, no. 1 (2004): 17–38.

Bellamy, Alex J., Paul Williams and Stuart Griffin. *Understanding Peacekeeping.* Cambridge: Polity Press, 2004.

Ben Solomon, Ariel. 'Iraqi Kurds Close to Declaring Independence'. *Jerusalem Post*, 9 June 2014.

Bengio, Ofra. *The Kurds of Iraq.* Boulder, CO: Lynne Rienner, 2012.

Beqiri, Besa. 'EULEX Becomes Fully Operational'. *Southeast European Times*, 7 April 2009.

Berger, Mark T. 'From Nation-Building to State-Building: The Geopolitics of Development, the Nation-State System and the Changing Global Order'. *Third World Quarterly* 27, no. 1 (2006): 5–25.

Bickerton, Chris J. 'Exporting State Failure'. *Arena Journal* 32 (2009): 101–23.

Bickerton, Christopher, Philip Cunliffe and Alexander Gourevitch, eds. *Politics without Sovereignty: A Critique of Contemporary International Relations*. Abingdon, UK: University College London Press, 2007.

Bilgin, Pinar and Adam David Morton. 'From "Rogue" to "Failed" States? The Fallacy of Short-Termism'. *Politics* 24 (2004): 169–80.

Blair, Tony. *Doctrine of the International Community*. Speech at the Chicago Economic Club, 24 April 1999, accessed 13 March 2009, www.pm.gov.uk/output/Page1297.asp.

Blair, Tony. *A Journey: My Political Life*. New York: Alfred A. Knopf, 2010.

Boege, Volker, Anne Brown, Kevin Clements and Anna Nolan. 'On Hybrid Political Orders and Emerging States: What is Failing – States in the Global South or Research and Politics in the West?'. In *Building Peace in the Absence of States: Challenging the Discourse on State Failure*, ed. Martina Fischer and Beatrix Schmelzle, 15–35. Berlin: Berghof Research Center, 2009.

Bojicic, Vesna. 'The Disintegration of Yugoslavia: Causes and Consequences of Dynamic Inefficiency in Semi-Command Economies'. In *Yugoslavia and After: A Study in Fragmentation, Despair and Rebirth*, ed. David A. Dyker and Ivan Vejvoda, 28–47. London, New York: Longman, 1996.

Bolton, Grace and Gezim Visoka. *Recognising Kosovo's Independence: Remedial Secession or Earned Sovereignty*. Southeast European Studies at Oxford Occasional Paper 11/10, 2010.

Boutros-Ghali, Boutros. *An Agenda for Democratization*. New York: United Nations, 1996.

Boutros-Ghali, Boutros, ed. *The Interaction between Democracy and Development*. Paris: United Nations Education, Scientific and Cultural Organisation, 2002.

Braithwaite, John, Hilary Charlesworth and Adérito Soares. *Networked Governance of Freedom and Tyranny: Peace in Timor-Leste*. Canberra: ANU E-Press, 2012.

Brajshori, Muhamet. 'Mitrovica: Temporary Fix, Long Term Problem'. *Southeast European Times*, 5 August 2011.

Bring, Ove. 1999. 'Should NATO Take the Lead in Formulating a Doctrine on Humanitarian Intervention?'. *NATO Review* 47, no. 3 (1999): 24–7.

Brown, Chris. *Sovereignty vs. Human rights in a Post-Western World*. Paper Presented at ESRC Seminar Series, 'Normative Challenges to International Society – Rising Powers and Global Responses', 2nd Seminar, 22 March 2013.

Buchanan, Allen. *Justice, Legitimacy and Self-Determination: Moral Foundations for International Law*. Oxford University Press: Oxford, 2004.

Bull, Hedley and Adam Watson, eds, *The Expansion of International Society*, Oxford: Clarendon Press; New York: Oxford University Press, 1984.

Bush, George H. *New World Order Speech*, 11 September 1990.

Bush, George W. *The State of the Union Address*, 29 January 2002.

Buzan, Barry, Ole Wæver and Jaap de Wilde. *Security: A New Framework for Analysis*. Boulder, CO: Lynne Rienner, 1998.

Campbell, David. *Writing Security*. Manchester: Manchester University Press, 1998.

Caspersen, Nina. *Unrecognized States: The Struggle for Sovereignty in the Modern International System*. Cambridge: Polity Press, 2012.

Cassese, Antonio. 'Ex Iniuria Ius Oritur: Are We Moving towards International Legitimation of Forcible Humanitarian Countermeasures in the World Community?'. *European Journal of International Relations* 10, no. 1 (1999): 23–30.

Chabal, Patrick and Jean-Pascal Daloz. *Africa Works: Disorder as Political Instrument*. Bloomington: Indiana University Press, 1999.

Chandler, David. *Empire in Denial: The Politics of State-Building*. London: Pluto Press, 2006.

Chandler, David. 'Human Security: The Dog That Didn't Bark'. *Security Dialogue* 39, no. 4 (2008): 427–38.

Chandler, David. *International Statebuilding: The Rise of Post-Liberal Governance*. London: Routledge, 2010.

Charountaki, Marianna. 'Turkish Foreign Policy and the Kurdistan Regional Government'. *Perceptions* 17, no. 4 (2012): 185–208.

Chen, Xi. *Social Protest and Contentious Authoritarianism in China*. Cambridge: Cambridge University Press, 2012.

Chesterman, Simon. *Just War or Just Peace? Humanitarian Intervention and International Law*. Oxford, New York: Oxford University Press, 2001.

Chopra, Jarat. 'Building State Failure in East Timor'. *Development and Change* 33, no. 5 (2002): 979–1000.

Chopra, Jarat. 'The UN's Kingdom of East Timor'. *Survival* 42, no. 3 (2000): 27–39.

Chopra, Jarat and Tanja Hohe. 'Participatory Intervention', *Global Governance* 10 (2004): 289–305.

Clark, Howard. *Civil Resistance in Kosovo*. London: Pluto Press, 2000.

Clark, Howard. 'The Limits of Prudence: Civil Resistance in Kosovo'. In *Civil Resistance and Power Politics: The Experience of Non-violent Action from Gandhi to the Present*, ed. Adam Roberts and Timothy Garton Ash, 277–294. Oxford: Oxford University Press, 2009.

Clinton, William J. *A National Security Strategy of Engagement and Enlargement, 1995–1996*. Washington, DC: Brassey's, 1995.

Collier, Paul. *Breaking the Conflict Trap: Civil War and Development Policy*. Washington, DC: World Bank World Bank and Oxford University Press, 2003.

'Condoleezza Blasts South Ossetia's Independence: "It's not Going to Happen"'. *The Tiraspol Times*, 6 March 2008.

'Containment: Iraqi No-Fly Zones'. BBC, 29 December 1998.

Cook, Steven A. 'Kurdistan – Just Being Independent'. *Middle East Voice*, 29 October 2013.

Cooley, Alexander and Hendrik Spruyt. *Contracting States: Sovereign Transfers in International Relations*. Princeton, NJ: Princeton University Press, 2009.

Cooper, Robert. 'The New Liberal Imperialism'. *Observer*, 7 April 2002.

Cotton, James. *East Timor, Australia and Regional Order: Intervention and its Aftermath in Southeast Asia*. London: Routledge, 2004.

'Council Joint Action 2008/124/CFSP of 4 February 2008, on the European Union Rule of Law Mission in Kosovo, EULEX Kosovo'. L 42/92, *Official Journal of the European Union*, 4 February 2008.

Danish Institute of International Affairs (DUPI). *Humanitarian Intervention: Legal and Political Aspects*. Copenhagen: DUPI, 1999.

de Wet, Erika. 'The Governance of Kosovo: Security Council Resolution 1244 and the Establishment and Functioning of EULEX'. *American Journal of International Law* 103, no. 1 (2009): 83–96.

'Debate: Would Independence for Kosovo Contribute to or Undermine International Stability?'. *NATO Review*, 2006, accessed 12 October 2011, www.nato.int/docu/review/2006/issue1/english/debate.html.

Deng, Francis Mading. 'State Collapse: The Humanitarian Challenge to the United Nations'. In *Collapsed States: The Disintegration and Restoration of Legitimate Authority*, ed. I. William Zartman, 207–19, Boulder, CO: Lynne Rienner, 1995.

Derks, Maria and Megan Price. *The EU and Rule of Law Reform in Kosovo*. The Hague: Netherlands Institute for International Relations, 2010.

DFID (UK Government's Department for International Development). *Why We Need to Work More Effectively in Fragile States*. London: DFID, 2005.

DFID (UK Government's Department for International Development). *Governance, Development and Democratic Politics: DFID's Work in Building More Effective States*. Glasgow: DFID, 2007.

Di John, Jonathan. 'Oil Abundance and Violent Political Conflict: A Critical Assessment'. *Journal of Development Studies* 43, no. 6 (2007): 961–86.

Diamond, Larry, Juan Linz and Seymour Martin Lipset, eds. *Democracy in Developing Countries: Comparing Experiences with Democracy*. Boulder, CO: Lynne Rienner, 1990.

Dobbins, James, Seth G. Jones, Keith Crane, Andrew Rathmell, Brett Steele, Richard Teltschik and Anga R. Timilsina. *The UN's Role in Nation-Building: From the Congo to Iraq*. Santa Monica, CA: RAND, 2005.

Dobbins, James, John G. McGinn, Keith Crane, Seth G. Jones, Rollie Lal, Andrew Rathmell, Rachel M. Swanger and Anga R. Timilsina. *America's Role in Nation-Building: From Germany to Iraq*. Santa Monica, CA: RAND, 2003.

Dorff, Robert H. 'Democratization, Failed States and Peace Operations: The Challenge of Ungovernability'. *American Diplomacy* 1, no. 2 (1996).

Doty, Roxanne Lynn. *Imperial Encounters: The Politics of Representation in North-South Relations.* Minneapolis: University of Minnesota Press, 1996.

Doyle, Michael W. 'Kant, Liberal Legacies, and Foreign Affairs'. *Philosophy and Public Affairs* 12, no. 3 (1983): 205–35.

Duffield, Mark. *Global Governance and the New Wars: The Merging of Development and Security.* London: Zed Books, 2001.

Duffield, Mark. 'Social Reconstruction and the Radicalization of Development: Aid as a Relation of Global Governance'. *Development and Change* 33, no. 5 (2002): 1049–71.

Dunn, James. *Timor: A People Betrayed.* Sydney: ABC Books, 1996.

Dunn, James. *Crimes against Humanity in East Timor, January to October 1999: Their Nature and Causes.* Dili, 2001, accessed 10 April 2006, www. etan.org/etanpdf/pdf1/dunn.pdf.

Dupont, Alan. 'The Strategic Implications of an Independent East Timor'. In *Out of the Ashes: The Destruction and Reconstruction of East Timor*, ed. James Fox and Dionisio Babo-Soares, 179–88. Adelaide: Crawford House Publishing, 2003.

'E Timor "Will Be Free within Three Years"'. *Guardian Weekly*, 16 August 1998.

'East Timor: An Interview with Prof. Jose Ramos Horta'. *CNN*, 14 January 1997, accessed 24 May 2013, www.hrsolidarity.net/mainfile.php/1997vol. 07no01/231.

'East Timor PM Mulls Closing Down Violent Martial Arts Groups'. *Agence France Presse*, 5 December 2011.

East Timor Peace Plan. Reports from the United Nations Association of New Zealand Seminar Entitled 'East Timor: A Time for Action'. Wellington, 8 June 1996.

Eide, Kai. *The Situation in Kosovo.* Report to the Secretary General of the United Nations, Brussels, 15 July 2004.

Elias, Norbert. *What is Sociology?* New York: Columbia University Press, 1978.

Economy Overview: Kurdistan Region of Iraq – Determined to Grow, accessed 16 September 2014, www.investingroup.org/publications/kurdistan/overview/ economy.

Erlanger, Steven. 'Albright Warns Serbs on Kosovo Violence'. *New York Times*, 8 March 1998.

Escobar, Arturo. *Encountering Development: The Making and Unmaking of the Third World.* Princeton, NJ: Princeton University Press, 1995.

'Ethnic Albanians Now Oppose EU Kosovo Mission'. *EurActiv*, 25 November 2008.

'EU Splits on Kosovo Recognition'. *BBC News*, 18 February 2008.

EULEX (European Union Rule of Law Mission Kosovo). *EULEX Programme Report 2011: Bolstering the Rule of Law in Kosovo: A Stock Take*, accessed 8

January 2013, www.eulex-kosovo.eu/docs/tracking/EULEX%20Programme Report%202011.pdf.

European Commission. *Key Findings of the 2010 Progress Report on Kosovo.* Brussels, 9 November 2010, accessed 23 September 2014, http://europa.eu/rapid/press-release_MEMO-10-554_en.htm.

European Parliament External Relations. 'Kosovo: A Special Case Say MEPs'. Press Service, Ref. 20080219IPR21734, 20 February 2008, accessed 16 May 2009, www.europarl.europa.eu/sides/getDoc.do?language=EN&type=IMPRESS&reference=20080219IPR21734.

European Union Office in Kosovo/European Union Special Representative in Kosovo. *Political and Economic Issues*, accessed 5 September 2012, http://eeas.europa.eu/delegations/kosovo/eu_kosovo/political_relations/index_en.htm.

'Ex-Rebel Becomes Kosovo's Prime Minister'. *MSNBC*, 9 January 2008.

Fearon, James D. and David D. Laitin. 'Neotrusteeship and the Problem of Weak States'. *International Security* 28, no. 4 (2004): 5–43.

Ferguson, James. *Anti-Politics Machine: Development, Depoliticization, and Bureaucratic Power in Lesotho*. Cambridge: Cambridge University Press, 1990.

Fernandes, Clinton. *The Independence of East Timor: Multi-Dimensional Perspectives – Occupation, Resistance, and International Political Activism*. Eastbourne: Sussex Academy Press, 2011.

Filkins, Dexter. 'The Fight of Their Lives'. *New Yorker*, 29 September 2014.

Foniqi-Kabashi, Blerta. 'International Community Urges Kosovo Leaders to Accept UN Chief's EULEX Plan'. *Southeast European Times*, 12 November 2008.

Foreign Policy. 'The 2012 Failed States Index – Interactive Map and Rankings'. 2012, accessed 25 July 2012, www.foreignpolicy.com/failed_states_index_2012_interactive.

Fowler, Michael Ross and Julie Marie Bunck. *Law, Power, and the Sovereign State: The Evolution and Application of the Concept of Sovereignty*. University Park, PA: Pennsylvania State University Press, 1995.

François, Monika and Inder Sud. 'Promoting Stability and Development in Fragile and Failed States'. *Development Policy Review* 24, no. 2 (2006): 141–60.

Freyre, Gilberto. *The Portuguese and the Tropics*. Trans. Helen M. D'O. Matthew and F. de Mello Moser. Lisbon: Executive Committee for the Commemoration of the Vth Centenary of the Death of Prince Henry the Navigator, 1961.

'From Chaos, Order: Rebuilding Failed States'. *The Economist*, 3 March 2005.

Fukuyama, Francis. *State-Building: Governance and World Order in the 21st Century*. Ithaca, NY: Cornell University Press, 2004.

Fukuyama, Francis. 'The End of History?'. *National Interest* 16 (1989): 3–18.

Gamage, Daya. 'Independence of Kosovo Sets No Precedent Anywhere Else in This World – US Secretary of State'. *Asian Tribune*, 7 March 2008.

Ghani, Ashraf and Clare Lockhart. *Fixing Failed States: A Framework for Rebuilding A Fractured World*. Oxford, New York: Oxford University Press, 2008.

Ghani, Ashraf, Clare Lockhart and Michael Carnahan. *Closing the Sovereignty Gap: An Approach to State-Building*. London: Overseas Development Institute, 2005.

Goldstone, Anthony. 'UNTAET with Hindsight: The Peculiarities of Politics in An Incomplete State'. *Global Governance* 10, no. 1 (2004): 83–98.

Gorani, Dukagjin. *Orientalist Ethnonationalism: From Irredentism to Independentism Discourse Analysis of the Albanian Ethnonationalist Narrative about the National Rebirth (1870–1930) and Kosovo Independence (1980–2000)*. PhD dissertation, Cardiff University, 2011.

Gorjão, Paulo. 'Regime Change and Foreign Policy: Portugal, Indonesia, and the Self-Determination of East Timor'. *Democratization* 9, no. 4 (2002): 142–58.

Gros, Jean Germain. 'Towards a Taxonomy of Failed States in the New World Order: Decaying Somalia, Liberia, Rwanda and Haiti'. *Third World Quarterly* 17, no. 3 (1996): 455–71.

Gross, Oren and Fionnuala Ní Aoláin. *Law in Times of Crisis: Emergency Powers in Theory and Practice*. Cambridge, New York: Cambridge University Press, 2006.

Guicherd, Catherine. 'International Law and the War in Kosovo'. *Survival* 41, no. 2 (1999): 19–34.

Gunter, Michael M. 'A De Facto Kurdish State in Northern Iraq'. *Third World Quarterly* 14 (1993): 295–319.

Gunter, Michael M. 'Kurdish Future in a Post-Saddam Iraq'. *Journal of Muslim Minority Affairs* 23, no. 1 (2003): 9–23.

Gunter, Michael M. 'Turkey's New Neighbor, Kurdistan'. In *The Future of Kurdistan in Iraq*, ed. Brendan O'Leary, John McGarry and Khaled Salih, 219–32, Philadelphia, PA: University of Pennsylvania Press, 2005.

Gunter, Michael M. *The Kurds Ascending: The Evolving Solution to the Kurdish Problem in Iraq and Turkey*. New York: Palgrave Macmillan, 2008.

Gurr, Ted Robert. *Peoples versus States: Minorities at Risk in the New Century*. Washington, DC: United States Institute of Peace, 2000.

Gusmão, José A. 'Xanana'. *Speech of His Excellency President Kay Rala Xanana Gusmão On the Occasion of the Handing Over of the Final Report of the CAVR to the National Parliament*, 28 November 2005.

Hadiz, Vedi R. 'Decentralization and Democracy in Indonesia: A Critique of Neo- Institutionalist Perspectives'. *Development and Change* 35, no. 4 (2004): 697–718.

Hadji, Philip S. 'The Case for Kurdish Statehood in Iraq'. *Case Western Reserve Journal of International Law* 41 (2009): 513–41.

Halliday, Fred. 'Can We Write a Modernist History of Kurdish Nationalism?'. In *The Kurds: Nationalism and Politics'*, ed. Faleh A. Jabar and Hosham Dawod, 11–20. London: Saqi, 2006.

Hameiri, Shahar. 'Failed States or a Failed Paradigm? State Capacity and the Limits of Institutionalism'. *Journal of International Relations and Development* 10 (2007): 122–49.

Hameiri, Shahar. *Regulating Statehood: State Building and the Transformation of the Global Order*. Basingstoke: Palgrave Macmillan, 2010.

Hamid, Triska. 'Corruption and Cronyism Hinder Kurdistan'. *Financial Times*, 5 September 2012.

Hammond, Philip. '"Good versus Evil" after the Cold War: Kosovo and the Moralisation of War Reporting'. *Javnost – The Public* 7, no. 3 (2000): 19–37.

Harden, Blaine. 'Yugoslav Regions Assert Independence: Secession of Slovenia, Croatia Prompts Calls for Army Intervention'. *Washington Post*, 26 June 1991.

Harrison, Graham. 'Post-Conditionality Politics and Administrative Reform: Reflections on the Cases of Uganda and Tanzania'. *Development and Change* 32, no. 4 (2001): 657–79.

Hedges, Chris. 'Notes from the Underground on Another Balkan Rift'. *New York Times*, 11 May 1997.

Hedges, Chris. 'Both Sides in the Kosovo Conflict Seem Determined to Ignore Reality'. *New York Times*, 22 June 1998.

Hellwig, Tineke and Eric Tagliacozzo, eds. *The Indonesia Reader: History, Culture, Politics*. Durham: Duke University Press, 2009.

Helman, Gerald B. and Steven R. Ratner. 'Saving Failed States'. *Foreign Policy* 89 (1992–3): 3–20.

Henry, Iain. 'Playing Second Fiddle on the Road to INTERFET'. *Security Challenges* 9, no. 1 (2013): 87–111.

Herring, Eric. 'From Rambouillet to the Kosovo Accords: NATO's War against Serbia and its Aftermath'. *International Journal of Human Rights* 4, no. 3–4 (2000): 224–45.

Hinsley, F.H. *Sovereignty*. Second edition, Cambridge: Cambridge University Press, 1986.

Holbrooke, Richard. 'Opportunity for Turks and Kurds?' *Washington Post*, 12 February 2007.

Holsti, Kalevi J. *The State, War, and the State of War*. Cambridge, New York: Cambridge University Press, 1996.

House of Commons Foreign Affairs Committee. *4th Report of the House of Commons Foreign Affairs Committee*, June 2000.

Human Rights Watch. *Genocide in Iraq: The Anfal Campaign against the Kurds.* New York: Human Rights Watch, 1993.

Huntley, Wade and Peter Hayes. 'East Timor and Asian Security'. In *Bitter Flowers, Sweet Flowers: East Timor, Indonesia, and the World Community*, ed. Richard Tanter, Mark Selden and Stephen Rosskamm Shalom, 173–85. Lanham, Maryland; Oxford: Rowman and Littlefield, 2001.

Huxley, Tim, *Disintegrating Indonesia? Implications for Regional Security.* Oxford: Oxford University Press, 2002.

Huysmans, Jef. 'The Jargon of Exception: On Schmitt, Agamben and the Absence of Political Society'. *International Political Sociology*, 2 (2008): 165–83.

ICG (International Crisis Group), *Unifying the Kosovar Factions: The Way Forward.* Balkan Report 58, Brussels, Tirana: ICG, 12 March 1999.

ICG (International Crisis Group). *Waiting for UNMIK: Local Administration in Kosovo.* Balkan Report 79, Pristina: ICG, 18 October 1999.

ICG (International Crisis Group). *After Milošević: A Practical Agenda for Lasting Balkans Peace.* Europe Report 108, Brussels: ICG, 1 April 2001.

ICG (International Crisis Group). *Collapse in Kosovo.* Europe Report 155, Pristina, Belgrade, Brussels: ICG, 2004.

ICG (International Crisis Group). *Kosovo: The Challenge of Transition.* Europe Report 170, Brussels: ICG, 17 February 2006.

ICG (International Crisis Group). *Iraq and the Kurds: The Brewing Battle over Kirkuk.* Middle East Report 56, Brussels: ICG, 18 July 2006.

ICG (International Crisis Group). *Kosovo Status: Delay is Risky.* Europe Report 177, Brussels: ICG, 10 November 2006.

ICG (International Crisis Group). *Kosovo's Status: Difficult Months Ahead.* Europe Briefing 45, Pristina, Brussels: ICG, 20 December 2006.

ICG (International Crisis Group). *Kosovo: No Good Alternatives to the Ahtisaari Plan.* Brussels: ICG, Europe Report 182, 14 May 2007.

ICG (International Crisis Group). *Georgia's South Ossetia Conflict: Make Haste Slowly.* Europe Report 183, Brussels: ICG, 7 June 2007.

ICG (International Crisis Group). *Cyprus: Reversing the Drift to Partition.* Europe Report 190, Brussels: ICG, 10 January 2008.

ICG (International Crisis Group). *Handing Back Responsibility to Timor-Leste's Police. Dili,* Asia Report 180, Brussels: ICG, 3 December 2009.

ICG (International Crisis Group). *Timor-Leste: No Time for Complacency.* Asia Briefing 87, Dili, Brussels: ICG, 2009.

ICG (International Crisis Group). *Iraq's Uncertain Future: Elections and Beyond.* Middle East Report 94, Brussels: ICG, 25 February 2010.

ICG (International Crisis Group). *Timor-Leste: Time for the UN to Step Back.* Asia Briefing 116, Dili, Brussels: ICG, 2010.

ICG (International Crisis Group). *North Kosovo: Dual Sovereignty in Practice.* Europe Report 211, Brussels: ICG, 14 March 2011.

ICG (International Crisis Group). *Timor-Leste: Stability at What Cost?* Asia Report 246, Brussels: ICG, 8 May 2013.

ICISS (International Commission on Intervention and State Sovereignty). *The Responsibility to Protect.* Report of the International Commission on Intervention and State Sovereignty, December 2001.

Idiz, Semih. 'Turkey Aids Fuel to Fight of Iraqi Kurds for Independence'. *Al-Monitor*, 19 July 2013.

ILO (International Labour Organisation). *Timor-Leste National Youth Employment Action Plan (NYEAP)*, 2009, accessed 9 May 2012, www.ilo.org/jakarta/whatwedo/publications/WCMS_116060/lang–en/index.htm.

IMF (International Monetary Fund). *Democratic Republic of Timor-Leste: 2013 Article IV Consultation*. IMF Country Report No. 13/338, Washington, DC, December 2013.

'In Cold Blood: The Massacre of East Timor'. Documentary, First Tuesday, 1992.

Independent International Commission on Kosovo. 2000. *The Kosovo Report: Conflict, International Response, Lessons Learned*. Oxford: Oxford University Press, 2000.

International Commission on the Balkans. *The Balkans in Europe's Future*. Sofia: Centre for Liberal Strategies, 12 April 2005, accessed 5 April 2007, www.balkan-commission.org/activities/Report.pdf.

International Court of Justice. *Case Concerning East Timor (Portugal v. Australia)*. International Court of Justice Reports, The Hague, 1995.

'Interview with Veton Surroi'. Posted to MINELRES (Minority Electronic Resources) by Kosovar Crisis Centre on 2 June 1998, accessed 6 April 2009, www.minelres.lv/minelres/archive/06021998-09:48:46-11994.html.

'Iraqi Kurds Inspired by Secession of South Sudan'. *Reuters*, 20 July 2011.

Isachenko, Daria. *The Making of Informal States: Statebuilding in Northern Cyprus and Transdniestria*. Basingstoke: Palgrave Macmillan, 2012.

Jackson, Robert H. 'Quasi-States, Dual Regimes, and Neoclassical Theory: International Jurisprudence and the Third World'. *International Organization* 41 (1987): 519–49.

Jackson, Robert H. *Quasi States: Sovereignty, International Relations, and the Third World*. Cambridge: Cambridge University Press, 1990.

Jakes, Lara. 'AP Interview: Iraqi Kurd Leader Hints at Secession'. *Associated Press*, 25 April 2012.

Jayasuriya, Kanishka. *9/11 and the New 'Anti-politics' of 'Security'*. Social Science Research Council Essays, 2002, accessed 26 October 2014, http://essays.ssrc.org/sept11/essays/jayasuriya.htm.

Jayasuriya, Kanishka. *Reconstituting the Global Liberal Order: Legitimacy, Regulation and Security*. Abingdon, UK, New York: Routledge, 2005.

Joint Assessment Mission. *East Timor, Building a Nation: A Framework for Reconstruction and Development*. Governance Background Paper, Washington, DC: World Bank, 1999.

Jolliffe, Jill. *East Timor: Nationalism and Colonialism*. St Lucia: University of Queensland, 1978.

Jones, Lee. '(Post-)Colonial State-Building and State Failure in East Timor: Bringing Social Conflict Back In'. *Conflict, Security and Development* 10 (2010): 547–75.

Jones, Lee. *ASEAN, Sovereignty and Intervention in Southeast Asia*. Basingstoke: Palgrave Macmillan, 2012.

Jones, Sidney. *Political Dynamics of the East Timor Issue in Post-Soeharto Indonesia*. Human Rights Watch, Report Prepared for the Asia 2000 Foundation, 3 September 1998.

Judah, Tim. *Kosovo: War and Revenge*. New Haven, London: Yale University Press, 2000.

Judah, Tim. *Kosovo: What Everyone Needs to Know*. Oxford: Oxford University Press, 2008.

Jwaideh, Wadie. *The Kurdish National Movement: Its Origins and Development*. Syracuse, New York: Syracuse University Press, 2006.

Kaijo, Sirwan. *The Rise of ISIS: A Golden Opportunity for Iraq's Kurds*. Carnegie Endowment for International Peace, 19 June 2014.

Kaldor, Mary. *New and Old Wars: Organised Violence in a Global Era*. Cambridge: Polity Press, 1999.

Kaldor, Mary. *Human Security: Reflections on Globalization and Intervention*. Cambridge: Polity Press, 2007.

Kane, Sean. *Iraq's Oil Politics: Where Agreement Might Be Found*. Peaceworks, United States Institute of Peace, 2010.

Kaplan, Robert. 'The Coming Anarchy'. *The Atlantic Monthly* 273, no. 2 (1994): 44–76.

Katzenstein, Suzanne. 'Hybrid Tribunals: Searching for Justice in East Timor'. *Harvard Human Rights Journal* 16 (2003): 245–78.

'KFOR Declares Gates 1 and 31 Military Zones, Angers Serbia'. *UNMIK Media Monitoring*, 29 July 2011.

King's College London. *A Review of Peace Operations: A Case for Change, East Timor Report*. London: King's College, 2003.

Kissinger, Henry. 'Reflections on a Sovereign Iraq'. *Kurdistan Observer*, 8 February 2004.

Kober, Avi. *Coalition Defection: The Dissolution of Arab Anti-Israeli Coalitions in War and Peace*. Westport, CT: Greenwood Publishing Group, 2002.

Kolsto, Pal. 'The Sustainability and Future of Unrecognized Quasi-States'. *Journal of Peace Research* 43, no. 6 (2006): 723–40.

'Kosovo Case Unique, Says Miliband'. *BBC News*, 18 February 2008.

'Kosovo Declared "Fully Independent"'. *BBC*, 10 September 2012.

'Kosovo Does Not Set Precedent, US Says'. *Taipei Times*, 20 February 2008.

'Kosovo is Ours'. *BBC World News*, 17 June 1999.

Krasner, Stephen D. *Sovereignty: Organized Hypocrisy*. Princeton, NJ: Princeton University Press, 1999.

Krasner, Stephen D. 'Sharing Sovereignty: New Institutions for Collapsed and Failing States'. *International Security* 29, no. 2 (2004): 85–120.

KRG (Kurdistan Regional Government). 'Ministries and Departments', accessed 8 September 2014, www.krg.org/p/p.aspx?l=12&s=030000&p=228.

KRG (Kurdistan Regional Government). 'The Kurdistan Parliament', accessed 6 September 2014, www.krg.org/p/p.aspx?l=12&p=229.

Kurtulmus, Ersun N. *State Sovereignty: Concept, Phenomenon and Ramifications*. New York: Palgrave Macmillan, 2005.

Lake, David A. 'Delegating Divisible Sovereignty: Sweeping a Conceptual Minefield'. *The Review of International Organizations* 2 (2007): 219–37.

Lao Hamutuk. 'Can the Petroleum Fund Exorcise the Resource Curse from Timor-Leste?', 1 June 2014, accessed 8 September 2014, www.laohamutuk. org/econ/exor/14ExorcisePaper.htm.

Le Billon, Philippe. 'Corruption, Reconstruction and Oil Governance in Iraq. *Third World Quarterly* 26, no. 4/5 (2005): 685–703.

Lemay-Hébert, Nicolas, 'The Bifurcation of the Two Worlds: Assessing the Gap between Internationals and Locals'. *Third World Quarterly* 32, no. 10 (2011): 1823–41.

Lemay-Hébert, Nicolas. 'The "Empty-Shell" Approach: The Setup Process of International Administrations in Timor-Leste and Kosovo, its Consequences and Lessons'. *International Studies Perspectives* 12 (2011): 190–211.

Lindstrom, Nicole. 'Between Europe and the Balkans: Mapping Slovenia and Croatia's "Return to Europe" in the 1990s'. *Dialectical Anthropology* 27 (2003): 313–29.

Lloyd, Grayson. 'The Diplomacy on East Timor'. In *Out of Ashes: Destruction and Reconstruction of East Timor*, ed. James J. Fox and Dionisio Babo Soares, 79–105. Canberra: Australian National University, 2000.

Loza, Tihomir. 'Kosovo Albanians: Closing Ranks'. *Transitions* 5, no. 5 (1998): 16–37.

Mac Ginty, Roger. 'Indigenous Peace-Making versus the Liberal Peace'. *Cooperation and Conflict* 43, no. 2 (2008): 139–63.

Magas, Branka. *The Destruction of Yugoslavia: Tracking the Break-Up 1980–92*. London and New York: Verso, 1993.

Mahdi, Kamil. 'Iraq's Oil Law: Parsing the Fine Print'. *World Policy Journal* 24, no. 2 (2007): 11–23.

Malcolm, Noel. *Kosovo: A Short History*. New York: New York University Press, 1998.

Maliqi, Shkelzen. 'Is Rugova Going to Be Arrested?' *AIM (Alternative Information Network)*, 15 March 1994, accessed 4 April 2009, www.aimpress.ch/dyn/ trae/archive/data/199403/40319–001-trae-pri.htm.

Maliqi, Shkelzen. 'The Albanian Movement in Kosovo'. In *Yugoslavia and After: A Study in Fragmentation, Despair and Rebirth*, ed. David A. Dyker and Ivan Vejvoda, 138–54. Abingdon, UK, New York: Routledge, 1996.

Maliqi, Shkelzen. 'Why Peaceful Resistance Movement in Kosova Failed', 22 March 2002, accessed 9 October 2014, http://shkelzenmaliqi.wordpress. com/2000/03/22/why-peaceful-resistance-movement-in-kosova-failed.

Matheson, Michael J. 'United Nations Governance of Postconflict Societies'. *American Journal of International Law* 95, no. 1 (2001): 76–85.

Mazower, Mark. *Governing the World: The History of an Idea, 1815 to the Present*. New York: Penguin, 2012.

McAdam, Douglas. *Political Process and the Development of Black Insurgency, 1930–1970*. Chicago: University of Chicago Press, 1999 [1982].

McAdam, Douglas. 'Conceptual Origins, Current Problems, Future Directions'. In *Comparative Perspectives on Social Movements: Political Opportunities, Mobilizing Structures, and Cultural Framings*, ed. Douglas McAdam, John D. McCarthy and Mayer Zald, 23–40. Cambridge: Cambridge University Press, 1996.

McAdam, Douglas, John D. McCarthy and Mayer N. Zald. 'Opportunities, Mobilizing Structures, and Framing Processes: Toward a Synthetic, Comparative Perspective on Social Movements'. In *Comparative Perspectives on Social Movements: Political Opportunities, Mobilizing Structures, and Cultural Framings*, ed. Douglas McAdam, John D. McCarthy and Mayer Zald, 1–21. Cambridge: Cambridge University Press, 1996.

McDowall, David. *A Modern History of the Kurds*. London: I.B. Tauris, 2007.

Meho, Lokman I. *The Kurdish Question in U.S. Foreign Policy: A Documentary Sourcebook*. Westport, CT: Praeger Publishers, 2004.

Mertus, Julie A. *Kosovo: How Myths and Truths Started a War*. Berkeley: University of California Press, 1999.

Metz, Helen Chapin. Iraq: 'A Country Study'. In *Iraq: Issues, Historical Background, Bibliography*, ed. Leon M. Jeffries, Hauppauge, New York: Nova Science Publishers, 2003.

Migdal, Joel. *State in Society: Studying How States and Societies Transform and Constitute One Another*. New York: Cambridge University Press, 2001

Milliken, Jennifer and Keith Krause. 'State Failure, State Collapse and State Reconstruction: Concepts, Lessons and Strategies'. *Development and Change* 33, no. 5 (2002): 753–74.

Morgenthau, Hans. *Politics among Nations: The Struggle for Power and Peace*. Fifth edition, New York: Alfred A. Knopf, 1972.

Mosse, David. 'Is Good Policy Unimplementable? Reflections on the Ethnography of Aid Policy and Practice'. *Development and Change* 35, No. 4 (2004): 639–71.

Mosse, David. 'Global Governance and the Ethnography of International Aid'. In *The Aid Effect: Giving and Governing in International Development*, ed. David Mosse and David Lewis, 1–36. London: Pluto Press, 2005.

Mudege, Netsayi Noris. *An Ethnography of Knowledge, The Production of Knowledge in Mupfurudzi Resettlement Scheme*. Leiden: Brill, 2008.

Natali, Denise. *The Kurds and the State: Evolving National Identity in Iraq, Turkey, and Iran*. Syracuse, NY: Syracuse University Press, 2005.

Natali, Denise. *The Kurdish Quasi-State: Development and Dependency in Post-Gulf War Iraq*. Syracuse, NY: Syracuse University Press, 2010.

National Commission on Terrorist Attacks upon the United States. 'Phase Two and the Question of Iraq', 3 October 2004.

'National Democratic Institute. Iraq Election Watch: KRG Parliamentary Elections'. 19 November 2013, accessed 25 July 2014, www.ndi.org/files/NDI-Iraq-Election-Watch-Ed7.pdf.

Neal, Andrew W. 'Foucault in Guantánamo: Towards an Archaeology of the Exception'. *Security Dialogue* 7, no. 1 (2006): 31–46.

Neal, Andrew W. *Exceptionalism and the Politics of Counter-Terrorism: Liberty, Security, and the War on Terror*. Abingdon, UK, New York: Routledge, 2010.

'New Focus on the Western Balkans'. Joint Article by Dr Dimitrij Rupel, President of the EU General Affairs and External Relations Council, Minister of Foreign Affairs of Slovenia, and Mr Bernard Kouchner, 2 April 2008.

O'Leary, Brendan and Khaled Salih. 'The Denial, Resurrection, and Affirmation of Kurdistan'. In *The Future of Kurdistan in Iraq*, ed. Brendan O'Leary, John McGarry and Khaled Salih, 3–43. Philadelphia, PA: University of Pennsylvania Press, 2005.

O'Connell, Mary Ellen. 'The UN, NATO, and International Law after Kosovo'. *Human Rights Quarterly* 22, no. 1 (2000): 59–87.

OECD (Organisation for Economic Co-operation and Development). *Preventing Conflict and Building Peace: A Manual of Issues and Entry Points*. Paris: OECD, 2005.

OECD (Organisation for Economic Co-operation and Development). *The Challenge of Capacity Development: Working towards Good Practice*. Paris: OECD, 2006.

OECD (Organisation for Economic Co-operation and Development). *Fragile States 2014: Domestic Revenue Mobilisation in Fragile States*. Paris: OECD, 2014.

OHCHR/UNMIT (Office of the United Nations High Commissioner for Human Rights/United Nations Integrated Mission in East Timor). *Report on Human Rights Developments: 1 July 2008 to 30 June 2009: Rejecting Impunity: Accountability for Human Rights Violations Past and Present*, 2009.

Olson, Robert. 'Turkish and Syrian Relations since the Gulf War: The Kurdish Question and the Water Problem'. In *The Kurdish Conflict in Turkey: Obstacles and Chances for Peace and Democracy*, ed. Ferhad Ibrahim and Gulistan Gurbey. Münster, New York: Lit Verlag, St Martin's Press, 2000.

Olson, Robert. *The Goat and the Butcher: Nationalism and State Formation in Kurdistan–Iraq since the Iraqi War*. Costa Mesa, California: Mazda Publisher, 2005.

Ortuoste, Maria Consuelo C. 2008. *Internal and External Institutional Dynamics in Member-States and ASEAN: Tracing Creation, Change and Reciprocal Influences*. PhD dissertation, Arizona State University.

OSCE (Organisation for Security and Cooperation in Europe). *Human Rights in Kosovo: As Seen, As Told. Volume II, 14 June – 31 October 1999*, 1999, accessed 8 May 2009, www.osce.org/kosovo/17781.

Osiander, Andreas. 'Sovereignty, International Relations, and the Westphalian Myth'. *International Organization* 55, no. 2 (2001): 251–87.

Otoo, Samuel, Natalia Agapitova and Joy Behrens. *The Capacity Development Results Framework: A Strategic and Results-Oriented Approach to Learning for Capacity Development.* Washington, DC: World Bank, 2009.

Ottaway, Marina and Stefan Meir. *States at Risk and Failing States.* Carnegie Endowment for International Peace: Policy Outlook, Democracy and Rule of Law Project, Washington, DC, 2004.

Özoğlu, Hakan. *Kurdish Notables and the Ottoman State: Evolving Identities, Competing Loyalties, and Shifting Boundaries.* Albany, NY: State University of New York Press, 2004.

Paris, Roland. 'Human Security: Paradigm Shift or Hot Air?' *International Security* 26, no. 2 (2001): 87–102.

Paris, Roland. 'International Peacebuilding and the "Mission Civilisatrice"'. *Review of International Studies* 28, no. 4 (2002): 637–56.

Paris, Roland. *At War's End: Building Peace after Civil Conflict.* Cambridge and New York: Cambridge University Press, 2004.

Paris, Roland. 'Saving Liberal Peacebuilding'. *Review of International Studies* 36, no. 2 (2010): 337–65.

Paris, Roland and Timothy D. Sisk. 'Introduction: Understanding the Contradictions of Postwar Statebuilding'. In *The Dilemmas of Statebuilding: Confronting the Contradictions of Postwar Peace Operations*, ed. Roland Paris and Timothy D. Sisk, 1–20. London: Routledge, 2009.

Paris, Roland and Timothy D. Sisk, eds. *The Dilemmas of Statebuilding: Confronting the Contradictions of Postwar Peace Operations*, London, New York: Routledge, 2009.

Parkinson, Joe and Adam Entous. 'How Kurds Came to Play Key Role in U.S. Plans to Combat Islamic State'. *Wall Street Journal*, 8 September 2014.

Pavkovic, Aleksandar. 'Kosovo/Kosova: A Land of Competing Myths'. In *Kosovo: The Politics of Delusion*, ed. Michael Waller, Kyril Drezov and Bulent Gokay, 3–10. London: Frank Cass, 2001.

Pellet, Alain. 'The Opinions of the Badinter Arbitration Committee: A Second Breath for the Self-Determination of Peoples Peace Conference on Yugoslavia'. *European Journal of International Law* 3 (1992): 178–85.

Pinto, Constâncio. *Statement before the United Nations Committee on Decolonization on Behalf of National Resistance of East Timorese Students, New York, July 1998*, accessed 19 November 2008, www.etan.org/etun/deco198/renetil.htm.

'President Bush Meets with President Barzani of Kurdistan Regional Government of Iraq'. White House Press Release, 25 October 2005.

'Press Statement by Dr Javier Solana, Secretary General of NATO'. Press Release, 23 March 1999, accessed 27 June 2007, www.nato.int/docu/pr/1999/p99–040e.htm.

Pugh, Michael. 'The Political Economy of Peacebuilding: A Critical Theory Perspective'. *International Journal of Peace Studies* 10, no. 2 (2005): 23–42.

Pugh, Michael, Neil Cooper and Mandy Turner. *Whose Peace? Critical Perspectives on the Political Economy of Peacebuilding*. Basingstoke, New York: Palgrave Macmillan, 2011.

Pula, Besnik. 'The Permanent State of Exception: International Administration in Kosovo'. In *World Hegemonic Transformations, the State, and Crisis in Neoliberal Capitalism*, ed. Yildiz Atasoy, 227–43. New York: Routledge, 2009.

Rakisits, Claude. 'The Gulf Crisis: Failure of Preventive Diplomacy'. In *Building International Community: Cooperating for Peace, Case Studies*, ed. Kevin Clements and Robin Ward, 58–103. St. Leonards, Australia: Allen & Unwin, 1994.

Ramos-Horta, José. *The Funu: The Unfinished Saga of East Timor*. Lawrencewill, NJ; Asmara, Eritrea: The Red Sea Press, 1987.

Rasmussen, Mikkel Vedby. *The Risk Society at War: Terror, Technology and Strategy in the Twenty-First Century*. Cambridge: Cambridge University Press, 2006.

Rees, Edward. *Under Pressure Falintil – Forças de Defesa de Timor-Leste: Three Decades of Defense Force Development in Timor-Leste, 1975–2004*. Geneva Center for the Democratic Control of Armed Forces (DCAF), Working Paper 139, 2004.

Rees, Edward. 'Time for the UN to Withdraw from East Timor?' *The Atlantic*, 21 December 2010.

Reno, William. *Corruption and State Politics in Sierra Leone*. New York: Cambridge University Press, 1995.

Rice, Susan E. *The New National Security Strategy: Focus on Failed States*. Brookings Policy Brief 116, Washington, DC, 2003.

Richmond, Oliver P. *The Transformation of Peace*. Basingstoke, New York: Palgrave Macmillan, 2005.

Richmond, Oliver P. 'The Problem of Peace: Understanding the "Liberal Peace"'. *Conflict, Security and Development* 6, no. 3 (2006): 291–314.

Richmond, Oliver P. *Peace in International Relations*, London: Routledge, 2008.

Richmond, Oliver P. 'Resistance and the Post-Liberal Peace'. *Millennium – Journal of International Studies* 38, no. 3 (2010): 665–92.

Richmond, Oliver and Jason Franks. *Liberal Peace Transitions: Between Statebuilding and Peacebuilding*. Edinburgh: Edinburgh University Press, 2009.

Riding, Alan. 'Separatists in Europe Indirectly Reinforce Unity in Yugoslavia'. *New York Times*, 7 July 1991.

Roberts, Adam. 'NATO's "Humanitarian War" over Kosovo'. *Survival* 41, no. 3 (1999): 102–23.

Robinson, Geoffrey. 'Human Rights History from the Ground Up: The Case of East Timor'. In *The Human Rights Paradox: Universality and its Discontents*, ed. Steve J. Stern and Scott Straus, 31–60. Madison, WI: University of Wisconsin Press, 2014.

Rolls, Mark. 'Indonesia's East Timor Experience'. In *Ethnic Conflict and Secessionism in South and Southeast Asia*, ed. Rajat Ganguly and Ian Macduff, 166–94. Thousand Oaks, CA: Sage, 2003.

Romano, David. *The Kurdish Nationalist Movement: Opportunity, Mobilization and Identity*. Cambridge, New York: Cambridge University Press, 2006.

Rotberg, Robert I. *When States Fail: Causes and Consequences*. Princeton, NJ: Princeton University Press, 2004

Roughneen, Simon. 'Potent Mix Brewing for Timorese'. *Asian Times*, 31 August 2011.

Rubin, Michael. 'Is Iraqi Kurdistan a Good Ally?'. *American Enterprise Institute (AEI) Middle Eastern Outlook*, January 2008.

Rubin, Michael. 'Why Won't Washington Support Kurdish Independence?'. *The Kurdistan Tribune*, 10 May 2014.

Rucht, Dieter, 'The Impact of National Contexts on Social Movement Structures: A Cross-Movement and Cross-National Comparison'. In *Comparative Perspectives on Social Movements*, ed. Douglas McAdam, John D. McCarthy and Mayer Zald, 185–204. Cambridge: Cambridge University Press, 1996.

'Rugova Calls for Kosovo "Protectorate"'. *BBC World News*, 24 June 1998.

Rummel, Rudolph J. 'Democracy, Power, Genocide, and Mass Murder'. *Journal of Conflict Resolution* 39, no. 1 (1995): 3–26.

Saeed, Yerevan. 'Barzani: Independence Will Come, and Peacefully'. *Rudaw*, 7 May 2015.

Sahin, Selver B. 'The Use of the "Exceptionalism" Argument in Kosovo: An Analysis of the Rationalization of External Interference in the Conflict'. *Journal of Balkan and Near Eastern Studies* 11, no. 3 (2009): 235–55.

Sahin, Selver B. 'How Exception Became the Norm: Normalizing Intervention as an Exercise in Risk Management in Kosovo'. *Journal of Balkan and Near Eastern Studies*, 5, no. 1 (2013): 17–36.

Scambary, James. *A Survey of Gangs and Youth Groups in Dili*. Report Commissioned by the Australian Agency for International Development (AusAID), 2006.

Schattschneider, Elmer Eric. *The Semisovereign People*. New York: Holt, Rinehart & Winston, 1960.

Schmitt, Carl. *Political Theology: Four Chapters on the Concept of Sovereignty*. Trans. George Schwab, Cambridge: MIT Press, 1985 [1922].

Sen, Amartya. 'Democracy As a Universal Value'. *Journal of Democracy* 10, no. 3 (1999): 3–17.

Shareef, Mohammed. *USA, Iraq and the Kurds: Shock, Awe and Aftermath*. Abingdon, UK, New York: Routledge, 2014.

Shurke, Astri. 'Peacekeepers As Nation-Builders: Dilemmas of the UN in East Timor'. *International Peacekeeping* 8, no. 4 (2001): 1–20.

Simma, Bruno. 'NATO, the UN and the Use of Force: Legal Aspects'. *European Journal of International Relations* 10, no. 1 (1999): 1–22.

Simpson, Brad. '"Illegally and Beautifully": The United States, the Indonesian Invasion of East Timor and the International Community, 1974–76'. *Cold War History* 5, no. 3 (2005): 281–315.

Snyder, Charles. 'Kosovo Case Unique, Says Miliband'. *BBC News*, 18 February 2008.

Snyder, Charles. 'Kosovo does Not Set Precedent, US Says'. *Taipei Times*, 20 February 2008.

Stansfield, Gareth. 'The Unravelling of the Post-First World War State System? The Kurdish Region of Iraq and the Transformation of the Middle East'. *International Affairs* 89, no. 2 (2013): 259–82.

State Failure Task Force. *State Failure Task Force: Phase III Findings*. Washington, DC, 2000.

Straw, Jack. *Failed and Failing States*. Speech Delivered at the European University of Birmingham, UK, 6 September 2002.

Sudetic, Chuck. 'Yugoslav Army Threatens Truce, 2 Republics Say'. *New York Times*, 10 July 1991.

Suhrke, Astri. 'Reconstruction as Modernisation: The "Post-Conflict" Project in Afghanistan. *Third World Quarterly* 28, no. 7 (2007), 1291–308.

Surroi, Veton. 'Kosovo – An Unfinished Political War'. *Koha Ditore*, UNMIK Local Media Monitoring, 24 March 2003.

Tarrow, Sidney. 'States and Opportunities: The Political Structuring of Social Movements'. In *Comparative Perspectives on Social Movements*, ed. Douglas McAdam, John D. McCarthy and Mayer Zald, 41–61. Cambridge: Cambridge University Press, 1996.

Taylor, John G. *Indonesia's Forgotten War: The Hidden History of East Timor*. London: Zed Books, 1991.

'Thaci Says Kosovo Backs EU Mission, Not Six-Point Plan'. *Radio Free Europe/Radio Liberty*, 23 December 2008.

'The Tiananmen in East Timor'. *New York Times*, 21 January 1992.

The White House. *The National Security Strategy of the United States of America*. Washington, DC: White House, 2002.

Timor-Leste Reception, Truth and Reconciliation Commission (CAVR). *Chega! The Report of the Commission for Reception, Truth, and Reconciliation in Timor-Leste*. Dili: CAVR, 2005.

Tol, Gönül. *Untangling the Turkey-KRG Energy Partnership: Looking Beyond Economic Drivers*. Global Turkey in Europe Policy Brief 14, 2014.

Torres, Magui Moreno and Michael Anderson. *Fragile States: Defining Difficult Environments for Poverty Reduction*. UK Department for International Development, Poverty Reduction in Difficult Environments Team Policy Division Working Paper 1, 2004.

'Turkey's AKP Spokesman: Iraq's Kurds Have Right to Decide Their Future'. *Rudaw*, 13 June 2014.

'Turkish Companies Dominate Northern Iraq'. *Anatolian News Agency*, 11 April 2013.

UK Government. *Building Stability Overseas Strategy*, 2012, accessed 6 June 2014, www.gov.uk/government/uploads/system/uploads/attachment_data/file/32960/bsos-july-11.pdf.

UN News Centre. 'Foes of Multi-Ethnic Democracy Still Threaten Kosovo's Progress – UN Envoy'. 10 February 2005.

United Nations. Transcript of Press Conference by Secretary-General Kofi Annan and Deputy-Secretary-General Louise Frechette at Headquarters, 30 June 1999, accessed 18 May 2008, www.un.org/News/Press/docs/1999/19990701.SGSM7055.html.

United Nations. *Secretary-General Informs Security Council People of East Timor Rejected Special Autonomy Proposed by Indonesia.* Security Council Press Release, SC/6721, 3 September 1999.

United Nations. *Report of the Secretary-General on the Situation in East Timor.* Security Council Document, S/1999/1024, 4 October 1999.

United Nations. *Report of the International Commission of Inquiry on East Timor to the Secretary-General.* UN Document A/54/726, S/2000/59, 31 January 2000.

United Nations. *Letter Dated 7 October 2005 from the Secretary-General Addressed to the President of the Security Council (Report on a Comprehensive Review of the Situation in Kosovo, Presented by Mr. Kai Eide, Special Envoy of the Secretary-General).* Security Council Document, S/2005/635, 7 October 2005.

United Nations. *2005 World Summit Outcome.* Resolution Adopted by the General Assembly, A/RES/60/1, 24 October 2005.

United Nations. *Progress Report of the Secretary-General on the United Nations Office in Timor- Leste.* Security Council Document, S/2006/24, 17 January 2006.

United Nations. *Report of the Secretary-General on Justice and Reconciliation for Timor-Leste.* Security Council Document, S/2006/580, 26 July 2006.

United Nations. *Resolution 1704.* S/RES/1704, 25 August 2006.

United Nations. *Report of the United Nations Independent Special Commission of Inquiry for Timor-Leste.* Geneva, 2006.

United Nations. *Letter Dated 26 March 2007 from the Secretary-General Addressed to the President of the Security Council (Report of the Special Envoy of the Secretary-General on Kosovo's Future Status*) Security Council Document, S/2007/168; (*Comprehensive Proposal for the Kosovo Status Settlement*) Security Council Document, S/2007/168/Addendum 1, Annex XI, 26 March 2007.

United Nations. *Repertoire of the Practice of the Security Council 1989–1992, Chapter 8, no. 22. Items Relating to the Situation between Iraq and Kuwait.* New York: UN, 2007.

United Nations. *Report of the Secretary-General on the United Nations Interim Administration Mission in Kosovo.* Security Council Document, S/2008/354, 12 June 2008.

United Nations. *Report of the Secretary-General on the United Nations Interim Administration Mission in Kosovo.* Security Council Document, S/2008/692, 24 November 2008.

United Nations. *Report of the Secretary-General on the United Nations Integrated Mission in Timor-Leste.* Security Council Document S/2009/504, 2 October 2009.

UNDP (United Nations Development Programme). *Human Development Report 1994.* Oxford: Oxford University Press, 1994.

UNDP (United Nations Development Programme). 'Strengthening Parliamentary Democracy in Timor-Leste (Parliament Project-Project No. 00014960)', revised project document for the period 2006–2009, unpublished working draft, January 2006.

UNDP (United Nations Development Programme). *Managing Natural Resources for Human Development: Developing the Non-Oil Economy to Achieve the MDGs.* Timor-Leste Human Development Report 2011.

UNDP (United Nations Development Programme). 'About Kosovo', accessed 16 December 2014, www.ks.undp.org/content/kosovo/en/home/countryinfo.

UNMIK (United Nations Interim Administration Mission in Kosovo). 'SRSG Hans Haekkerup Addresses North Atlantic Council'. UNMIK Press Release, UNMIK/PR/515, 28 February 2001.

UNMIK (United Nations Interim Administration Mission in Kosovo). 'SRSG Michael Steiner Addresses Permanent Council of the OSCE'. UNMIK Press Release, UNMIK/PR/774, 11 July 2002.

UNMIK (United Nations Interim Administration Mission in Kosovo). 'Standards for Kosovo'. UNMIK/PR/1078, 10 December 2003.

UNMIK (United Nations Interim Administration Mission in Kosovo). 'Harri Holkeri's Address to the UN Security Council'. UNMIK Press Release, UNMIK/PR/1119, 6 February 2004.

UNOSEK (United Nations Office of the Special Envoy of the Secretary-General for the Future Status Process for Kosovo). Press Conference by UN Special Envoy for the Future Status Process for Kosovo Martti Ahtisaari, in Pristina, 2 February 2007.

'UN Preparing to Leave Kosovo, Jessen-Petersen Says'. *Deutsche Presse-Agentur (German Press Agency)*, 1 June 2006.

US Department of Defense. 'Cohen Declares Iraq No-Fly Zones "Successful"', 10 March 1999.

US State Department. *Trafficking in Persons Report 2011*, accessed 13 January 2013, www.state.gov/g/tip/rls/tiprpt/2011/index.htm.

USAID (US Agency for International Development). *Fragile States Strategy.* Washington, DC: USAID, 2005.

Vali, Abbas. 'The Kurds and their "Others": Fragmented Identity and Fragmented Politics'. *Comparative Studies of South Asia, Africa and the Middle East* 18, no. 2 (1998): 83–94.

Vickers, Miranda. *Between Serb and Albanian: A History of Kosovo.* London: Hurst, 1998.

Voller, Yaniv. 'Kurdish Oil Politics in Iraq: Contested Sovereignty and Unilateralism'. *Middle East Policy* 20 (2013): 68–82.

Voller, Yaniv. *The Kurdish Liberation Movement in Iraq: From Insurgency to Statehood*. Abingdon, UK: Routledge, 2014.

Wæver, Ole, 'Securitization and Desecuritization'. In *On Security*, ed. Ronnie D. Lipschutz. New York: Columbia University Press, 1995.

Wainwright, Elsina. *New Neighbor, New Challenge: Australia and the Security of East Timor*. Canberra: Australian Strategic Policy Institute, 2002.

Walsh, Pat. 'From Opposition to Proposition: The National Council of Timorese Resistance (CNRT) in Transition'. 1999, accessed 22 November 2013, http://members.pcug.org.au/~wildwood/CNRTPat.ht.

Watts, Nicole F. 'Democracy and Self-Determination in the Kurdistan Region of Iraq'. In *Conflict, Democratization, and the Kurds in the Middle East: Turkey, Iran, Iraq, and Syria*, ed. David Romano and Mehmet Gurses, 141–68. New York: Palgrave Macmillan, 2014.

Weatherbee, Donald E. 'Portuguese Timor: An Indonesian Dilemma'. *Asian Survey* 6, no. 12 (1966): 683–895.

Weber, Cynthia. *Simulating Sovereignty: Intervention, the State and the Symbolic Exchange*. Cambridge: Cambridge University Press, 1995.

Weber, Max. *From Max Weber: Essays in Sociology*. Ed. Hans Heinrich Gerth and C. Wright Mills, New York: Oxford University Press, 1946.

Weldemichael, Awet Tewelde. *Third World Colonialism and Strategies of Liberation: Eritrea and East Timor*. Cambridge: Cambridge University Press, 2013.

Weldes, Jutta. 'Constructing National Interests'. *European Journal of International Relations* 2, no. 3 (1996): 275–318.

Weller, Marc. 'The International Response to the Dissolution of the Socialist Federal Republic of Yugoslavia'. *The American Journal of International Law* 86, no. 3 (1992): 569–607.

Wendt, Alexander and Michael Barnett. 'Dependent State Formation and Third World Militarization'. *Review of International Studies* 19, no. 4 (1993): 321–47.

Wheeler, Nicholas J. and Tim Dunne. 'East Timor and the New Humanitarianism'. *International Affairs* 77, no. 4 (2001): 805–27.

'Why are So Many Kurdish Women Setting Themselves on Fire?'. *The Economist*, 18 March 2014.

Wilde, Ralph. 'From Danzig to East Timor and Beyond: The Role of International Territorial Administration'. *American Journal of International Law* 95, no. 3 (2001): 583–606.

Wilde, Ralph. 'Representing International Territorial Administration: A Critique of Some Approaches'. *European Journal of International Law* 15, no. 1 (2004): 71–96.

'Will Turkey Midwife An Independent Iraqi Kurdish State?'. *Al Monitor*, 16 July 2014.

Williams, Gregory P. 'When Opportunity Structure Knocks: Social Movements in the Soviet Union and Russian Federation'. *Social Movement Studies* 9, no. 4 (2010): 443–60.

Williams, Paul R. and Francesca Jannotti Pecci. 'Earned Sovereignty: Bridging the Gap between Sovereignty and Self-Determination'. *Stanford Journal of International Law* 40 (2004): 1–40.

Wilson, Bu V. E. 'Smoke and Mirrors: Institutionalising Fragility in the Policia Nacional Timor-Leste'. In *Democratic Governance in Timor-Leste: Reconciling the Local and National*, ed. David J. Mearns, 98–115. Darwin: Charles Darwin University Press, 2008.

Wilson, Bu V. E. *The Exception Becomes the Norm in Timor-Leste: The Draft National Security Laws and the Continuing Role of the Joint Command*. Australian National University Centre for International Governance and Justice Issues Paper 11, 2009.

'Wisner: Kosovo Status Agreement is Close'. *Southeast European Times*, 27 October 2006.

Wolfowitz, Paul J. 'Timor-Leste: The Challenge of Keeping Peace for Development', Dili, 9 April 2006.

'Women Demand Greater Role in New Kurdistan Government'. *Rudaw*, 1 December 2013.

Woodward, Susan L. 'The West and the International Organisations'. In *Yugoslavia and After: A Study in Fragmentation, Despair and Rebirth*, ed. David A. Dyker and Ivan Vejvoda, 155–76. London, New York: Longman, 1996.

Woodward, Susan L. 'Failed States: Warlordism and "Tribal" Warfare'. *Naval War College Review* 52 (1999): 55–67.

World Bank. *The State in a Changing World*. New York: Oxford University Press, 1997.

World Bank. *Post-Conflict Reconstruction: The Role of the World Bank*. Washington, DC: World Bank, 1998.

World Bank. *Building Effective States, Forging Engaged Societies*. Report of the World Bank Task Force on Capacity Development in Africa. Washington, DC: World Bank, 2005.

World Bank. *Capacity Building in Africa: An OED Evaluation of World Bank Support*. Washington, DC: World Bank, 2005.

World Bank. 'Definitions of Fragility and Conflict, 2009', accessed 3 April 2011, http://go.worldbank.org/NEK8GNPSO0.

'Xanana Gusmao's Paper to NZ Conference'. 9 September 1998, accessed 24 May 2011, www.etan.org/et/1998/september/sept8-14/9xpaper.htm.

Yannis, Alexandros. 'The Concept of Suspended Sovereignty in International Law and Its Implications in International Politics'. *European Journal of International Law* 13, no. 5 (2002): 1037–52.

Zartman, I. William. 'Introduction: Posing the Problem of State Collapse'. In *Collapsed States: The Disintegration and Restoration of Legitimate Authority*, ed. I. William Zartman, 1–11. Boulder, CO: Lynne Rienner, 1995.

Zartman, I. William. 'Putting States Back Together'. In *Collapsed States: The Disintegration and Restoration of Legitimate Authority*, ed. I. William Zartman, 267–73. Boulder, CO: Lynne Rienner, 1995.

Zedalis, Rex. *Oil and Gas in the Disputed Kurdish Territories: Jurisprudence, Regional Minorities and Natural Resources in a Federal State*. Abingdon, UK: Routledge, 2012.

Index

For Product Safety Concerns and Information please contact our EU
representative GPSR@taylorandfrancis.com
Taylor & Francis Verlag GmbH, Kaufingerstraße 24, 80331 München, Germany